COGNITIVE-BEHAVIORAL THERAPY
FOR BIPOLAR DISORDER

Cognitive-Behavioral Therapy for Bipolar Disorder

MONICA RAMIREZ BASCO
A. JOHN RUSH

Foreword by
Robert M. Post

THE GUILFORD PRESS
New York   London

Printed in the United States of America

This book is printed on acid-free paper.

Last digit is print number: 9   8   7   6   5   4

Library of Congress Cataloging-in-Publication Data

Basco, Monica Ramirez
    Cognitive-behavioral therapy for bipolar disorder / Monica Ramirez
Basco, A. John Rush
      p. cm.
    Includes bibliographical references and index.
    ISBN 1-57230-090-6
    1. Manic-depressive illness—Treatment.   2. Cognitive therapy.
I. Rush, A. John.   II. Title.
    [DNLM: 1. Bipolar Disorder—therapy.   2. Cognitive Therapy—
methods. 3. Bipolar Disorder—diagnosis.   4. Bipolar Disorder—
psychology.   WM 207 B298c 1996]
RC516.B36   1996
616.89′50651—dc20
DNLM/DLC
For Library of Congress   96-13739
                                                                              CIP

To those who have shaped our views, our practices,
and our dedication to the care
of those who suffer from mental illness

To Aaron T. Beck, MD,
mentor, inspiration, and friend

To our patients

To our families, Michael A. Basco and sons;
Dee Miller, A. J. Rush, and Matthew J. Rush; and
Pedro and Isabel Ramirez

Acknowledgments

We wish to acknowledge the support of the MacArthur Foundation in the development of this manual. In addition, support was provided by the Mental Health Connections Research Program and the University of Texas Southwestern Medical Center at Dallas.

We also wish to express our appreciation for the careful reading, critique, and support of this book by Melanie M. Biggs, PhD, University of Texas Southwestern Medical Center at Dallas; Jesse H. Wright, MD, PhD, University of Louisville; Dean Schuyler, MD, Rockville, Maryland; and Patricia L. Baltazar, PhD, El Segundo, California. Their contributions facilitated the development of this book.

Finally, we wish to express appreciation for the ongoing administrative support of David Savage, B. J. Bailey-Smith, and Fast Word, Inc., of Dallas, Texas, for their secretarial and technical support, and to Kenneth Z. Altshuler, MD, Stanton Sharp Distinguished Chair, Professor and Chairman, Department of Psychiatry, University of Texas Southwestern Medical Center, for his administrative support. We are grateful to Marcia Mofson for her review of the life events literature. We are also indebted to Kitty Moore of Guilford for her helpful advice and encouragement throughout the writing of this book.

Foreword

The current volume is heralded as a much-needed and long-overdue synthesis of specific techniques designed to optimize the pharmacotherapeutic and psychotherapeutic management of patients with bipolar affective disorder. While multiple articles, chapters, and books have been written on the psychotherapy of the anxiety disorders, unipolar depression, and a variety of neurotic and psychotic psychiatric illnesses, little has directly focused on effective therapeutic strategies for patients with bipolar affective illness. This gap has occurred despite increasing recognition of the morbidity and mortality of this disorder with the only FDA-approved agent for long-term prophylaxis being lithium carbonate.

This volume is all the more critical and needed in light of the wide range of clinical outcomes possible in the illness. There is increasing awareness of potential links between extraordinary productivity and creativity in individuals with bipolar illness on the one hand, and the potential for catastrophic impact of the illness on the other. There is a seven to ten times higher risk of three or more comorbid psychiatric illnesses with bipolar illness compared to any other psychiatric illness, and bipolar illness is overrepresented by patients with extremely poor outcomes, in some instances paralleling that of schizophrenia on long-term follow-up. Patients with bipolar illness fill the ranks of the homeless and are among the incarcerated because of encounters with the legal system. While the empirical evidence is not yet in that psychotherapy facilitates and optimizes pharmacotherapy and improves prognosis, it will be readily apparent to the reader that this volume provides a wealth of techniques and practical and specific approaches which are highly likely to enhance the successful treatment of the bipolar patient.

Basco and Rush have drawn upon their experience in the psychotherapies of other serious mental illnesses, particularly unipolar depression, and have modified and honed these well-documented and tested approaches to make them most optimally applicable to patients with bipolar illness. Their perspective implicitly and, in some instances, explicitly integrates and acknowledges the progress and understanding of the neurobiology of the affective disorders and their complex impact on multiple structures in the central nervous system. For example, as in the case of the unipolar recurrent affective disorders, bipolar illness is often associated with major alterations in endocrine systems such as hypercortisolemia and peptide deficits such as lower somatostatin in spinal fluid during episodes of depression. These are noteworthy in that the associated endocrinopathics of hypercortisolemia of Cushing's disease and low somatostatin of Alzheimer's are associated with substantial cognitive impairment. Some patients with bipolar illness, moreover, have psychomotor slowing and defects in concentration that are directly proportional to the degree of decrease in metabolism in the frontal lobes noted on PET scans, while other patients have cognitive and memory difficulties based on a pattern of metabolic hyperactivity in their temporal lobes. Given these altered neural substrates in the bipolar illnesses, it becomes necessary to approach the psychotherapy of the illness on a systematic basis utilizing the tools not only of the supportive psychotherapy but more focused techniques adapted from cognitive and behavioral approaches to the illness. If frontal and limbic substrates are impaired during episodes of affective illness, psychotherapeutic and rehabilitative techniques need to be brought into play and utilized in ways that can be effective despite these transient impairments.

This is exactly what Basco and Rush have detailed in a practical sequential approach to the illness. The traditional verbal modes of dynamic psychotherapy are supported with a variety of visceral, cognitive, and behavioral techniques involving written and practice assignments. Not only do these enhance the likelihood of their being accurately perceived and understood, but they also speak to more fundamental therapeutic mechanisms pertinent to the defects present in the affective disorders. That is, in the well-state, patients are often amenable to corrective cognitive and emotional experiences based on a realistic appraisal of the self and the environment and its implications for the future. Contrarily, the depressed patient is unable to appropriately assess these variables as part of these deficits in self-appraisal which are among the definitional aspects of depression. Given this persistent and recalcitrant negative view of the self and the future and the added deficits of psychomotor impairment and lack of energy in bipolar illness, not only are typical social interactions of inadequate support, but more traditional dynamic-based psychotherapies appear to have less of an impact as well. Many of the specific techniques outlined in this volume are targeted in such a way that practice, repetition, and practical approaches to incremental improvement are programmed and strongly integrated into the therapeutic process.

Thus, the different types and structures involved in learning and memory problems associated with the affective disorders are being specifically addressed and tuned by this targeted psychotherapy. "Representational" memory is the type that is involved in one trial learning and is thought to be mediated by the structures in the medial temporal lobe and limbic area of the brain. In contrast "habit" memory is based on repetition, not dependent on medial temporal lobe structures, but on the striatum, and functions in the relatively more automatic or unconscious basis, and thus makes unlearning a more protracted task. An example of representational memory might be recalling a single experience in the past and the events and emotions associated with it, while habit memory would be like that acquired when one learns to ride a bicycle or drive to work by the same route each day and to have these processed rather automatically and perhaps unconsciously.

Many of the traditional techniques of insight-oriented psychotherapy appear more specifically tuned to temporal lobe based representational memory processes, while one of the paradigmatic aspects of bipolar episodes and their recurrence is their increasing autonomy from psychosocial stresses and events in the environment as precipitants of episodes. As such, bipolar illness would appear to have many of the components of "habit" memory, occurring on a relatively automatic basis and immune to single cognitive corrective experiences. In contrast, many of the behavioral techniques utilized in this manual appear highly specifically targeted to such automatic biochemical and memory-like systems. Multiple modalities are brought into play besides the verbal conceptual mode; in particular, outlines, balance sheets, work sequences, visual material, and perhaps most importantly, repetitive practice sessions are utilized. If bipolar illness with relatively autonomous mood fluctuations is operating on a model more akin to "habit" memory systems, it is sensible to utilize corrective therapeutic techniques pertinent to the types of deficits induced.

Just as the neuropharmacology of manic-depressive illness may ultimately have to be specifically adjusted as a function of different types and stages of affective illness and dramatically change as more intimate knowledge of the central nervous system neurotransmitter defects are elucidated, increasing refinements in psychotherapeutic approaches may also be brought into play in a parallel fashion. The current manual provides an extraordinarily scholarly, clinically, and empirically based approach to this enterprise. As greater knowledge of the systems involved in the illness becomes available and the greater and lesser utilities of the specific techniques described in this volume become known, the next

generation of focused psychotherapies of bipolar illness will more naturally evolve from this initial effort.

Thus, we strongly endorse and applaud this first systemization of
psychotherapeutic approaches directly targeted to patients with bipolar
illness. Not only will such a systemization facilitate the testing of the
techniques described and lead to their eventual perfection, but in the
meantime it provides a wealth of clinical techniques and strategies which
will most certainly enhance the psychotherapeutic and pharmacological
approaches to bipolar illness. The field is indebted to Basco and Rush for
such an outstanding and systematic approach to the psychotherapy of
bipolar illness.

ROBERT M. POST

Preface

This book represents an integration of our individual clinical experiences and research. Dr. Basco's original clinical training was in cognitive-behavioral therapy (CBT) with a special emphasis on the CBT approach to the treatment of marital and family problems. After joining the Department of Psychiatry at the University of Texas Southwestern Medical Center at Dallas, she was a research cognitive therapist for studies on major depression, and she spent several years studying the special interpersonal and psychosocial problems of patients with mood disorders. At the same time, she was a member of the University of Texas Southwestern Medical Center multidisciplinary research team studying the intensive treatment of insulin-dependent diabetes mellitus (IDDM), in the national Diabetes Control and Complications Trial. Dr. Basco developed and tested cognitive-behavioral interventions for enhancing patient compliance with a complex diabetes treatment regimen.

Similarities between bipolar disorder and IDDM, such as the chronic nature of the illness, the need for daily medication management, the importance of symptom monitoring and early intervention, the difficulty that patients experience in following treatment recommendations, and the psychological adjustment to a chronic illness, led her, with Dr. Rush's assistance, to develop cognitive and behavioral interventions for bipolar disorder. These methods relied heavily on the work of Aaron T. Beck, MD (Beck, Rush, Shaw, & Emery, 1979), which has been adapted for bipolar disorder.

Dr. Rush, a student of Aaron Beck, spent over two decades in the study and treatment of mood disorders and coauthored *Cognitive Therapy of Depression* (Beck et al., 1979), the first cognitive therapy treatment manual. With grants from the National Institute of Mental Health, he has evaluated the efficacy of cognitive therapy in the acute phase treatment of depression. Over the years, Dr. Rush has adapted cognitive and behavioral approaches to the treatment of bipolar disorder as an adjunct to pharmacotherapy. He proposed a conceptual model for the use of these methods to improve treatment adherence based on his three years as a consultant to the multicenter National Heart and Lung Institute trial of cholestyramine in the prevention of strokes and heart attacks (Rush, 1988).

This manual integrates pharmacotherapy and psychotherapy to maximize the benefits of both treatment modalities for addressing the complex problems associated with bipolar disorder. Psychological treatments alone are not recommended in the treatment of this chronic, recurring, and devastating mood disorder. Indeed, we believe that efficacious, concurrent pharmacotherapy is essential to the conduct of this psychotherapeutic treatment. Careful diagnosis of the illness, including current symptoms and prior course, should precede the use of these methods. The book provides a conceptual basis for implementing this treatment as well as step-by-step instructions.

As experienced clinicians know, a therapeutic alliance is essential before any therapeutic interventions can be delivered effectively; this is also true for this structured treatment manual. In addition, the therapeutic methods must be adapted to and tailored for each individual patient. Some steps may be skipped. Additional steps, which we have not specified, may be called for. Indeed, as with most psychotherapeutic interventions, the artfulness with which the therapy is applied is critical to its efficacy. Along with cognitive-behavioral techniques, each chapter discusses general therapeutic and patient management issues relevant to addressing specific symptoms or problems of bipolar disorder.

While the clinical issues raised throughout the book likely apply to many different psychiatric and general medical illnesses, the specific cognitive and behavioral techniques described were developed specifically for individuals with bipolar disorder. In fact, some of the treatment recommendations in this book are not specific to a cognitive approach but are common to all forms of psychotherapy and to the pharmacological treatment of bipolar disorder. The chapter summaries highlight both the general clinical management issues and specific cognitive and behavioral approaches in each chapter. Mastery of both specific interventions and the therapeutic relationship skills is essential for optimal management of patients with bipolar disorder.

This book was written for mental health professionals who treat patients with bipolar disorder: psychiatrists and other physicians, psychologists, social workers, counselors, and nurses. We have tried to define terms clearly and to provide sufficient examples to make this manual useful to people from many professional disciplines and with varying levels of experience and training. While this is not a patient handbook, we also tried to make the text understandable for patients. We attempted to provide a review of the clinical features and an overview of the pharmacological treatment of bipolar disorder. For a more in-depth review of the psychology, biology, pharmacology, and phenomenology of bipolar disorder we recommend the classic work by Goodwin and Jamison (1990), *Manic Depressive Illness.*

We have attempted to introduce each component of the intervention systematically so that each builds on the others. The chapters provide the rationale for each therapeutic method, as well as detailed descriptions of when and how to execute each intervention. At the beginning of each chapter, we have provided session-by-session instructions, including suggested homework assignments. Modifications may be needed to address the special needs of individual patients, however. The sessions are numbered and descriptively labeled. More than one session outline may appear at the beginning of a chapter if the content and methods for those sessions are described within the chapter. The sessions are presented in sequential order.

The book consists of twelve chapters. The first three chapters are informational in nature. Chapter 1 contains a discussion of the cognitive-behavioral approach to the maintenance treatment of bipolar disorder. Chapter 2 provides an overview of the diagnosis, course, and characteristics of bipolar disorder. Chapter 3 reviews common psychopharmacological approaches to the treatment of symptoms of bipolar disorder. This overview of medications for manic and psychotic symptoms, as well as the pharmacological management of depression, was written as an introduction to inform clinicians who are not experts in psychopharmacology. When medication questions arise in the course of managing these patients, expert psychopharmacological consultation is essential. The first three chapters are also designed to provide information that clinicians can and should share with patients, since patient education is very important in the successful maintenance treatment of bipolar disorder. Chapter 1 includes a discussion of the various methods for educating patients.

Chapter 4 is dedicated to symptom monitoring, which sets the stage for using cognitive-behavioral techniques to combat symptoms. Clearly, awareness of the onset of symptoms must precede remediation.

Chapter 5 centers on the enhancement of treatment adherence. This chapter precedes those providing more detailed descriptions of specific cognitive-behavioral techniques because medication adherence is essential to symptom control. Chapters 6 and 7 cover specific interventions aimed at the cognitive symptoms of depression and mania, while Chapters 8 and 9 specify techniques to address behavioral symptoms of depression and mania. We have selected a small subset of cognitive therapy techniques from the Beck et al. (1979) manual for our treatment package because we believe that the selected techniques are useful for most bipolar patients. Rather than overwhelming clinicians with a plethora of cognitive therapy techniques, we provide illustrative examples of how to adapt this approach and selected techniques to issues commonly encountered in the treatment of bipolar disorder.

The recurring episodes of depression and mania in bipolar disorder always strain and often devastate interpersonal relationships. In addition, they can lead to loss of employment, financial ruin, and other hardships. Likewise, the occurrence of psychosocial problems unrelated to bipolar disorder can cause considerable emotional turmoil, disrupt sleep, and preoccupy patients. Such problems often keep patients from taking medication or engaging in other treatment-related activities. Many problems faced by people with bipolar disorder are interpersonal in nature. For example, they may find it particularly difficult to get along with family members, resolve problems with coworkers, communicate with employers, or maintain friendships. Therefore, we have dedicated Chapters 10 and 11 to understanding and facilitating interpersonal communication and solving problems of daily living. Chapter 12 provides some clinical vignettes of applications of this treatment package with individuals suffering from bipolar illness.

Although we have used real clinical examples throughout this book, we have changed the identifying information to protect patient privacy. In some cases, we have merged the experiences of several patients into one example. We know that each patient has a unique presentation of symptoms, response to treatment, and life circumstances. Therefore, we have tried to incorporate several different kinds of examples in an effort to capture the diversity of people with this disorder, as well as the variations in the expression of the illness.

This treatment manual is intended to be used in its entirety with each patient. We strongly recommend that information on the diagnosis and treatment of bipolar disorder be presented to patients and family members at the outset of treatment. Even if they seem knowledgeable about their disorder, it is important to present it to them. The goal is to engage patients as active participants in their own management by informing them about the nature of the illness, treatment options, and specific treatment plans. An informed patient is an ally in the conduct of cognitive and behavioral methods. We believe that remaining interventions should be delivered in the sequence presented, though patients may benefit from some interventions more than others.

We believe that optimal results from this approach to bipolar disorder depend on a comprehensive integration of pharmacotherapy, good clinical management, and specific techniques presented herein. Thus, we view this manual as a treatment package, though some may prefer to use only a subset of the methods outlined.

The strategies and tactics presented in this book are based on our collective clinical experiences and the available research with cognitive and behavioral methods in mood and other general medical disorders. While we have used these procedures clinically and refined them over time, the reader is cautioned that this adjunct to the pharmacological treatment of bipolar disorder has not been formally tested in randomized controlled clinical trials. Thus, whether it is effective, and for whom, is not known. We hope that this treatment manual will provide a basis for formal studies of the efficacy and effectiveness of CBT for bipolar disorder.

Contents

COGNITIVE-BEHAVIORAL THERAPY
FOR BIPOLAR DISORDER

Cognitive-Behavioral Therapy for Bipolar Disorder: An Overview

---

SESSION 1. OVERVIEW
OF COGNITIVE-BEHAVIORAL THERAPY

Purpose of the Session

The purpose of this session is to provide patients and their family members with a rationale for cognitive-behavioral treatment of bipolar disorder and with an overview of the treatment process, including the goals of therapy. Providing information about the treatment procedures will help patients prepare for the coming months. In addition, the family members and friends, if present, will learn what will be provided and what is expected of patients. Perhaps more important, this and the remaining educational sessions provide opportunities for the clinician to establish an alliance with patients and their family members.

Goals of the Session
1. Provide an overview of the treatment process.
2. Discuss patients' rights.
   a. High-quality clinical care.
   b. Confidentiality.
3. Clearly specify patients' responsibilities in the treatment process.
4. Clearly specify the clinician's responsibilities in the treatment process.
   a. High-quality care.
   b. Availability for emergencies when needed.
   c. Honest feedback to patients.

(cont.)

(continued from page 1)

5. Discuss families' responsibilities.
   a. Symptom detection.
   b. Encouragement and support of patients.

Procedure

1. Introduce relevant clinical staff members to patients and significant others. Provide cards with the primary clinician's name and phone number, the clinic's phone number, and where to call for after-hours emergencies.
2. Review the treatment plans. Discuss responsibilities of patients, clinicians, and family members.
3. Review the purpose of providing homework assignments and provide copies of the assigned reading material.

Recommended Reading

Thompson, Stancer, and Persad (1984). *Manic Depressive Illness: A Guide for Patients and Families.*

Bipolar disorder is a severe, chronic, and disabling mental illness. It afflicts nearly 1% of adults in the United States (Robins et al., 1984). While some individuals may experience only a single episode of mania and depression in their lifetimes, over 95% of people with bipolar disorder have recurrent episodes of depression and mania throughout their lives (see reviews by Goodwin & Jamison, 1990, and Zis & Goodwin, 1979). The probability of experiencing new episodes of depression or mania actually increases with each subsequent episode (Gelenberg, Carroll, Baudhuin, Jefferson, & Greist, 1989; Keller, Shapiro, Lavori, & Wolfe, 1982) despite treatment. There is also evidence that the time between episodes decreases during the course of the illness (Angst, 1981; Kraepelin, 1921/1976; Roy-Byrne, Post, Uhde, Porcu, & Davis, 1985; Zis, Grof, Webster, & Goodwin, 1980). This means that individuals will spend more time ill and less time well as the disorder progresses. Approximately 25% of people with bipolar disorder attempt suicide (Weissman, Leaf, Bruce, Bruce, & Florio, 1988).

The marked changes in mood, personality, thinking, and behavior inherent in bipolar disorder often have profound effects on interpersonal relationships. Affective lability (Goodwin & Jamison, 1990), financial extravagance (Akiskal, Djenderedjian, Rosenthal, & Khani, 1977), fluctuations in levels of sociability (Akiskal et al., 1977; Murphy & Biegal,

1974; Winokur, Clayton, & Reich, 1969), sexual indiscretions (Akiskal et al., 1977; Spalt, 1975; Winokur et al., 1969), and violent behaviors are all clearly a source of turmoil, conflict, and concern to those who suffer from this illness and their significant others.

To attempt to control the course of this illness, lifelong or maintenance (i.e., prophylactic) pharmacological treatment is generally indicated. Maintenance pharmacotherapy may not altogether eliminate recurrences of mania or depression. It can, however, decrease the frequency, duration, and severity of episodes of both depression and mania (Baastrup & Schou, 1967) and decrease patient suffering, hospitalization, and cost, and improve psychosocial functioning.

A common problem in the treatment of bipolar disorder is that people do not always take their medications regularly. When patients do not adhere to their medication regimens, that is, when they do not consistently take their medications over time, the effectiveness of maintenance pharmacotherapy is greatly compromised. Depending on the study design, it is estimated that 15–46% of patients with this disorder fail to fully comply with treatment (Connelly, 1984; Connelly, Davenport, & Nurnberger, 1982; Danion, Neureuther, Krieger-Finance, Imbs, & Singer, 1987; Kucera-Bozarth, Beck, & Lyss, 1982; Schwarcz & Silbergeld, 1983). Dropping out of treatment altogether is also common (Prien et al., 1984; Prien, Caffey, & Klett, 1973; Prien, Klett, & Caffey, 1973; Stallone, Shelley, Mendlewicz, & Fieve, 1973).

Traditional maintenance pharmacotherapy can also fail when symptom breakthroughs are not identified early enough and/or not appropriately treated and, therefore, become full episodes of depression or mania. The occurrence of subsyndromal or mild mood symptoms increases the risk of recurrences of depression and mania fourfold in those with bipolar disorder (Keller et al., 1991).

Symptom breakthroughs can be precipitated by environmental, organic, or unknown factors. Sleep disruption, for example, caused by somatic events such as medical illness, or by travel or schedule changes, is one of several mechanisms that may underlie symptom breakthroughs (Wehr, Sack, & Rosenthal, 1987). Psychosocial stressors also can precipitate the onset of episodes of illness in bipolar disorder (e.g., Aronson & Shukla, 1987; Bidzinska, 1984; Dunner, Murphy, Stallone, & Fieve, 1979; Glassner & Haldipur, 1983; Kennedy, Thompson, Stancer, Roy, & Persad, 1983; Kraepelin, 1921/1976), though perhaps more commonly in earlier episodes of depression and mania than in later ones (Goodwin & Jamison, 1990; Post, 1992). Environmental and other factors may interact. For example, preoccupation with psychosocial problems may cause patients to forget to take medication, may cause sleep disruption due to worry, or may be accompanied by severe and prolonged emotional distress that leads to relapses or recurrences of depression or mania. By implication, early identification might allow early intervention and, perhaps, prevention of an episode or quicker containment of symptoms.

USE OF PSYCHOSOCIAL TREATMENTS

A psychotherapeutic intervention, such as cognitive-behavioral therapy (CBT), can add to and enhance medical management by helping patients improve their adherence to pharmacotherapy, identifying subsyndromal symptoms such that early intervention may prevent a full relapse or recurrence or perhaps limit the length of a new episode, providing patients with techniques that may help combat subsyndromal symptoms, and teaching patients strategies for coping with common social and interpersonal stressors that may be triggers or exacerbating factors in depression or mania.

Some preliminary evidence indicates that psychotherapeutic interventions can augment the prophylactic effect of medication through improvement in treatment adherence and psychosocial functioning. In a 12-month study of the maintenance treatment of bipolar disorder, Davenport, Ebert, Adland, and Goodwin (1977) found that patients assigned to a couples psychotherapy group had fewer instances of rehospitalization and fewer marital failures, as well as better social functioning and family interaction, than did patients in a lithium maintenance group or community-based aftercare. Other long- and short-term group therapies, when combined with pharmacotherapy, have also been found to reduce the frequency and length of episodes and/or hospitalization in patients with bipolar disorder (Benson, 1975; Powell, Othmer, & Sinkhorn, 1977; Shakir, Volkmar, & Bacon, 1979; Wulsin, Bachop, & Hoffman, 1988). Shakir et al. (1979) found that long-term group psychotherapy for 15 patients with bipolar disorder reduced the frequency and length of hospitalizations and increased the number of patients continuously employed. Similarly, Powell et al. (1977) found that providing group therapy for patients with bipolar disorder limited relapse to only 15% of the 40 group participants over a 12-month period.

Some preliminary evidence suggests that CBT may improve treatment adherence in bipolar disorder. Cochran (1984) found that bipolar patients assigned to a 6-week cognitive therapy intervention were significantly less likely than the standard care group to be rated as having major adherence problems, terminating lithium against medical advice, having nonadherence-precipitated episodes, or being hospitalized. Although this was a short-term intervention and the results pertain to only 3- and 6-month posttreatment follow-up, Cochran's (1984) finding provides some evidence for the utility of individual CBT in increasing adherence as an adjunct to pharmacotherapy in the treatment of bipolar disorder.

CBT has been shown to be effective in acute or short-term (e.g., Murphy, Simons, Wetzel, & Lustman, 1984; Rush, Beck, & Kovacs, 1977) and possibly longer-term (e.g., Blackburn, Evanson, & Bishop, 1987) treatments of major depression. While never tested with prodromal symptoms of mania, CBT has been shown to be successful in treating the physical, cognitive, and behavioral symptoms associated with depression.

Bipolar disorder is generally considered a biologically driven illness, yet there is considerable evidence that psychosocial stressors can result from both the impaired judgment and functioning during episodes of illness and can also actually precipitate recurrences of depression and mania (e.g., Ambelas, 1979; Clancy, Crowe, Winokur, & Morrison, 1973; Dunner et al., 1979; Glassner, Haldipur, & Dessauersmith, 1979; Kennedy et al., 1983; Thomsen & Hendrie, 1972). (See Chapter 10 for a more thorough discussion.)

The onset of depression or mania causes changes in mood (e.g., sadness, elation, or irritability), changes in thinking or perceptions (e.g., worry, grandiosity, self-criticism), and changes in physiological processes (e.g., sleep, appetite, energy). These changes quickly manifest in behavioral changes such as increases or decreases in activity, productivity, or social interaction. These behavioral changes can and often do interfere with an individual's psychosocial functioning. The resulting problems— often financial or interpersonal—cause stress even after the episode has eased up. Psychosocial problems, in turn, produce symptoms such as insomnia and emotional distress. These symptoms can prolong the episode or leave bipolar patients vulnerable to relapse.

Mr. Bell is a 45-year-old computer salesman whose livelihood is completely dependent upon his ability to make new contacts and sell his products. When depressed, he has little energy and not much interest in being around people. He views himself as nonproductive and sees little hope for improvement. He "knows" that his wife is disappointed in him and that he is a "lousy salesman." Mr. Bell has trouble sleeping and when his alarm goes off at 6:00 A.M., he ignores it. During the day, he tries to complete some paperwork at home but finds it hard to concentrate. With great effort, he is able to complete the sales he has started, but cannot bring himself to call the new sales leads. It does not take long for Mr. Bell's decline in work activity to affect his income and ability to meet his financial obligations. He and his wife begin to argue over money. As the stress increases, his symptoms of depression worsen.

When Mr. Bell is hypomanic, the picture is quite different. His confidence in his sales ability is heightened. He inspires customers' confidence in him and his products. He sells day and night, hardly having time for social or family activities. "I am the greatest salesman in the world," he boasts to his friends. With confidence in future productivity, Mr. Bell buys a new Cadillac, a diamond ring for his wife, and season tickets to the Dallas Cowboys football games. Unfortunately, his sales frenzy does not last. His thinking becomes increasingly confused and his behavior disorganized. His confidence turns to impatience and rudeness with customers. Sales decline. Conflict with his wife ensues. Mania dominates his life and leaves him with the same despair he experiences with depression.

In Mr. Bell's case, the changes in behavior and subsequent decline in psychosocial functioning leave him with financial and marital problems. Even if symptoms remit with treatment, the remaining psychosocial problems create worry, stress, and hardship. The continued stress makes patients vulnerable to relapse. Thus, the cycle depicted in Figure 1.1 can repeat itself in time.

Traditional pharmacotherapy attempts to intervene at two places in the cycle. The first is to control symptoms during an acute episode of depression or mania. This is indicated by point B in Figure 1.2. The second point of intervention is prevention of relapses or recurrences of depression or mania through maintenance treatment. This is represented by point A in Figure 1.2. When prevention fails, the target of intervention is remediation of symptoms to forestall a full recurrence of depression or mania.

CBT can help at all phases. It can strengthen the acute, continuation, and maintenance phase pharmacotherapies by enhancing medication compliance and by offering patients additional nonpharmacological strategies for combating symptoms. This is shown at points A and B on Figure 1.3. CBT techniques for cognitive restructuring can also help to reduce dysfunctional cognitions and associated emotions that can lead to maladaptive changes in behavior (point C). If behavioral changes have occurred, CBT techniques can be used to increase activity when the lethargy or stagnation of depression keeps people from completing daily work, social, or family obligations. CBT methods for reduction, organization, and proper evaluation of activities can help to contain the increased volume and potentially dangerous nature of activities inspired by hypomania and mania. This is represented by point D on Figure 1.3. Structured problem-solving techniques can be used to prevent the development of serious psychosocial problems (point E). Once they have occurred, CBT methods can be used to help resolve problems and/or control the behavioral, affective, physical, or cognitive symptoms of depression and mania while problems of daily living are addressed (point F).

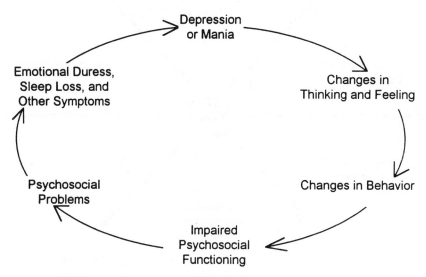

FIGURE 1.1. The phenomenological course for bipolar disorder.

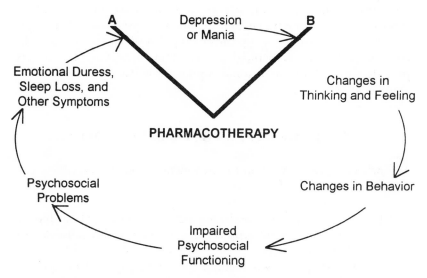

FIGURE 1.2. The targets of pharmacotherapy for bipolar disorder.

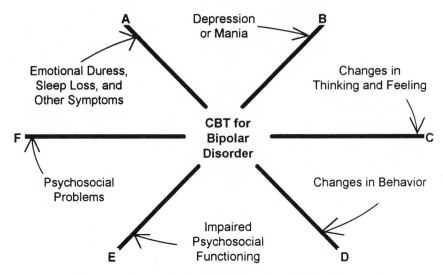

FIGURE 1.3. The targets of CBT interventions for bipolar disorder.

In summary, CBT for the maintenance phase treatment of bipolar disorder augments rather than replaces the pharmacological management of this illness. Teaching patients to monitor and control the subsyndromal symptoms of bipolar disorder, to reduce the obstacles to treatment adherence, and to cope with psychosocial stressors that can exacerbate the symptoms of the disorder may enhance the effectiveness of pharmacological treatments. The CBT techniques provide patients with additional coping strategies when medication alone is not enough.

GOALS OF CBT FOR BIPOLAR DISORDER

The primary goals of CBT in the treatment of bipolar disorder are as follows:

1. To educate patients and their significant others about bipolar disorder, treatment approaches, and common difficulties associated with the illness.
2. To teach patients a method for monitoring the occurrence, severity, and course of manic and depressive symptoms.
3. To facilitate compliance[1] with prescribed medication regimens.
4. To provide nonpharmacological strategies, specifically cognitive-

behavioral skills, for coping with the cognitive, affective, and behavioral problems associated with manic and depressive symptoms.

5. To assist patients in coping with stressors that may interfere with treatment or precipitate episodes of mania and/or depression.

The CBT approach to the treatment of bipolar disorder is based on several underlying assumptions. The first assumption is that the thoughts, feelings, and behaviors of people are tightly connected, each influencing the other. Shifts in mood and changes in cognitive processing with the onset of depression and mania inevitably influence behavior. The behavioral responses can reinforce the faulty information processing and affective states that stimulated the behavior—a kind of self-fulfilling prophecy. For example, Mr. Bell, who believes he is the best salesman in the world, is driven by the increased energy, motivation, activity, and confidence of his hypomanic state. Under these circumstances, he is selling products at an accelerated rate and volume. For the time being he *is* the best salesman in the world. Similarly, his blunted affect, low motivation, and impaired concentration when depressed prevent him from doing his job. His low productivity validates his view that he is incompetent. For the time being he *is* a "lousy salesman."

This vicious cycle, if left unchecked, can greatly exacerbate symptoms. Even when medication treatments are not optimally effective, interventions that break this escalating cycle can help to reduce symptomatology.

Ms. Galindo's mood seemed to change from week to week. Her roommate was never certain if she would come home to find her sitting in the corner of her darkened room or dancing in the halls. Ms. Galindo usually took medication for this problem, but it did not always prevent breakthrough symptoms of hypomania or depression. When she was in a good mood, she wanted to live each day to its fullest. She painted or worked on her pottery until the early hours of the morning, slept a few hours, and awakened to start again. She painted more and more and slept less and less until she became irritable, paranoid, and disorganized. Her belief that staying awake would help to prolong the euphoria was false. Her behavior (painting more and sleeping less) that followed from this belief and her exuberant mood served to push her further into mania. Her roommate knew the sequence of symptoms and the routine for getting Ms. Galindo to the hospital.

CBT is based on the notion that feelings, thoughts, and behaviors are interrelated. That is, they influence one another.

When Ms. Galindo felt blue (feelings), she reminisced about the past. She thought about the mistakes she had made and the people she had hurt (thoughts). She looked at herself, her life, and the distance she had to go to achieve her goals. She felt hopeless: "What's the use? I'll never make it." She stayed in her room, missed her classes, called in sick to work, and rejected help from her roommate (behavior). Ms. Galindo's mood and negative thinking appeared to evolve together. The more she thought about her bad experiences, the sadder she felt. The deepening of her gloom seemed to open the floodgates from which more negative thoughts flowed. Each bad thought seemed to pull another right behind it. Her sadness turned to hopelessness and then to despair. Her behavioral changes included isolation from others, not eating, poor hygiene, and failure to fulfill work and school responsibilities. Her inactivity had many consequences, such as missed deadlines, risk of termination of employment, and physical weakness. These consequences only seemed to worsen her mood, thus perpetuating the cycle of mood, cognitive, and behavioral changes.

In CBT, patients are taught to recognize the affective, cognitive, and behavioral patterns that worsen their symptoms. Once the pattern is recognized, CBT techniques can be used to "break the cycle" by modifying cognitive or behavioral responses. These symptoms can also serve as cues to seek better pharmacological control of symptoms.

The second underlying assumption of CBT for bipolar disorder is that patients who understand what it means to have bipolar disorder will be able to play a more active role in and make more informed decisions about their treatment. Therefore, patient education is introduced before CBT techniques are taught. Third, identification of the early warning signs of mania or depression provides an opportunity for early intervention and containment of symptoms. Education coupled with symptom monitoring tasks provides a vehicle for early identification of symptoms. Fourth, the addition of cognitive and/or behavioral interventions expands the patient's armamentarium against relapse. Milder prodromal symptoms may not require additional medications if they can be controlled with psychotherapeutic interventions. Fifth, enhanced medication compliance allows patients to receive the maximum benefit from treatment. CBT is of little use for bipolar patients when pharmacotherapy fails. Sixth, improved management of psychosocial problems that stress bipolar disorder patients and exacerbate symptoms may help to prevent relapses or recurrences of mania or depression. Seventh, the CBT approach emphasizes the teaching of skills for coping with the symptoms and consequences of bipolar disorder. That is, it assumes that not all problems will be solved during therapy sessions. Instead, presenting problems are used to facilitate the teaching of CBT techniques. This increases the patient's ability to cope with symptoms and problems between sessions. Thereby therapy becomes more than a series of crisis intervention visits.

CBT for bipolar disorder differs from the more traditional forms of cognitive therapy in several ways: (1) patients are usually not acutely ill during the psychoeducational and skills training sessions, (2) skills will be taught in a didactic fashion, (3) only a few basic cognitive-behavioral techniques will be taught, and (4) the agenda for each session is protocol driven as opposed to patient driven.

The bipolar CBT package is delivered over a 12-month period with weekly sessions. As with traditional cognitive therapy, homework is given at the end of each session. The chapters of this book match the sequence of therapy sessions. However, information and interventions for several therapy sessions may be covered in a single chapter. For example, in sessions 3 and 4, information on antimanic and antidepressant medications are introduced respectively. The information to be conveyed to patients is summarized in Chapter 3 on medication treatments for bipolar disorder. Table 1.1 lists the phases of treatment, session topics, and the chapters where the interventions are covered.

THE THERAPEUTIC ALLIANCE

Commitment

Working with patients who have bipolar disorder can be fascinating, challenging, and rewarding. It can also be difficult and frustrating. Although clinicians try to maintain positions of neutrality and objectivity, when faced with their patients' severe symptom fluctuations that seem unresponsive to even the most creative interventions they often find themselves passengers on an emotional roller coaster. Those times when clinicians perceive their efforts as futile; when they are intimately in touch with their powerlessness in the face of this chronic illness; when they feel most like throwing in the towel, referring patients elsewhere, and leaving on a 2-week trip to Hawaii are the times when individuals with bipolar disorder need their therapists the most.

These patients know that their futures are uncertain. They are likely to have experienced many problems in the past, and they know that there is more to come and that they will need help again. They want psychiatrists and psychotherapists who will help them through the difficult times. They need people who will tolerate their emotional outbursts, paranoia, periodic noncompliance, and financial hardships. Patients can sense the level

TABLE 1.1. Phases of Treatment and Session Topics

Phase	Topic	Chapter
Patient education		
Session 1	Overview of cognitive-behavioral therapy	1
Session 2	What is bipolar disorder?	2
Session 3	Mood-stabilizing medications	3
Session 4	Antidepressant medications	3
Session 5	Individual symptoms of bipolar disorder	4
Session 6	Symptom monitoring	4
Treatment compliance		
Session 7	Treatment compliance	5
Cognitive-behavioral interventions		
Session 8	Biased thinking	6
Session 9	Cognitive changes in depression	6
Session 10	Logical analysis of negative automatic thoughts	6
Session 11	Cognitive changes in mania	7
Session 12	Behavioral aspects of depression	8
Session 13	Behavioral changes in mania	9
Psychosocial problems		
Session 14	Psychosocial problems	10
Session 15	Assessment of psychosocial functioning	10
Session 16	Problem-solving skills development	10
Sessions 17–20	Resolution of psychosocial problems	11
Maintenance treatment		
1–4 sessions/month as clinically indicated	Review and utilization of CBT skills	

of their care provider's commitment to the therapeutic relationship. They grow anxious when they feel that support is being withdrawn. Clinicians may sometimes have difficulty hearing the anxiety underlying angry outbursts. They may misinterpret fear of abandonment as entitlement, demands, or symptoms of the illness needing immediate intervention, especially if they have treated the same person for many years and through many episodes of illness. Health care providers can begin to feel as burned out as family members often feel. Although patients with bipolar disorder may behave in an irritable and sometimes obnoxious manner, they are in distress when symptomatic. The withdrawal of support, attention, or affection from family, friends, or health care providers intensifies the pain. Clinicians' commitment to the therapeutic relationship is essential.

This is not to say that changes are not necessary at times. However, when treatment begins with a person with bipolar disorder, one is usually signing on to long-term care.

Collaboration

CBT hinges upon a strong collaborative relationship between patients and clinicians. Although CBT appears to be structured, the choice of intervention and the method of applying each technique must be tailored to the special problems, needs, and abilities of each individual. To accomplish this and to maximize the effectiveness of each intervention, active patient involvement is essential. This level of involvement can be difficult to achieve if both the patient and the clinician have been socialized into accepting the model of patient as passive recipient of care.

Clinicians can do several things to foster collaborations with patients—some behavioral, others attitudinal. For example, clinicians may invite patients to give opinions about treatment. Clinicians may ask what patients think will be efficacious and what has or has not been successful in dealing with symptoms or problems in the past. The underlying attitude that complements this behavior is one of respect for patients' opinions. Unfortunately, health care workers sometimes inaccurately assume that those with chronic psychiatric illnesses do not have the mental capacity to understand or to contribute to the development of their treatment plans, so they do not encourage these patients to contribute or, worse, dismiss patients' contributions.

When suggesting a new intervention, be it pharmacological or nonpharmacological, clinicians are wise to solicit patients' opinions. The underlying principle is that patients have a right to disagree with clinicians' ideas. Discussing their concerns and taking time to negotiate mutually acceptable treatment plans demonstrate clinicians' respect for this right. Except perhaps for those who are acutely ill, usually several treatment options are available.

Patients sometimes reject the option that clinicians prefer. Collaboration can mean implementing the patient's preferred strategy instead of the clinician's.

> Mr. Hubbard had several breakthrough symptoms of dysphoric mania during treatment. He and his psychiatrist decided that a trial of valproic acid might be helpful. They differed, however, on whether the medication change should take place in the hospital or on an outpatient basis. Mr. Hubbard preferred the latter; the psychiatrist and therapist, the former. Since there was no clear-cut evidence that hospitalization was

necessary, Mr. Hubbard's right to choose was respected and he was not pressured to go into the hospital (although such pressure would likely have been effective). The medication change was difficult for Mr. Hubbard and ultimately failed to reduce symptom breakthroughs. With perfect hindsight, he felt that hospitalization would have been better, but he was grateful for the respect for his right to choose.

The bottom line is that, when engaged in a collaborative treatment effort, patients sometimes make choices that in the short run may be unhelpful or even hurtful. In the long run, however, clinicians' respect for their patients' opinions and willingness to give patients' ideas the benefit of the doubt will build trust.

Humor

Therapy needs to be taken seriously, but humor can be a way to share a sense of togetherness with the patient. The process should balance the pain of addressing problems and the discomfort of self-exploration with the interest and excitement of an adventure. Patients need something to look forward to. Particularly with CBT, where patients are asked to explore and evaluate their distortions in thinking, gentle humor can be facilitative when the therapist is laughing with the patient, never at the patient. Humor, however, must feel comfortable and natural for the therapist. Joke telling by clinicians is not recommended, but allowing the patient to share a joke can help strengthen rapport and can indicate comfort and trust in the patient. Many patients have wonderful senses of humor, an asset that serves them well in other environments. This strength can be put to use in therapy.

It is usually best to let the patient take the lead when introducing humor into the session. Allow them to poke fun at you when you have done something amusing. Do not try to act funny to elicit laughs. This will give the impression that you will not take problems seriously. Allow patients to see you make errors, get confused, lose your keys, spill your coffee, and get tongue-tied, and chuckle along with them.

> Mrs. Paul had been coming to weekly therapy session for 3 months. She was comfortable with her therapist and seemed to enjoy and benefit from the sessions. She arrived early to one of her sessions to find the therapist searching through the office for something.
>
> THERAPIST: Hello, Mrs. Paul. I'll be with you in just a moment.
> PATIENT: Take your time; I'm a little early. Did you lose something?
> THERAPIST: Yes, I seemed to have misplaced my calendar. I don't know

what appointments I have today. I'll just have to sit here and wait to see who will walk through the door at the top of each hour.

PATIENT: Oh. That's too bad.

THERAPIST: It's a good thing my head is screwed on real tight or I might lose that too.

PATIENT: (*Laughs.*) You know what's nice? You are the first therapist I've had that I didn't think was perfect.

THERAPIST: (*Looks confused.*) Thanks . . . I think. (*Both laugh.*)

In this example, humor models for the patient a tolerance for and even an expectation of imperfection in oneself. It can communicate several other important messages as well: "It's OK to make a mistake. Even therapists make mistakes." "I do not expect myself to be perfect; therefore, I do not expect you to be perfect." "It is important to keep things in perspective. Small events deserve small amounts of emotion. Big events deserve more." "Errors do not have to spoil your whole day."

Humor is not helpful when it is critical, mean, disruptive, overly time consuming, distracting, or not well received by the patient. Obviously, if it is in poor taste, targets other patients, or is used at inappropriate moments, such as when the topic of the session is serious and painful for the patient, humor is unacceptable. Jokes do not lighten an intense therapeutic exchange the way comic relief distracts the audience during a sad movie. If you are new to the use of humor in therapy, get supervision from a more experienced clinician.

WORKING WITH OTHER HEALTH CARE PROVIDERS

Clinicians from a variety of disciplines—psychiatrists, psychologists, nurses, and counselors—can use the cognitive-behavioral approach to the maintenance phase treatment of bipolar disorder. It is not uncommon for persons with bipolar disorder to receive some form of care from more than one health care provider, usually a psychiatrist and a therapist or counselor. Clinicians who have engaged in this type of joint treatment find it particularly important to know what the other health care providers are doing, as patients find it confusing and stressful when they receive conflicting information from two different health care professionals. Family members may add to the confusion and stress by offering a third set of suggestions or beliefs.

The cognitive-behavioral therapist can help to be supportive of medication management, just as the psychiatrist can reinforce and encourage the use of CBT methods. In many cases, however, neither clinician may be aware of the other's strategies, goals, conceptualizations of the problems, and philosophies of care. The therapist providing CBT can expand the treatment collaboration by engaging the other health care providers in a team effort, provided that the patient is open to this process. The therapist, with the permission of the patient, can get the ball rolling by letting the other health care providers know what CBT offers, how it works, and how it may be helpful. Encouraging the patient to share the work in CBT with other health care providers or social workers and forwarding periodic progress notes enhance this process. The amount of contact between clinicians will vary with the severity of the patient's symptoms (i.e., more contact when symptoms are severe, as in acute exacerbations, and less contact when the patient's condition is relatively stable).

At times, some patients may attempt to form an alliance with one health care provider against another. This behavior, while likely unintentional, can cause frustration and distress for members of the treatment team. Strain can also develop in the working relationship when one clinician disagrees with another's treatment decisions. In working with other health care providers, clinicians should strive to convey consistent messages to patients. When concerns arise about another's clinical practices, it is best not to voice criticism in the presence of the patient. Clinicians can generally resolve these disagreements more effectively, first by giving each other the benefit of the doubt that there is a rationale for practice choices and, second, by taking time to discuss concerns directly with the other health care provider.

GETTING STARTED

When faced with problems, people usually try to cope in some way. Their behaviors may be effective or ineffective, passive or direct, planned or reactive. CBT uses patients' strengths and experiences to help build a repertoire of coping skills. To begin this process, it is helpful to take inventory of patients' strengths or coping resources. Table 1.2 lists some of the resources that people may use to cope with special problems and daily demands. Throughout the course of treatment, a cumulative list placed in the chart can refresh clinicians' and patients' memories of coping strategies that have been effective in the past. When developing an intervention to address new problems or symptoms, clinicians can begin by building on these strengths.

Before treatment focuses on specific problems or symptoms, it can be time efficient and valuable for patient–clinician rapport to ask what coping strategies have already been tried. This provides an opportunity for the clinician to assess patients' usual coping behaviors and avoids the

TABLE 1.2. Coping Resources

1. Intelligence	14. Health insurance
2. Education	15. Good physical health
3. Skills training	16. Physical strength or stamina
4. Problem-solving ability	17. Energy
5. Frustration tolerance/patience	18. Motivation
6. Creativity	19. Assertiveness
7. Interpersonal/social skill	20. Confidence
8. Communication ability	21. Good reality testing
9. Sense of humor	22. Ability to mobilize resources
10. Friends or supportive family members	23. Ability to ask for help
11. Ability to get along with coworkers	24. Common sense
12. Ability to maintain employment	25. Chocolate
13. Financial resources	

pitfall of reinventing the wheel with new interventions. Asking how they have dealt with problems in the past communicates several important relationship messages. It says that the clinician is interested in what patients have to say, views them as competent individuals who are capable of action in response to problems, and does not view himself or herself as one who "knows what is best" for everyone or as one who has "all the answers." These relationship messages can help to develop a collaborative working relationship. In addition, assessment of previous coping strategies and an analysis of the reasons that these interventions succeeded or failed will help in future treatment planning.

To enhance collaboration with patients, provide them with a road map of your plans for therapy. Explain how CBT works, that it is *not* a replacement for medication, and what they can expect to learn during the course of treatment. Suggestions are given in each chapter for introducing interventions to patients. In the beginning, an overview of the treatment goals and methods is sufficient.

PATIENT EDUCATION

Although few clinicians would disagree with the importance of educating people about their general medical illnesses and treatment, people with psychiatric illnesses do not always receive sufficient information about their disorders or their treatment. Either party may be responsible for this gap in communication. Symptoms such as impaired concentration, racing thoughts, distractibility, and anxiety may not always be apparent to clinicians, but can reduce a person's comprehension or retention of information. Likewise, clinicians may not effectively convey information or may not take sufficient time to educate patients. The jargon used in daily interactions among coworkers is often confusing to patients (e.g., "You are having a breakthrough of hypomania" or "You may be having a recurrence of major depression"). Patients can sometimes recall a diagnosis given in the past, but may not understand what it means. They will not always ask for clarification because they are embarrassed to acknowledge that they did not understand a word or expression used to describe their illness or treatment. Sometimes health care workers fail to provide adequate information because they believe that the patient is incapable of understanding, is disinterested, or has already been informed by a previous clinician.

Sometimes the information provided about diagnosis or treatment is too general or too vague. Patients may think that they understand what their doctors have said, and the doctors may think that they have provided perfectly clear explanations, but both may be wrong. A simple example is, "You need to watch your diet and get some exercise." This common recommendation lacks sufficient detail to alter a person's behavior in the grocery store or at the dinner table.

> After being told to take better care of his body, Mr. Chavez left the office feeling irritated. He said, "That doctor expects me to buy a membership at one of those fancy health clubs. I can't afford that." Mr. Chavez incorrectly assumed that his doctor was recommending a health club. The doctor had made no specific recommendations about the kind of exercise appropriate for the patient, but thought Mr. Chavez understood that all he needed to do was to walk for 15 to 20 minutes three to four times per week.

Despite good intentions, learning does not occur if information is not clearly sent and received.

In busy clinics or practices there is often little time for patient education. By necessity, clinicians must curtail their visits in order to see a large number of patients. While there may be many reasonable explanations for poor patient education, there are few legitimate excuses.

Why Patient Education Is Important

There is some evidence that patient education can improve adherence to treatment and ease adjustment to the illness. Peet and Harvey (1991) randomized 60 lithium clinic patients to either participate in an educational group that viewed a 12-minute videotaped lecture on lithium and received a written transcript or to receive standard pharmacotherapy. Measurements of patients' attitudes toward lithium and understanding of lithium treatment before and after the educational video showed a significant improvement after the educational lectures.

Van Gent and Zwart (1991) provided educational sessions to 14 bipolar disorder patients and their partners. After five educational sessions and a 6-month follow-up, the patients' partners demonstrated more understanding of the illness, of lithium, and of social strategies for coping with their partners' symptoms. Patients' serum lithium levels did not change in the year following the education program from the levels achieved during the program. This suggests that the education program may have helped to prevent the deterioration in compliance over time often found in lithium-treated patients.

Altamura and Mauri (1985) and Youssel (1983) also tested the effectiveness of patient education in improving treatment compliance in depressed outpatients. Both studies indicated that patients who received information about their illness were more likely to follow the prescribed treatment regimen.

In a more elaborate patient education study, Seltzer, Roncari, and Garfinkel (1980) provided nine lectures for inpatients on their diagnosis, course of treatment, medication, side effects, relapse, and importance of social support. Based on diagnosis and current medication type, 44 patients with schizophrenia, 16 with bipolar disorder, and 7 with major depression were placed in either education groups or a no education control group. Compliance was measured through pill counts or medication blood levels. Five months later, patients in the education groups demonstrated greater treatment adherence and were less fearful of side effects and drug dependency than were those in the control group. The noncompliance rate for educational group members was 9%, while the noncompliance rate for the control group was 66%.

These studies provide some examples of the value of patient education. It is difficult to say if the type of effect observed (e.g., decreased side effects, better compliance) is dependent on the type of information provided to patients. Psychiatric patients, like all other patients, can be better participants in the treatment process if they understand the nature of the disorder and their role in its treatment.

Why Family Education Is Important

When Mr. Chen had his first episode of mania, his wife was frightened and confused. She had no experience with mental illness and did not know what to make of her husband's strange behavior. At first, she thought he was just being "a little hyper." In fact, his new attitude was a nice change from his otherwise serious demeanor. His talkativeness and humor were appealing. He seemed interested in doing everything. He would wake up in the early morning and work in the garage on various projects until it was time to go to work. He did not seem to tire. His sex drive was revitalized, and his enthusiasm was unending. These benign activities did not last for long, however. Soon he wanted to make changes that caused some concerns. They were a middle-income family with one child in high school and a second beginning college. They had saved some money for their son's college tuition, but relied on their current income to meet their present needs. Mr. Chen wanted to sell their house and buy a larger one in a new neighborhood. He talked about quitting his job and opening a business in his garage. Mrs. Chen thought that he was just dreaming until he came home in the middle of the workday with $1,000 worth of equipment to start his new business. Mr. Chen's functioning began to deteriorate. He missed work to set up his new workshop in the garage. In fact, he spent every waking moment on his new projects. He slept little and became very irritable. Mrs. Chen had trouble understanding him, as he talked in torrents and jumped from subject to subject. When she saw him in the garage in the nude, shouting at someone she could not see, she knew that he was ill. She called her family doctor, who helped her to get her husband to the hospital. After an evaluation of his condition, Mr. Chen was admitted to an inpatient psychiatric unit. It all happened so fast that Mrs. Chen wondered if she had done the right thing.

Family members will have many questions about the symptoms of mania and depression, the treatment, and the prognosis for the future. Educating family members about bipolar disorder serves two functions. First, it helps the family members cope with their own pain and suffering and prepares them for difficult times to come. Second, it enlists them as active participants in the treatment process.

Those who live with, have regular contact with, or who may be in a position to assist patients with treatment should be involved in the education process. Spouses, children, and parents are good candidates. Sometimes friends of the family are included as well. The real question is, who does the patient want involved in the treatment? It is necessary to tailor the involvement of significant others to the special needs of each individual. As always, it is important for the clinician to protect the confidentiality of patient information and to seek patients' permission before communicating clinical information to significant others.

When to Educate Patients and Their Family Members

Every contact with patients and their family members is an opportunity to educate them about living with bipolar disorder. The most obvious time is when the initial diagnosis is made. Often this occurs in an emergency room or inpatient unit when the patient is acutely ill. As patients' mental statuses clear, the education process begins. The treatment team must be prepared to answer questions such as:

- "What has happened to me?"
- "What caused this?"
- "Why do I have to take this medication?"
- "Do I have to take this medication for the rest of my life?"
- "When can I get out of the hospital?"
- "When will I be back to normal?"
- "Is it going to happen again?"

After patients' discharge from the hospital, the education process continues. Because, as was mentioned earlier, the symptoms experienced during the acute phase of treatment may have interfered with patients' abilities to grasp all the provided information, clinicians responsible for outpatient follow-up care can probe for how much information was retained and fill in any gaps. As with most things, learning can be facilitated by using everyday experiences to illustrate the concepts being taught. Each outpatient visit offers an opportunity for clinicians to inquire about the experiences their clients may have had with the symptoms of bipolar disorder and the treatment.

It is common for patients to change health care providers several times during the course of their lives. At each transition point, the education process begins again. Even if individuals previously received care from prominent clinicians with reputations for educating patients and their significant others, those who later care for patients should never assume that further education is unnecessary. Furthermore, as research continues to expand our understanding of the psychobiology and treatment of mood disorders, there will be new information to share.

Clinicians differ in their treatment philosophies. For example, some psychiatrists teach patients to make changes in their medication regimen when breakthroughs of depression or mania seem imminent. Others prefer to discuss any change in dosage with patients before any such adjustment. Patients may not know that there are different strategies for controlling symptoms of bipolar disorder, depending on their symptoms; their lifestyles; and the preferences, training, and comfort of the physicians. They may logically assume that a new psychiatrist will provide the same care as the former one. When treating new patients, clinicians can reduce misunderstandings by sharing their treatment philosophy. If that philosophy of care does not match the patients' needs, it is best to discuss this early in treatment and, if necessary, refer them elsewhere.

How to Educate Patients and Their Family Members

Some people take time to read about the illness, attend lectures, and converse with others about the special problems associated with bipolar disorder. Although seemingly well informed, these individuals may, nevertheless, need clarification or additional information. Pamphlets and self-help books can provide a great amount of information. To check their understanding of the material, clients and their significant others should have opportunities to ask questions about and discuss any new informational pamphlets that they may have read. Several books, pamphlets, and videotapes are available to facilitate the education process. While useful and highly recommended, these materials should be viewed as supporting the education process between clinicians and patients/families. The process will vary depending on the clinical setting and the resources available for patient education, but clinicians who are primarily responsible for care should take time to inform patients and their significant others about their diagnoses and treatment of bipolar disorder. Written materials may not be available in the hospital or clinic, but they can be acquired from bookstores or the National Depressive and Manic Depressive Association (DMDA), the National Mental Health Association (MHA), the National Alliance for the Mentally Ill (NAMI), and other consumer organizations. The telephone numbers and addresses of these organizations appear in the Appendix and can be shared with patients so that additional educational materials can be sought out. Organizations such as NAMI and the DMDA also have meetings one to four times each month that often include presentations by mental health professionals. Patients and their family members generally find these educational opportunities very helpful.

If the patient or family members have examined videotaped or written information, the health care provider should set aside time to answer questions and to translate the information presented into an individualized plan for the patient's care.

CHAPTER SUMMARY

Bipolar disorder is a chronic and recurrent mental illness. Maintenance treatment aimed at prevention of future episodes of depression and mania is critical, but often fails because of poor medication compliance and lack of recognition and aggressive treatment of subsyndromal symptom breakthroughs.

The goals of CBT are to:

1. Engage patients as active participants in their care by providing them with information about the illness, treatment approaches, and common difficulties associated with the illness.
2. Sensitize patients to the onset of depression and mania so that early identification and early treatment of subsyndromal symptoms can occur to avoid full recurrences of illness.
3. Facilitate medication compliance.
4. Provide nonpharmacological interventions to augment control of the cognitive and behavioral symptoms of depression and mania.
5. Prevent and resolve psychosocial stressors.

The affective, cognitive, and physiological changes in depression and mania lead to behavioral responses that can create problems for patients. These problems are often stressful and can exacerbate symptoms. CBT aims at breaking the cycle between cognitive and affective changes and problematic behavioral responses to decrease symptoms and minimize the psychosocial sequelae of this illness. The intervention begins with an assessment of patients' strengths and an introduction to CBT methods. This is followed by intensive education about the illness, its symptoms, its course, and available treatments.

When initiating CBT, establishing a collaborative working relationship is essential. This is enhanced by an environment where patients have opportunities to ask questions, give suggestions, and even disagree with their therapists. Humor can be facilitative if used judiciously. Finally, when patients are receiving care from another mental health professional, open communication between health care providers can help avoid confusion for patients and can reinforce one another's treatment efforts.

NOTE

1. Some argue that noncompliance is an accusatory label that assigns blame to patients (e.g., Meichenbaum & Turk, 1988). A "kinder and gentler" word such as *nonadherence* is recommended in lieu of noncompliance. This semantic switch attempts to refocus clinicians' views on noncompliance from resistance by patients to a collaborative error. Despite the change in terminology, however, most clinicians continue to view noncompliance or nonadherence as the fault of the patient. We believe that a semantic face-lift is insufficient to change clinicians' views on noncompliance. Therefore, while we use the words *compliance* and *adherence* interchangeably, we will attempt to introduce a different perspective—one that makes compliance a shared responsibility of both patients and clinicians.

TWO

Recognition and Diagnosis of Bipolar Disorder

SESSION 2. WHAT IS BIPOLAR DISORDER?

Purpose of the Session

In this session, the therapist will provide information regarding the definition and etiology of bipolar disorder. This process will help to clarify misconceptions patients or family members may have regarding the nature of bipolar illness.

Goals of the Session

1. Provide descriptive definitions and examples of depression, mania, and bipolar disorder.
2. Briefly review the biological aspects of affective disorders.
3. Discuss the relationship between psychosocial factors, such as stress, and recurrences of depression and mania.

Procedure

1. Elicit feedback on the reading assignment from the previous session. If the homework was not completed, use the compliance intervention (Chapter 5) and add the reading materials to the next homework assignment.
2. Discuss how the diagnosis of bipolar disorder is defined. Provide examples of symptoms. Ask patients and family members to describe their experiences with mania, depression, and any other symptoms.
3. Assign reading material as homework.

Recommended Reading

American Psychiatric Association (1990). *Facts about Manic Depression.*

Bipolar disorders fall within the mood disorders group in the fourth edition of the *Diagnostic and Statistical Manual of Mental Disorders* (DSM-IV; American Psychiatric Association, 1994). The central feature of these disorders is a mood disturbance that occurs along with a number of additional diagnostic and associated symptoms that cause significant disability or distress. These mood disturbances include episodes of major depression, mania, hypomania, and mixed episodes.

Mood disorders are generally underrecognized in practice. In fact, fewer than one in three people with mood disorders are in treatment today. Perhaps because the mood disturbances are "explained away" by both the individual and the practitioner as "normal" responses to life events, these illnesses are not detected early or accurately and, therefore, are not properly diagnosed and treated. Since it is clear that life stresses precipitate episodes of mood disorders, their occurrence should increase clinicians' suspicions that mood disorders may be present.

This chapter provides a brief synopsis of the diagnostic issues relevant to bipolar disorders. This summary is not a substitute for proper diagnostic training. For further detailed information on diagnosis, the reader is encouraged to consult DSM-IV (American Psychiatric Association, 1994) and, for background, *DSM-IV Made Easy* (Morrison, 1995).

MOOD EPISODES

Major depressive episodes are characterized by a change in mood, usually extreme sadness (although sometimes with anxiety or irritability) or an inability to experience pleasure or enjoyment. These changes in mood are accompanied by several other symptoms including:

- Disturbances in sleep (oversleeping or insomnia).
- Disturbances in appetite or weight regulation (increase or decrease).
- Inability to concentrate or make decisions.
- Thoughts of death or suicide.
- Feelings of guilt or extreme self-criticism.
- Low energy level or fatigue.
- Psychomotor changes (agitation or retardation).

These episodes are associated with significant disability or distress. In 10–15% of people, the depressive episodes come with hallucinations or delusion (i.e., psychotic depression). These major depressive episodes last 6–18 months; 9–12 months is a reasonable average.

Although most of these episodes remit naturally, even without treatment, they unfortunately return over time. In fact, the more previous episodes of major depression, the more likely another episode will occur. depressive disorder, Seventy-five percent of the time the episodes remit fully. In 5% of people, the episodes last longer than 2 years. In 20% of people, the episodes may end in 12 months, but between full episodes of major depression residual depressive symptoms, distress, and disability are present.

Risk factors for having a major depressive episode include being female and having a positive history in a close biological relative of major depressive disorder, bipolar I or bipolar II disorder, or (in women) postpartum (1–6 months following childbirth) depression. Factors that can precipitate or prolong major depressive episodes include life stresses, many kinds of general medical illnesses, substance or alcohol abuse, poor social support, and some other psychiatric disorders, such as anorexia nervosa, bulimia, and obsessive–compulsive disorder.

Manic episodes are almost the opposite of major depressive episodes. Instead of feeling sad, people often feel euphoric, extremely happy, and extraordinarily enthusiastic about a very wide range of ideas and activities. The diagnostic criteria of the American Psychiatric Association (1994) for a manic episode include a discrete period of abnormally and persistently elevated, expansive, or irritable mood lasting at least 7 days when at least three of the following symptoms or signs are also present in the same period:

- Inflated self-esteem/grandiosity.
- Marked decrease in need for sleep.
- Much more talkative than usual (pressure speech) or flight of ideas (rapidly racing thoughts).
- Marked distractibility.
- Increased goal-directed activity/psychomotor agitation.
- Excessive involvement in pleasurable activities without regard for obvious and frequent negative consequences.

These episodes, by definition, are severe enough to substantially impair function or require hospitalization to prevent harm to self or others.

Early in a manic episode, these individuals often feel euphoric, but over time mood often changes to intense feelings of hostility or anger. Sometimes those in a manic episode have poor judgment about the ultimate success of new and risky projects and get into trouble with the law, with investments, or with other people. Because they have an excessive level of energy when in a manic episode, these individuals do not feel the need to sleep and do not sleep very much.

Speech and thinking increase in amount and in speed as the mania worsens. In more severe manic episodes there may be a nearly continuous flow of very rapid speech. Sometimes during a manic episode, people are very humorous, but more often their humor is sarcastic, hostile, insensitive, or even bizarre. The manic person may jump from topic to topic, either based on obvious associations between the topics or based on the presence of distracting stimuli, such as background noise or even pictures on the wall. Sometimes, speech may be grossly disorganized and incoherent.

Initially in manic episodes, there is often an increase in goal-directed activities (e.g., excessive planning of, or participation in, multiple occupational, political, or religious activities). For example, there is often a marked increase in interpersonal activities such as efforts to renew old acquaintances or call friends at all hours of the day and night. Manic individuals are usually unaware of how intrusive, domineering, or demanding their behavior actually appears to others. Often, judgment is so impaired that it leads to foolish or dangerous activities that are out of character (e.g., buying sprees, reckless driving, significant financial misjudgments, or sexual indiscretions). Manic episodes lead to substantial dysfunction at work or at home. Thus, even though people, when in a manic episode, may initially feel very good, they usually have increasing difficulty in carrying out their routine, daily obligations.

Sometimes manic episodes are associated with psychotic symptoms (hallucinations or delusions). Hallucinations refer to the presence of voices or visions that others do not hear or see. Delusions are fixed false beliefs that cannot be changed with logical argument or objective evidence. For example, a manic person may think she is the Virgin Mary. When psychotic, coherent thinking, logical conversation, and planning become difficult to impossible, hospitalization is virtually always needed for the patients' own protection.

Manic episodes are time limited. They usually last between a few weeks and several months, averaging perhaps 1–3 months. However, the length of these episodes can be highly variable even in the same individual over time.

MOOD DISORDERS

Unipolar Disorders

Mood disorders can be divided into bipolar (two poles) and unipolar (one pole) disorders. Bipolar disorders are distinguished from unipolar disorders by the presence of manic, hypomanic, or mixed manic episodes. Unipolar disorders include major depressive disorder (which may be single or recurrent), dysthymic disorder, and depressive disorder, not otherwise specified (NOS). Most individuals with major depressive disorder have periods of wellness interspersed with episodes of major depression that, if untreated, last somewhere between 9 and 18 months. If a person has had only a single major depressive episode, the chances of a second are 50–60%. If the person has already had two episodes of major depression, the chance of a third is approximately 70%. With three episodes, the chance of another is about 90% (National Institutes of Health/National Institute of Mental Health, 1985).

Recurrent major depression is common in close relatives of people with bipolar I disorder, bipolar II disorder, or recurrent major depressive disorder. Approximately 12% of first-degree relatives (mother, father, brother, sister, or children) of people with bipolar disorder have major depressive disorder. Another 12% have bipolar disorder (Rush et al., 1991).

People with dysthymic disorder have a chronic course of symptoms that are less severe than are those associated with major depression. These individuals do not function to their potential and are often distressed and disabled for a long period of time. They often have a chronically negative outlook, poor concentration, low energy, little interest, and low self-esteem. Although their symptoms are not severe enough to warrant a diagnosis of major depressive disorder within the first 2 years of the onset of the illness, such individuals usually go on to develop episodes of major depression (i.e., major depressive disorder) after some years. Without treatment, full recovery from dysthymic disorder is rare. The episodes of major depression tend to come and go, but the dysthymic symptoms usually persist between these episodes.

Bipolar Disorders

Bipolar disorders are mood disorders that are typically lifelong episodic conditions. They feature two kinds of mood episodes of differing polarity—major depressive and manic episodes. Manic episodes may also be expressed in a less severe form (hypomanic episodes) or mixed with depressive symptoms (mixed manic episodes). All three types of episodes are viewed as being on the manic pole. These recurrent mood episodes (major depressive, manic, hypomanic, or mixed manic) are interspersed over time with periods of well-being or euthymia. Bipolar disorders include bipolar I, bipolar II, cyclothymic, and bipolar disorder, not otherwise specified (NOS).

Bipolar I disorder is characterized by one or more manic episodes. Clues that may alert the practitioner to suspect the ultimate development of bipolar disorder in patients presenting with major depressive disorder are:

- A family history of bipolar disorder.
- Early onset (in the teens) of the first major depressive episode.
- High frequency of recurrent major depressive episodes (i.e., more than two per year).
- Very prominent psychomotor retardation or hypersomnia when in major depressive episodes.

Some people with bipolar I disorder experience not only classic major depressive and manic episodes, but mixed episodes as well. In mixed manic episodes, the symptoms of both major depressive and manic episodes are present at the same time (i.e., in the same day). In some cases, the patients feel extremely gloomy, depressed, and suicidal at one time during the day, but are extremely euphoric and convinced of the success of virtually everything to be undertaken at another time in the day. In other cases, they meet the criteria for mania, but are irritable and the valance of their rapid thinking is negative. They are often hopeless, believe that they are worthless, cry frequently, and contemplate suicide. That is, these patients feel both depressive and manic symptoms nearly simultaneously. Mixed manic episodes are extremely disabling and often psychotic. Mixed episodes only account for approximately 6–10% of all mood episodes in bipolar disorders, but they lead to great dysfunction, suffering, and often suicide attempts.

Bipolar I disorder is usually characterized by one or more major depressive episodes and one or more manic or mixed manic episodes. Bipolar I disorder affects approximately 0.6–1% of the population (about 1 in 100), which is about the same percentage affected by idiopathic (unexplained) epilepsy. It occurs in men and women equally. The usual age at onset of the first episode of illness is between 18 and 30 years of age.

A recently recognized variant of bipolar I disorder is bipolar II disorder. Bipolar II disorder features one or more major depressive episodes interspersed with one or more hypomanic episodes. Hypomanic episodes are similar to manic episodes in symptom features except they are less severe. In fact, in hypomanic episodes there may be a marked increase in productivity or periods of extreme well-being. Hypomanic episodes are not just a few good days. During a hypomanic episode, people are clearly different from their usual selves. There is, as in manic episodes, decreased need to sleep, rapid thinking, euphoria or irritability, and a significant to marked increase in activity. When in a hypomanic episode, they may feel fine and even be quite productive, though close friends can see clearly that they are different from their normal selves. There may be only mild functional disability. In fact, greater confidence and optimism may lead these individuals to try new, and sometimes risky, activities. Hypomanic episodes usually tend to last days to weeks although some may be more prolonged. They alternate with asymptomatic periods (normal functioning) and periods of major depression. It is possible for someone to develop bipolar II disorder initially but later develop full-blown manic episodes. About 10% of those with bipolar II disorder develop bipolar I disorder over the first 5 years of the illness. The diagnosis of bipolar II disorder is changed to bipolar I disorder once a person has had one manic or mixed episode.

Bipolar I and II disorders are the most severe forms of bipolar disorder, but other types do occur. For example, in cyclothymic disorder, an illness that falls within the bipolar group, people have brief spells of hypomania (i.e., some mild manic symptoms) interspersed with brief spells of mild depression (i.e., symptoms that are not of sufficient number or duration to meet the criteria for major depressive episodes). There is rarely a time when no symptoms are present. Although these individuals may function adequately from time to time, they may also have substantial functional disability. They face day-to-day problems that result from being unpredictably "up" or "down," and it is difficult for them to make plans. Although by definition, cyclothymic symptoms last a minimum of 2 years, cyclothymic disorder is chronic, often lasting many years. About 15–25% of patients with cyclothymic disorder go on to develop bipolar I or II disorder (i.e., patients either develop full mania or full major depressive episodes). Cyclothymic disorder affects less than 0.5% of the population.

Bipolar disorder, NOS, is a residual category for patients with a bipolar type of mood disorder that does not clearly fit the bipolar I, bipolar II, or cyclothymic disorder categories.

COURSE OF ILLNESS FOR BIPOLAR DISORDER

Individuals with bipolar I or II disorder experience, in addition to episodes of major depression and episodes of mania, periods of normalcy that may last weeks, months, or even years. Figure 2.1 illustrates the different courses of illness of bipolar I disorder. The manic, hypomanic, or major depressive episodes do not necessarily follow a predictable order. Some people have two or three episodes of mania followed by one or two episodes of depression. In others, episodes of mania alternate somewhat more predictably with episodes of major depression, or manic episodes predictably follow depressive episodes.

Over a lifetime, a person with untreated bipolar I disorder suffers approximately 8–12 major depressive episodes and approximately 4–8 manic episodes. Over time, the length of both the depressive and manic episodes often increases, while the length of euthymic (symptom-free) periods decreases. That is, the individual may spend even more time being ill than well, as the illness progresses.

The course of bipolar I or II disorders have several variations. In some cases, especially in northern latitudes, the major depressive episodes are tied to the seasons of the year. Typically, the depressive episodes

1. Depression Following Manic Episodes

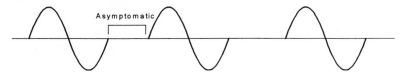

2. Manic and Depressive Episodes Independent of Each Other

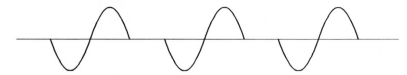

3. Manic, Hypomanic, and Depressive Episodes

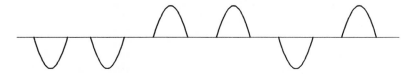

4. Depressive Episodes Precede Manic Episodes

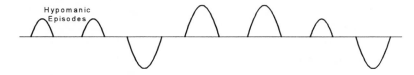

5. Rapid Cycling (at least 4 mood episodes per year)

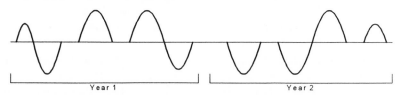

FIGURE 2.1. Examples of bipolar courses of illness.

occur consistently in the fall and remit in the spring, probably because of the shift in the light–dark cycle (Bauer & Dunner, 1996). This pattern usually recurs from year to year so that the fall of each year brings a major depressive episode. The seasonal form of bipolar disorder seems more likely in patients with bipolar II disorder (10%) than bipolar I disorder (1–3%).

Another pattern is called "rapid cycling." This pattern occurs in 5–15% of patients with either bipolar I or bipolar II disorder. By definition, a rapid cycling pattern involves four or more episodes of illness (major depressive, manic, mixed manic, or hypomanic) within a 12-month period. Women are more likely to have a rapid cycling pattern than men. Some evidence indicates that thyroid dysfunction can cause a rapid cycling pattern. In addition, some antidepressant medications may induce rapid cycling in some patients with bipolar I or II disorder. The prognosis for those with rapid cycling bipolar disorder is poorer than the prognosis for those without a rapid cycling pattern. Treatment for bipolar I or II disorder with a rapid cycling pattern is more likely to include the use of anticonvulsant medications. Lithium alone is not as effective as for those without a rapid cycling pattern.

Women with bipolar I or II disorder are at a greater risk for developing a major depressive, manic, or mixed manic episode during the postpartum period (i.e., 1 to 6 months following childbirth). Perhaps 10% of women with bipolar I or II disorder have such postpartum precipitated episodes. If a woman experiences a psychotic postpartum depressive or manic episode after the birth of one child, the risk of repeating this pattern with each subsequent birth is over 50%. Careful treatment with medication beginning immediately after delivery may prevent these postpartum episodes.

ESTABLISHING THE DIAGNOSIS OF BIPOLAR DISORDER

To establish the diagnosis of bipolar I or II disorder, clinicians should be trained and experienced in recognizing and diagnosing psychiatric conditions, as well as general medical conditions that may cause a mood disorder which looks like but is not, in fact, bipolar I or II disorder. In addition, an accurate history is essential to making the diagnosis. It is best to obtain this history from both the patient and a close friend or relative who has known the patient well for at least several years. The most common problem in obtaining an accurate history is that people do not recognize or report manic or hypomanic episodes. In fact, they often do not seek treatment when manic or hypomanic; they seek treatment when depressed. But the nature of the depressive episode itself does not distinguish between bipolar I and II and major depressive disorders. By carefully questioning their past history of symptoms, a far clearer and more accurate history can be obtained, which is essential.

Misdiagnosis has serious consequences. The wrong medicine may be given, the prognosis can be wrong, and the overall management of the patient will suffer. The three most common diagnostic errors are (1) mistaking recurrent major depressive episodes for normal reactions to life's difficulties, (2) failing to detect manic or hypomanic episodes, and (3) judging the patient to have schizophrenia instead of bipolar disorder with psychotic, manic, mixed manic, or major depressive episodes.

Finally, it is very common for patients with bipolar disorder to episodically (or less commonly, chronically) abuse alcohol, stimulants (amphetamines, cocaine), or other substances. In some, this is an attempt to -medicate. For others, these substances precipitate specific episodes. Thus, the presence or history of substance abuse should not discount the diagnosis of bipolar disorder. On the other hand, if all of the manic or hypomanic episodes are caused by substance abuse and largely end when the abuse stops, the diagnosis Of bipolar disorder should not be made.

THE MEANING OF HAVING BIPOLAR DISORDER

The diagnosis of bipolar disorder carries substantial personal meaning to people, meanings that differ based on each individual's background and experience. Patient concerns regarding the meaning of the diagnosis and its consequences deserve clinical attention prior to embarking on formal treatment and during the longer-term course of managing the disorder.

Managing the meaning of diagnosis is not different for patients with bipolar disorder than for patients with other chronic, severe general medical conditions, such as diabetes or heart disease. A careful discussion of the meaning of the condition is essential to attain compliance and optimal long-term management. Thus, it is advisable for the practitioner to set aside time to discuss this, both when the condition is initially recognized and treated and subsequently once it is more stabilized.

Patients often inquire about written information on their disorder (see the Appendix for a listing of information resources). In addition, support groups such as the National Depressive and Manic Depressive Association, with over 100 chapters across the United States, provide ongoing patient education and support for those with bipolar and unipolar mood disorders.

The initial fears associated with the diagnosis of bipolar disorder include being chronically and totally disabled. Patients should be reassured that in the vast majority of cases, with diligent medication and psychological management, a return to a normal level of functioning is likely. However, in some cases, especially when the disorder is detected rather late in its course, only partial rather than complete remission may be expected, even under optimal treatment conditions. In all circumstances, people with this illness should be given a clear-cut picture of what to expect, whether it is full or partial remission.

A second common concern is that life events or stresses may precipitate new episodes of illness. This fear is based on a recognition by some patients that past life events have precipitated episodes of illness or is based on reading that life events can precipitate episodes early in the course of the disorder. Patients should be assured that life events and stresses, while they play a role in the precipitation of new episodes, are not to be feared if medication management is well conducted. On the other hand, patients should not engage in activities likely to reduce the efficacy of medications, such as excessive alcohol ingestion, abuse of substances—especially stimulants—and engaging in behaviors that create chronically erratic sleep–wake cycles. Patients can travel through time zones but should plan on a day or two to recover from jet lag before returning to work.

Patients often ask if they need to be on medication forever. The general answer is yes. Patients with recurrent mood episodes (i.e., more than a total of two manic, hypomanic, or major depressive episodes) are very likely to have subsequent episodes. The earlier the onset of the bipolar I and II disorder, the more likely it is to be recurrent. In addition, many believe that a stronger family history of mood disorders indicates a greater likelihood of recurrence (new episodes) throughout one's lifetime. Thus, patients should, by and large, plan to take medication for many years. For a few patients some clinicians may gradually discontinue medication under tightly controlled clinical conditions, after many years of being entirely stable, to determine whether the patient can go without medication. For the vast majority of patients, these discontinuation trials, even if the medication is gradually tapered, eventually lead to new episodes.

On the other hand, patients may tend to unilaterally discontinue medication to see if they need it. This all-too-common practice may cause subsequent episodes, especially if medicine is abruptly stopped. The new episodes may be even more difficult to treat. Thus, from a medication management point of view, bipolar I or II disorders are very similar to many cases of diabetes in which a medication is required for a lifetime and its careful regulation is essential to obtaining a good outcome.

Patients often ask about getting married and having children. It is advisable to inform one's potential spouse about general medical and psychiatric health issues prior to marriage. This information typically does not result in a discontinuation of the relationship. The potential spouse should be invited to talk with the patient's doctor and to get all the facts before deciding what to do. Furthermore, the issue of having children is one of personal consideration. The risk of an affected off-spring is especially high if both parents have bipolar disorder. Thus, it is best for single patients with bipolar disorder who are seeking a spouse to find one who does not suffer from recurrent major depressive or bipolar disorder.

Questions as to medication management during pregnancy are also common. Because this information is constantly changing, patients should seek experienced psychopharmacological consultation before deciding to become pregnant. There is a small but still significant risk of damage to the fetus if the mother is taking lithium or anticonvulsants in the first trimester of pregnancy. It is also possible in many cases to become pregnant while remaining off medication without having manic or de-pressive episodes, especially in the first trimester, to minimize the risk of fetal damage. Certain mediations carry a greater risk than others. Again, expert consultation is recommended. Following delivery there is a sub-stantial risk of a manic, mixed manic, or major depressive episode with or without psychosis. Studies are now ongoing to define how to best manage women in this high-risk postpartum period. Some evidence indicates that immediate reinstitution of antimanic and/or antidepres-sant medications may prevent or shorten these postpartum episodes. Other evidence suggests that immediate use of postpartum estrogen, to reduce the rapidity of estrogen withdrawal that occurs in the immediate postpartum period, may also prevent these episodes.

Patients often ask about whether or not they should discontinue medication when they are receiving general anesthesia or under surgical conditions. Patients should inform their physicians, both the surgeon and anesthesiologist, about the medication they are taking and follow their advice. In many circumstances, medications need not be discontinued, depending on the type of surgery and type of anesthesia.

Patients also often ask whether their prior manic, mixed manic, or major depressive episodes have psychologically damaged their children. In general, studies indicate that such episodes, in and of themselves, do not increase the likelihood of children developing major depressive or bipolar disorder. That is, the risk for children is a genetic rather than an environmental one. On the other hand, severe and sustained mood episodes over a prolonged period of time are not believed by anyone to be a benefit to children. Prior episodes cannot be undone. However, developing a stable, well state is of substantial benefit, undoubtedly to both the patient and those close to the patient, including spouse and children.

Patients often ask about whether they should report their illness on job application forms. The recently enacted Americans with Disabilities Act makes it illegal for most potential employers to ask about prior psychiatric or other medical disabilities. Thus, patients need not complete the section if it still appears on employment applications. For some jobs, however, this information may be required and, therefore, must be reported. In some instances, the employer will be fully understanding of prior psychiatric or other general medical conditions, whereas in other instances they will not be.

Finally, patients ask about whether they should have their children checked for bipolar disorder. Since the condition has an onset at midadolescence to about age 30, it is unusual, though possible, for children under the age of 12 to develop bipolar disorder. If the child is functioning normally and has no symptoms, there is no basis for an independent evaluation. If, however, the child or adolescent is having some symptoms or is performing very erratically in school over a sustained period of time, it is advisable to have him or her checked by a child/adolescent psychiatrist to determine if there are early signs of bipolar disorder. At present, no laboratory tests exist to confirm the diagnosis in children/adolescents prior to the full clinical expression of the condition. Since the risk of developing a severe bipolar or unipolar mood disorder is only 25% in each offspring, the likelihood that a given child is affected is low, but not zero. At least by the time children have attained adulthood they should know that this illness is present in their family and that they are at an increased risk for developing the condition. Most importantly, should it occur, early treatment is both effective and essential.

ANSWERS TO COMMON QUESTIONS
PATIENTS ASK ABOUT BIPOLAR DISORDER

Is bipolar disorder genetic? Most bipolar disorders are genetic. The vast majority of patients with bipolar disorder have a family history of it, strongly suggesting that the condition is inherited. However, there are exceptions. For example, bipolar type condition can result from specific neurological disorders, such as multiple sclerosis, head injury, brain tumors, or, occasionally other general medical conditions such as thyroid or adrenal diseases.

What is the risk of developing bipolar disorder if your parent has bipolar disorder? The risk of developing bipolar disorder is approximately 12% for a person who has a parent with bipolar disorder. Each child of that parent has the same risk and has a 12% chance of developing recurrent major depressive disorder at some time in his or her life. Taken together, then, there is an approximately 24% chance of a serious recurrent mood disorder of some kind in each offspring of a patient with bipolar disorder (Rush et al., 1991). These risk figures are applicable to either bipolar I or II disorder.

What is the biological basis for depressive and manic episodes? Substantial scientific investigation into this question is currently under way. It has already been well established that profound biological changes occur during both manic and major depressive episodes. Laboratory tests reveal abnormalities in sleep physiology, neurotransmitters, neuroendocrine function, and neuropsychological function (ability to organize, retain, process, and use information). Many of these abnormalities disappear once the manic or depressive episode ends, although they return with a new episode. It is suspected (some data suggest) that the more mood episodes a patient has had, the more difficult/complex the treatment and the less full or complete the recovery between episodes. Therefore, it is important to diagnose bipolar disorders early and to treat this illness vigorously to prevent more episodes. This early and vigorous treatment not only prevents new episodes, reducing suffering and disability, but also prevents complications.

What is the role of life events or stresses in bipolar disorder? There is good evidence that stressful life events precipitate depressive or manic episodes in those with bipolar disorder, especially early in the course of illness (Post, 1992). Over time, however, the illness often takes on "a life of its own" as a recurring condition independent of life events. Yet, even after the illness is established, stressful life events may still make the episodes worse or prolong their duration.

What life events are most problematic? Extreme sleep deprivation can precipitate manic episodes. Even a marked dysregulation in sleep (e.g., staying up all night or crossing time zones) can precipitate, maintain, or worsen manic episodes. Excessive use of alcohol or stimulants (e.g., cocaine or amphetamines) is very likely to precipitate episodes of mania, mixed mania, or (during withdrawal) major depressive episodes. Thus, drugs of abuse are clearly precipitating or maintaining factors. The menstrual cycle may exacerbate depressive or manic episodes in some women. The biological changes that surround childbirth also are precipitants of manic, mixed manic, or major depressive episodes in some patients with bipolar disorder.

Interpersonal events (grief, divorce, job difficulties) can also inter-fere with patients' ability to participate in treatment optimally. For instance, patients who are busy or distracted may forget to take medica-tion. If blood levels are appropriately maintained, however, symptom worsening is unlikely.

If I have bipolar disorder, should I have children? This is a personal decision. Since statistics indicate that most of your children (three out of four) will not have a major mood disorder, chances favor having children. Also, early detection and effective treatment are available, so even if a child develops the condition, a normal functioning life can usually be expected. However, if both parents have bipolar disorder, the chances of an affected child go to roughly 50%. In this case, a considered judgment with professionals is recommended.

CHAPTER SUMMARY

There are two major groups of mood disorders, unipolar and bipolar disorders. Bipolar disorder occurs in two common forms. Bipolar I disorder involves episodes of mania and major depression. Bipolar II disorder involves episodes of major depression and hypomania, but not mania. Both bipolar I and II disorders are recurrent and are typically characterized by asymptomatic (euthymic) periods of well-being between episodes of illness (even without treatment). Both together are relatively common (approximately 1.0–1.8% of the population) and appear to be largely genetic. That is, there is a tendency for relatives of patients with either form of bipolar disorder to develop either a bipolar or unipolar (recurrent major depressive) disorder.

A primary goal of treatment is to prevent subsequent episodes of illness. An essential element in the management of bipolar disorder is medication. Careful, diligent attention to medication management usu-ally results in a return to normal psychosocial functioning.

Medication Treatments
for Bipolar Disorder

SESSION 3. MOOD-STABILIZING MEDICATIONS

Purpose of the Session

During this session, the therapist will discuss the use of anti-manic and mood-stabilizing medications such as lithium and anticonvulsants. Patients and their significant others may have questions and concerns about the long-term use of mood-stabilizing drugs and their intended effects. This session aims at providing such information and clarifying any misconceptions about medication.

Goals of the Session

1. Review the pharmacology, toxicity, side effects, and positive effects of lithium or other mood-stabilizing medications that have been prescribed for the patient.
2. Review the interaction of illicit drugs and alcohol use with psychotropic medication use and with symptoms of bipolar illness.
3. Correct any misconception about the use of antimanic medications, including issues of addiction and dependence.
4. Identify medication issues and questions that patients should discuss with their physicians.

Procedure

1. Assess treatment compliance.
2. Elicit feedback on the reading assignment from the previous session (if completed). Allow time for questions regarding the

(cont.)

(continued from page 39)

material. If the homework was not completed, use the compliance intervention (Chapter 5) and add the mood graph to the next homework assignment.
3. Discuss commonly used antimanic medications such as lithium, valproic acid, or carbamazepine, including benefits, side effects, and interactions with other medications and drugs of abuse.
4. Assign reading material.

Recommended Reading
Schou (1989). *Lithium Treatment of Manic–Depressive Illness.*

SESSION 4. ANTIDEPRESSANT MEDICATIONS

Purpose of the Session
The purpose of this session is to provide general information regarding the use of antidepressant medications. Antidepressants are commonly prescribed in addition to mood-stabilizing medications to help shortcut possible recurrences of depression or to treat depressive symptoms. This session reviews the appropriate use of such medications.

Goals of the Session
1. Review the pharmacology of antidepressant medication including when its use is indicated, expected effects, toxicity, and side effects.
2. Correct any misconceptions about antidepressant medications.
3. Identify issues or concerns that patients should discuss with their physicians.

Procedure
1. Assess treatment compliance.
2. Elicit feedback on the reading assignment from the previous session (if completed). Allow time for questions regarding the material. If the homework was not completed, use the compliance intervention (see Chapter 5) and add the reading materials to the next homework assignment.
3. Discuss commonly prescribed antidepressant medications,

(cont.)

(continued from page 40)

including their benefits, side effects, and interactions with other medications and with the symptoms of bipolar disorder. Discuss potential mania-inducing effects of antidepressant medications.
4. Assign reading material.

Recommended Reading

Gold (1986). "Treatment that Works," in *Good News About Depression.*

This chapter provides general information on the nature, use, side effects, and commonly encountered issues surrounding the use of medication for bipolar disorder. We feel that the information is important for patients to know and that the prescribing physician should always be responsible for providing it. On the other hand, nonphysician clinicians who are interacting with patients with bipolar disorder should also be generally informed about common medication issues. In particular, the nonphysician can reinforce the need for careful medication adherence by patients, clarify issues of concern to the patient, help to identify early symptom breakthrough or side effects, and, importantly, encourage the patient when appropriate to seek medical counsel and possible medication revisions. Just as the management of diabetes requires lifestyle adjustments, careful symptom monitoring, and occasional medication dose or type changes, much of which nonphysicians can play a key role in, so too with bipolar disorder, where the nonphysician clinician can contribute in a major way to optimal medication management.

However, it should be made clear to patients that questions will arise that the prescribing physician must answer. It is not the responsibility of nonphysicians to provide in-depth pharmacological consultation to patients. Rather, by helping patients to identify questions and problems, symptoms, and possible side effects, the clinician can ensure both the timely and efficient use of physician time in addressing these key patient concerns.

The subsequent information is a snapshot circa 1995 of medication used for bipolar disorder. Advances and consequent changes in this information occur frequently and rapidly (e.g., new antimanic or antidepressant medications are discovered). The reader is cautioned, therefore, that the following is a synopsis only and that at least some of the information, herein, is likely to change sooner rather than later.

COMMON MEDICAL ISSUES

- If a woman wants to get pregnant, does she have to stop or change medication? If yes, when and how should this be done?
- What will happen to the symptoms after delivery?
- Can a new mother breast-feed her newborn? Does she have to stay off medications?
- When under a lot of stress and experiencing symptoms, how severe should the symptoms become before calling the doctor to discuss medication adjustment or changes?
- Is it safe to take over-the-counter medications to deal with sleep problems caused by stress?
- How will grief after the death of a family member affect the symptoms of bipolar disorder?
- When should other health care professionals be informed about the psychiatric medication being taken? Is it necessary to tell the dentist before receiving anesthesia? Should the obstetrician/gynecologist be informed?
- Should a patient see the psychiatrist or family doctor about side effects from medications?

Medications are used in bipolar disorder to treat manic (antimanic or mood-stabilizing agents) or depressive (antidepressant agents) episodes or both. The diligent use of medication requires patient collaboration. With such collaboration, pharmacotherapy is extremely likely to control symptoms in patients suffering from either bipolar I or bipolar II disorder. Most patients are able to return to their usual level of function and to avoid subsequent hospitalizations, as well as prolonged, significant disability. Improperly administered treatments, however, will fail to control symptoms, thereby leading to a poorer long-term course (prognosis), and may also lead to undesirable side effects.

Physicians caring for patients with bipolar disorder select from a range of effective antimanic and antidepressant medications to initiate treatment. Typically, a single mood stabilizer (lithium, valproate, or carbamazepine) is the initial treatment. As with the treatment of other general medical conditions (e.g., arthritis, diabetes, heart disease, hypertension), medication selection is, in part, a trial-and-error effort. Some patients respond well to and find few side effects with one medication while other patients do better on different medicine. The best way to see which medicine is right for a particular patient is to try out the medications. Thus, one medication is prescribed and the tolerability and beneficial effects are evaluated. This medication, if tolerated but only partially successful, is augmented with a second medication, or, if unsuccessful, is switched to another medication. Again, the benefits and tolerability are evaluated. This stepwise sequence, over time, leads to medication or a combination of medications that provides optimal symptom control with minimal side effects.

This series of suggested steps requires substantial collaboration between physician and patient. Because medications do not work fully for several weeks, the selection of an optimal treatment for a particular patient usually requires the evaluation of symptomatic outcomes over periods of weeks. Once the patient's condition is stabilized, treatment visits for medication become less frequent. However, continued monitoring of symptoms is needed to ensure that stabilization persists or that a timely revision in the medication type or dosage is undertaken to address symptom breakthrough should it occur.

PHASES OF TREATMENT

There are three phases to treatment (Figure 3.1). For patients in an episode of mania, hypomania, or major depression, the first and most important objective is to control or eliminate the symptoms so they can return to a normal level of interpersonal, occupational, and social functioning. This so-called acute phase treatment may be as brief as 6 weeks or as long as 6 months. Longer time periods are sometimes necessary to sort through several different medications to find the medication or combination of medications that provides optimal benefit with minimal side effects.

The next phase, continuation treatment, lasts from 4 to 9 months. The objective of the continued use of medication is to maintain the asymptomatic state by preventing the return of the most recent mood episode. In addition, the use of psychosocial or rehabilitative treatments (or, in some cases, the passage of time with the adaptation of patients and others in their environment to the asymptomatic state) leads to improved psychosocial functioning during this phase of treatment.

The third phase, maintenance treatment, is a critical and essential step for all patients with bipolar disorder. The goal of maintenance treatment is to prevent new mood episodes (i.e., mania, hypomania, or depression). Like patients with other chronic medical

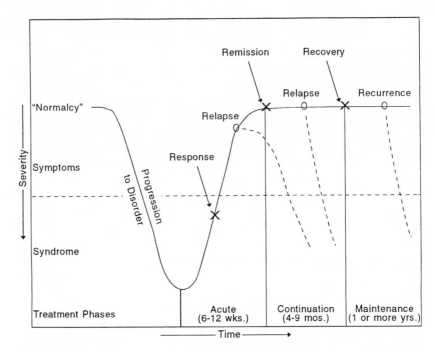

FIGURE 3.1. Phases of treatment. From Kupfer (1991). Copyright 1991 by Physicians Postgraduate Press. Reprinted by permission.

conditions, such as diabetes or arthritis, patients with bipolar disorder are maintained on medication(s) to control the symptoms of their illness for prolonged periods of time. Maintenance treatment may last 5 years, 10 years, or, for most patients with bipolar disorder, a lifetime. Prolonged symptom control also results in continued optimal functioning on a day-to-day basis.

For all phases of treatment and all medications (whether antimanic or antidepressant), patients must take the prescribed medication(s) on a daily basis. Unlike aspirin, for example, which is taken for the treatment of headache only when a person actually has a headache, medications for bipolar disorder must be taken regularly—on both good days and bad days—at the same dosage.

PRINCIPLES OF MEDICATION MANAGEMENT

To obtain optimal patient adherence, it is helpful for clinicians to explain to patients with bipolar disorder several general principles about the effective use of antimanic and antidepressant medications:

1. The objectives of medication treatment are, first, to control symptoms and, second, to maintain the asymptomatic state for prolonged periods of time. These objectives usually require some adjustment of medication type, dosage, or both.

2. To obtain optimal benefit, patients should diligently follow the prescribed treatment and carefully monitor their symptoms and side effects.

3. If side effects develop, patients and their families, who are often the first to notice the problems, should report them to the physician as soon as possible to avoid prolonged discomfort. Most people will not take medications that cause significant side effects for very long. Therefore, if side effects are not minimal, even patients with a recurring severe illness, such as bipolar disorder, are likely to discontinue the medications. Therein lies a major danger—the manic or depressive episodes will return and hospitalization may be needed. Clearly, patients should be strongly encouraged to report side effects early so that physicians can deal with them aggressively and prevent poor patient adherence.

4. Other prescribed medicines, as well as drugs of abuse (e.g., cocaine, amphetamines, alcohol, hallucinogens, narcotics), will affect the efficacy of the prescribed medications and may increase side effects. For optimal control of bipolar disorder, patients should report all other medications they are taking for both general medical and psychiatric disorders to ensure that none are contraindicated or adversely interact with drugs prescribed for bipolar disorder.

5. Antimanic medications (lithium, carbamazepine, and valproic acid) may have teratogenic effects (i.e., affect adversely the development of the fetus). Lithium may be the least teratogenic of these three medications. When clinically possible, women should not become pregnant while taking these medications.

6. Sometimes adjunctive medications (such as sleeping pills or antianxiety medicines) are used to augment the effect of antimanic medications.

7. These adjunctive medications are appropriately used for short periods to manage a breakthrough of symptoms of mania or depression. While safe, these adjunctive medications are often not necessary over prolonged periods of time.

The key to the medication management of bipolar disorder involves early detection and careful monitoring of symptoms and side effects, diligent adjustment of the dosages or types of medications, and early detection and reporting of potential symptom breakthrough as well as side effects. Each step requires an active collaborative relationship between physician and patient, as well as significant others, to work together for long-term successful management of this condition.

USE OF ANTIMANIC MEDICATIONS

The antimanic medications most commonly used for the acute, continuation, and maintenance phases of treatment include lithium, certain anticonvulsants (e.g., carbamazepine, valproate), or, in selected cases, neuroleptic (antipsychotic) medications. Not only are virtually all these medications effective in the acute phase treatment of mania (i.e., they resolve the manic episode), but they also prevent relapses and recurrences of hypomanic or manic episodes. Sometimes, but less predictably, they also prevent or lessen the severity of relapses/recurrences of major depressive episodes. Lithium may have more antidepressant activity than does either carbamazepine or valproate. The neuroleptics have minimal antidepressant activity. All of these medications may cause lethargy in some people. Antimanic medications are often used in combination with antidepressant medications or other antimanic medications in the acute phase treatment of the depressed or manic phases, respectively, of the illness.

In continuation and maintenance phases, the antimanic or mood-stabilizing medications that were successful in acute treatment phase are typically continued, though efforts are usually made to reduce or eliminate neuroleptic medications. Some evidence suggests the need to curtail the use of antidepressant medications as well, in continuation and maintenance phase treatments, since, for some, these medications may increase the cycling nature of these disorders or cause manic or hypomanic symptom breakthrough (Altshuler et al., 1995).

Lithium

The most commonly used and best studied antimanic medication is lithium. An Australian physician, John Cade, discovered its use in 1949 when treating a severely disabled, manic patient in a state hospital who returned to normal functioning. (In fact, the patient died only recently, in his 80s, having had a successful career while he continued to take lithium.) Lithium is a salt and is quite inexpensive. It appears in very minimal amounts in everyone's body; therefore, allergies to it are very rare. Table 3.1 shows the available lithium preparations.

Differentially effective for different types of manic and depressive episodes, and for different phases of bipolar disorder, lithium is used in all phases of treatment but is best understood in the acute phase treatment for manic episodes. Patients with typical manic episodes generally respond rapidly, within 1–3 weeks. The response rate in patients who take lithium alone for the acute phase treatment of mania is approximately 50–75% (Goodwin & Jamison, 1990). By contrast, patients with dysphoric manic episodes or rapid cycling manic episodes seem to have lower response rates to lithium alone—less than 50% of these patients improve significantly. If lithium alone is not fully effective in the acute phase treatment of mania, it is often combined with other medications (e.g., neuroleptics or other antimanic drugs) to achieve fuller symptom remission. The depressed phase of bipolar illness may also respond to lithium alone, although the response may not occur until the third or fourth week of treatment.

Lithium must be taken at a dosage that results in a blood level within a specific therapeutic range (i.e., 0.8–1.2 mEq/liter, as determined by measurements on blood samples drawn 8 to 10 hours after the last oral dose. The oral dosage needed to obtain this level varies among different individuals. When beginning lithium, levels are usually checked often (e.g., every 1–2 weeks). Once a therapeutic level is attained, periodic blood level determinations are still essential to ensure each patient is taking the optimal amount of lithium over the longer term.

Specific clinical situations that also call for lithium level checks include the following: after a change in dose (5–10 days later); during

TABLE 3.1. Lithium Preparations

Generic name (trade name)	Strength	Type
Lithium carbonate (Eskalith, Lithane)	300 mg	Capsules
Lithium carbonate (Lithotabs)	300 mg	Tablets
Lithium carbonate (Eskalith-CR)	450 mg	Sustained-release tablets
Lithium carbonate (Lithium Citrate Syrup)	8 mEq/5 cc = 1 teaspoon (equivalent to a 300-mg pill)	Liquid

major weight changes (e.g., diet); during treatment with diuretics; during a change in mood (both to check compliance and because lithium levels decrease in mania and increase in depression); during general medical illnesses, including the flu; or if lithium toxicity is suspected (Preston, O'Neal, & Talaga, 1994).

In continuation and maintenance phases of treatment, the preferred blood levels of lithium are usually the same as those found to be effective in acute phase treatment. Alone, lithium is an effective continuation or maintenance phase treatment for 30–60% of patients with bipolar disorder. Other patients, however, may experience some breakthrough of manic or depressive symptoms on lithium alone in these later phases of treatment, even if the lithium level is appropriate.

The difficulty with lithium is that patients may take too little or too much. Too little lithium provides little or no therapeutic benefit. On the other hand, too much lithium causes side effects (see Table 3.2), the most common of which are thirst, excessive urination, weight gain, fatigue, and dry mouth. The most distressing side effects are weight gain, cognitive effects, excessive urination, nausea, and fatigue. In some cases, lithium may affect the thyroid gland or kidneys. Lithium decreases the production and release of thyroid hormone by the thyroid gland, and 1–3% of patients who take it develop hypothyroidism (i.e., low thyroid function). Women are at higher risk than men for lithium-induced hypothyroidism. Lithium may also affect the tubular system in the kidney, interfering with the kidneys' ability to concentrate urine and, thus, increasing both the amount and frequency of urination in some patients. This increased urination is not life threatening, since it is not due to progressive destruction of the kidney.

When more than therapeutic amounts of lithium are used, they may

TABLE 3.2. Signs of Lithium Toxicity

Mild	Moderate	Severe
Mild apathy, lethargy	Increased lethargy	Somnolence
Weakness	Confusion, drowsiness	Gross confusion
Unsteady balance	Gross ataxia	Profound loss of balance
Nausea	Vomiting	Urinary incontinence
Decreased concentration	Slurred speech	Random muscle twitching
Worsening hand tremor	Muscle twitching	Coma
Diarrhea		

produce toxic reactions. The earliest signs are usually a tremor (often progressing from a fine to a coarse tremor), diarrhea, nausea, and poor balance (ataxia). If the clinician recognizes the toxic reaction at this stage and reduces the dosage, damage is rare. At higher levels (i.e., above 1.8 mEq/liter), mental confusion, impaired alertness, cardiac arrhythmias, unconsciousness, and death can occur. Immediate recognition and treatment of these more severe signs and symptoms is essential.

There are no absolute contraindications to the use of lithium, but several general medical conditions and concurrent uses of certain medications require caution. Impaired kidney function is a relative contraindication, because the kidney clears lithium from the body. It is best to avoid lithium in cases of dementia, because these patients seem particularly sensitive to the effects of lithium on the central nervous system. Lithium may worsen the muscular weakness seen with myasthenia gravis. Thiazide diuretics and some other medications taken in conjunction with lithium increase lithium levels, thus requiring even more careful monitoring for safe therapy.

Treatments with lithium or valproate are the only therapies that the Food and Drug Administration (FDA) has approved for mania. Suggestive data indicate that several other medications (alone or in combination with lithium) are effective and safe, however. In general, these agents are reserved for patients who do not tolerate or respond well to lithium or valproate.

Anticonvulsants

Japanese and American investigators in the 1970s and early 1980s found the anticonvulsant carbamazepine effective for mania. In addition to carbamazepine (Tegretol), valproate (Depakote, Depakene) has also been recently found to be an effective antimanic agent (Bowden et al., 1994). Once again, patients can take too little or too much of either of these anticonvulsant medications, but clinicians can monitor the anticonvulsant blood levels. The side effects of these anticonvulsants differ from those of lithium. Both anticonvulsants can have central nervous system side effects such as dizziness, poor coordination, or double vision, but these appear more likely with carbamazepine. If properly regulated, however, anticonvulsants usually have very few side effects for most patients.

These anticonvulsants may be effective acute phase treatments in 30–60% of patients with mania. They also appear to be effective (though less well studied) in the continuation and maintenance phases of treatment. That is, they appear to prevent relapses or recurrences of mania or hypomania, but they may not be as effective in preventing relapses or recurrences of depressive episodes. Either medication may be relatively more effective than lithium in the acute phase treatment of dysphoric mania and rapid cycling forms of mania. Thus, carbamazepine or valproate may be first-line alternatives to lithium in the dysphoric or rapid cycling bipolar disorders. Both medications also appear to work very well if added to lithium when lithium alone is not fully effective.

The average oral dosage for carbamazepine is 800–1,000 mg/day, although therapeutic effects can be seen at dosages from 400 to 1,200 mg/day. Most laboratories report the therapeutic blood level to be 4–12 mEq/liter for carbamazepine, even though the relationship between blood level and therapeutic response is not well established (Post et al., 1983). Because of its short half-life, patients usually take it two to three times per day. This schedule maintains a more constant blood level and minimizes side effects. Although carbamazepine is free of many of the side effects of lithium, it can cause a variety of side effects of potential concern. As always, the risks and benefits must be weighed. The most common side effects of carbamazepine (i.e., dizziness, poor or unsteady balance, double vision, sedation, nausea) are typically dose related. A rare, but very important, possible side effect is a decrease in the ability of bone marrow to produce white blood cells to fight infection and platelets to help blood to clot. The incidence of this bone marrow suppression (agranulocytosis) is estimated to be between 1/40,000 and 1/125,000 patients (Post et al., 1983).

Carbamazepine also induces liver enzyme activity such that the metabolism of carbamazepine itself is actually increased. Therefore, over time (3–8 weeks), a fixed oral dosage of carbamazepine may result in subtherapeutic medication levels. In most cases, the dose of carbamazepine may need to be raised to maintain a therapeutic blood level. In addition, other oxidatively metabolized drugs (such as tricyclic or other antidepressants or birth control pills) may have their circulating levels lowered when carbamazepine is added, which secondarily may require a dose adjustment of these medication as well.

There is now strong evidence that valproate (valproic acid; Depakote, Depakene) is effective in the acute phase treatment of mania, even in cases where lithium is ineffective or only partially effective (e.g., dysphoric mania, rapid cycling pattern; Rosenbaum, Fava, Nierenberg, & Sachs, 1995). Other potential predictors of response to valproate in treating bipolar disorder are (1) rapid cycling (four or more episodes per year) (McElroy, Keck, Pope, & Hudson, 1988) and (2) a mildly abnormal electroencephalogram (McElroy, Keck, & Pope, 1987).

The amount of valproate prescribed should be sufficient to attain blood levels of 50–120 µg/dl, although blood levels may not correlate with therapeutic efficacy (McElroy et al., 1987). Valproate potentiates the effects of gamma-aminobutyric acid (GABA), an important inhibitory neurotransmitter in the central nervous system. Enhancing the effects of GABA potentially decreases electrical activity (i.e., has an antiseizure effect). Like lithium, GABA may affect the messenger systems inside cells (McElroy et al., 1988).

Valproate is well tolerated and usually has fewer, milder side effects than does carbamazepine, the most common of which are nausea, diarrhea, mild tremor, and sedation. Weight gain and hair loss are less common, but troublesome. The enteric-coated form (Depakote) may reduce or eliminate the nausea. Although the bone marrow suppression associated with carbamazepine does not occur with valproate, a rare, severe liver condition has been reported in children treated for seizures with valproate. In adolescents and adults, however, valproate has not caused these severe liver problems.

Antipsychotic Medication

Sometimes, antipsychotic (neuroleptic) drugs are used in the acute phase treatment of mania. Drugs such as haloperidol (Haldol), thioridazine (Mellaril), and chlorpromazine (Thorazine) are often combined with lithium or the anticonvulsants to help control hallucinations (voices or visions) or delusions (fixed irrational beliefs), to induce sleep, to reduce inappropriate grandiose thinking, or to decrease irritability or impulsive behaviors that are frequently part of manic episodes. These medications are seldom needed in the treatment of hypomanic episodes, however. Although antipsychotic medications are not always necessary in continuation or maintenance phase treatments, quite a few patients may require small dosages of these medications over prolonged periods to ensure that their delusions, hallucinations, or other symptoms of mania do not return.

Antipsychotic medications reduce psychomotor agitation, but may be less effective for some other core features of manic episodes. Acute akathisia (motor and subjective restlessness), cognitive impairment (e.g., trouble concentrating), anticholinergic side effects (e.g., blurred vision, dry mouth, and difficulty urinating, especially for men), and, after chronic use, tardive dyskinesia (an involuntary movement disorder) are common problems in the use of these medications. These problems can be reduced or avoided by using the lowest necessary doses of the neuroleptics whenever clinically feasible.

Clonazepam is often used as an adjunctive medication in the acute phase treatment of mania. Clonazepam helps to induce sleep, reduce psychomotor agitation, and slow rapid thinking and pressured speech. It may reduce the need for a neuroleptic drug. Furthermore, it has a longer duration of action than do other benzodiazepines. Lorazepam (available for intramuscular use) has a rapid onset of action and is often used in combination with neuroleptics to control acute agitation, hostility, and psychosis.

As noted above, combination drug therapy is common in the management of bipolar disorder (e.g., lithium and antipsychotic medications are frequently used together). However, few prospective studies have evaluated the safety and efficacy of various combinations. Since toxic as well as nontoxic, but troubling, side effects may be increased when combinations of medications are used, careful monitoring of both the clinical responses and side effects is especially important.

A few other agents currently under investigation may be useful in the treatment of manic episodes that are otherwise difficult to treat. For example, clozapine, a new antipsychotic medication, may be particularly helpful for patients whose bipolar disorder has failed to respond to lithium and the anticonvulsants (Suppes, Phillips, & Judd, 1994).

USE OF ANTIDEPRESSANT MEDICATIONS

Like the antimanic medications, antidepressant medications can play a role in acute, continuation, and/or maintenance phases of treatment. Table 3.3 indicates the antidepressant medications as divided into drug classes based on their major neurochemical effects which are thought to account for their therapeutic action. The first antidepressants were the tricyclic (three-ring) antidepressant (TCA) compounds, including imipramine, amitriptyline, desipramine, doxepin, and nortriptyline, and the monoamine oxidase inhibitors (MAOIs; phenelzine and tranylcypromine), both discovered in the 1950s. Newer antidepressant medications, introduced in the early 1970s, sometimes called the heterocyclic (multiring) or unicyclic (one-ring) agents, include amoxapine, maprotiline, trazodone, and bupropion. The newest group of antidepressants, called the selective serotonin reuptake inhibitors (SSRIs), includes fluoxetine, sertraline, paroxetine, and fluvoxamine (approved in the United States as a drug for obsessive–compulsive disorder, but also has established antidepressant activity). In addition to these specific antidepressant medications, some antimanic medications, as noted earlier, especially lithium and the anticonvulsants, have some antidepressant activity in selected patients.

No one antidepressant medication is known to be preferentially effective in bipolar disorder. Furthermore, in prescribing any antidepressant drug, it is possible to make several major mistakes: (1) starting the dosage too high, (2) increasing the dosage too quickly, (3) not increasing the dosage enough, or (4) not giving the medication for a sufficient length of time to determine its full effect. All antidepressant medications can induce manic or hypomanic episodes in patients with bipolar disorder, particularly if the patient is not taking a mood-stabilizing agent along with the antidepressant drug. Because all the antidepressant medications appear to be equally effective, and all take several weeks to work fully, side effects play a key role in selecting among these various treatments. Again, a trial-and-error approach is often used to select the most effective, best tolerated antidepressant for a particular patient. In general, if a patient fails to respond to one class of drugs, he or she will often tolerate

TABLE 3.3. Antidepressant Medications

Drug	Initial dose[a]	Usual dose range[a]
Norepinephrine reuptake inhibitors		
Desipramine (Norpramin, Pertofrane)	25–50	100–250
Maprotiline (Ludiomil)	25–50	100–225
Nortriptyline (Pamelor, Aventyl)	10–25	50–150
Protriptyline (Vivactil)	10	15–60
Serotonin reuptake inhibitors		
Fluoxetine (Prozac)	10–20	10–30
Fluvoxamine (Luvox)	50	100–300
Paroxetine (Paxil)	10–20	20–40
Sertraline (Zoloft)	50	100–150
Dopamine reuptake inhibitors		
Bupropion (Wellbutrin)	100–150	300–450
Mixed norepinephrine/serotonin reuptake inhibitors		
Amitriptyline (Elavil, Endep)	25–50	100–250
Doxepin (Adapine, Sinequan)	25–50	100–300
Imipramine (Tofranil)	25–50	100–250
Trimipramine (Surmontil)	25–50	100–300
Venlafaxine (Effexor)	37.5	125–275
Mixed action drugs		
Amoxapine (Asendin)	50–100	150–400
Clomipramine (Anafranil)	25	150
Nefazodone (Serzone)	100	250–500
Trazodone (Desyrel)	50	150–300
Monoamine oxidase inhibitors		
Phenelzine (Nardil)	15	60–90
Tranylcypromine (Parnate)	10	40–60

[a]μg/day.

and respond to a different class. Interestingly, intolerance (i.e., develop-ment of intolerable side effects) to one agent in a class does *not* necessarily mean the patient will not tolerate another drug in the same class.

The side effects of an antidepressant medication are usually due to its chemical effects that are not related to its therapeutic benefit. Side effects that result from increased activity of the cholinergic neurotrans-mitter system (so-called anticholinergic side effects) include dry mouth, blurred vision, constipation, mild sedation, and difficulty urinating. Some patients, especially older ones, are particularly sensitive to these anticholinergic side effects, which are especially common with some tricyclic and heterocyclic antidepressants (e.g., amitriptyline, imipramine, nortriptyline, maprotiline). Table 3.4 lists the side effects of each drug, grouped by the above classes. The SSRIs have fewer anticholinergic side effects but more gastrointestinal, sleep, and sexual dysfunction problems. Other new drugs (e.g., venlafaxine, nefazodone, bupropion) also have fewer anticholinergic side effects.

In managing patients who are taking antidepressants, it is important to help them to distinguish depressive symptoms from side effects due to the antidepressant drug. It is wise for a physician to discuss side effects with patients before prescribing an antidepressant. For example, depres-sion often comes with a dry mouth, trouble sleeping, and sexual dysfunc-tion. But some medications, as noted above, can cause these symptoms as side effects. Therefore, it is important for patients to note the specific symptoms they have *before* beginning an antidepressant, so, if after taking the medication for a while they begin to report the same symptoms as side effects, a record of the type and severity of symptoms prior to the medication is available. A careful tracking of these symptoms over time often helps patients to distinguish side effects from lack of therapeutic effect. Patients should know (1) which side effects are more likely and which are less likely, (2) which side effects are dangerous, (3) which side effects will gradually disappear over time, and (4) what methods can be used to counter side effects if they occur.

Side effects are typically seen early (i.e., when the drug is initiated) or when the dose is raised. Lower doses are associated with fewer side effects. Also, it is generally wise *not* to try to reduce side effects by adding another drug, since this increases the chances of undesired interaction between drugs. Lowering the dose or more gradually raising the dose is often an excellent first step. Switching to another drug is sometimes required, if dose adjustments do not result in better tolerance and good efficacy. Longer-term side effects are especially important in selecting among the available antidepressants. In general, the newer drugs (i.e., bupropion, venlafaxine, the SSRIs, nefazodone) have fewer side effects in the short and longer run than older medications.

TABLE 3.4. Side-Effect Profiles of Antidepressant Medications

Drug	Central nervous system			Orthostatic hypotension	Cardiovascular		Other	
	Anti-cholinergic[a]	Drowsiness	Insomnia/agitation		Cardiac[a] arrhythmia	Gastrointestinal distress	Weight gain (6 kg)	Sex
Major effects on the norepinephrine system								
Desipramine	1	1	1	2	2	0	1	1
Maprotiline	2	4	0	0	1	0	2	1
Nortriptyline	1	1	0	2	2	0	1	1
Protriptyline	2	1	1	2	2	2	0	0
Major effects on both the norepinephrine and serotonin systems								
Amitriptyline	4	4	0	4	3	0	4	2
Doxepin	3	4	0	2	2	0	3	2
Imipramine	3	3	1	4	3	1	3	2
Trimipramine	1	4	0	2	2	0	3	2
Venlafaxine	0	1	1	0	1	2	1	1
Major effects on the dopamine system								
Bupropion	0	0	2	0	1	1	0	0
Major effects on multiple systems								
Amoxapine	2	2	2	2	3	0	1	2
Clomipramine	2	3	1	2	2	2	3	1
Nefazodone	0	3	0	0	1	2	0	0
Trazodone	0	4	0	1	1	1	1	4
Major effects on monoamine oxidase								
MAOIs	1	1	2	2	0	1	2	3
Selective blocking of serotonin reuptake								
Fluoxetine	0	0	2	0	0	3	0	3
Fluvoxamine	0	2	1	0	1	3	1	2–3
Paroxetine	0	0	2	0	0	3	0	3
Sertraline	0	0	2	0	0	3	0	3

Note. 0 = absent or rare; 1,2 = in between; 3,4 = relatively common. [a]Dry mouth, blurred vision, urinary hesitancy, constipation.

Generally, TCAs show only a partial clinical effect during the first several weeks of treatment. Typically, the starting dosage is low and is titrated up gradually to minimize side effects. Thus, the clinician gradually increases the dosage over 7–14 days to the lower end of the therapeutic range. If there is no response at all after 2 or 3 weeks and side effects are minimal, the medication dosage is gradually raised up to the maximum shown in Table 3.3. If there is no response after 6 weeks of gradually increasing dosages, the clinician may use a number of different strategies. The simplest is to obtain a blood level measurement of the antidepressant to determine if the dosage is adequate. (This level is meaningful only for some medications, however.) If a patient does not respond to a full trial of a TCA, many physicians prescribe a drug from a different class of antidepressants.

Some TCAs are sedating (although not all to the same extent), and most physicians recommend that the sedating medications be taken at bedtime so whatever sedation occurs is maximized during sleep. Once-daily dosing with TCAs is as effective as divided dosages because the medicine stays in the body for several days before being fully metabolized and excreted. Once-daily dosing is preferred to optimize adherence.

Like the TCAs, heterocyclic and unicyclic medications are given initially in a low dosage that is raised over days to several weeks, depending on the patient's response and side effects. Some non-TCAs such as bupropion must be given in divided doses. For bupropion, no more than 150 mg at any one time is recommended because higher dosages increase the risk of seizures.

The TCAs, as well as the heterocyclic and unicyclic drugs, cause side effects. Some side effects are common, but only minimally bothersome; others may be common early in treatment, but disappear over time. As with any medical treatment, it is necessary to weigh the risk and severity of side effects against the benefit of medication treatment.

Sedation is a common side effect, associated not only with many of the TCAs, as mentioned earlier, but also with trazodone. Dizziness on standing (postural hypotension) is a relatively common side effect that is manifested by a drop in blood pressure when the person changes position, especially when standing up. Sexual side effects are less common, but may include a decreased ability to maintain an erection and/or an orgasm. Trazodone, in particular, can cause priapism—a prolonged painful erection that occurs without sexual stimulation in 1 in 6,000 males. Some patients feel increased anxiety and restlessness with some of the more activating agents, such as bupropion, desipramine, or protriptyline. Some TCAs, especially amitriptyline and imipramine, may cause patients to crave carbohydrates or sweets and to gain weight. In fact, long-term weight gain occurs in 10–15% of patients who take TCAs over 9 to 12 months. The newer heterocyclic and unicyclic drugs, and the SSRIs are less likely to cause weight gain in the long run than are the TCAs.

Bupropion, amoxapine, maprotiline, and trazodone are just as effective as the TCAs, but differ in some side effects. Bupropion, for example, has less weight gain, dry mouth, blurred vision, and sedation. Like the TCAs, these medications are used in the acute phase treatment of a depressive episode and may be used in continuation or maintenance treatment to prevent depressive relapses or recurrences.

Norepinephrine Reuptake Inhibitors

The norepinephrine reuptake inhibitors include desipramine, maprotiline, nortriptyline, and protriptyline, of which desipramine and nortriptyline are most commonly prescribed. Three of these agents are TCAs (all but maprotiline which has $3\frac{1}{2}$ rings). All have significant anticholinergic side effects and a lethal dose of these drugs may be as little as a 2-week supply. These drugs need to be adjusted from their initial dose to a final therapeutic range. In general, strong evidence suggests that a higher dose is more effective. These are well-established agents. There is evidence that they are effective when the MAOIs or the SSRIs fail.

The long-term side effects of these drugs, while modest, importantly include weight gain. In addition, some patients find that the therapeutic dose is simply too sedating to tolerate over a prolonged period of time.

Serotonin Reuptake Inhibitors

In acute and longer-term (continuation and maintenance phases) treatment, these agents (fluoxetine, sertraline, paroxetine, and fluvoxamine) appear equally effective in treating depression, at least mild to moderately severe depressions, as other classes of drugs. They are effective for the depressed phase of bipolar disorder. There is no scientific evidence that these drugs increase suicidal thinking or attempts, in spite of the suggestions to the contrary in the media. They are rarely associated with weight gain. They can, as do other antidepressant medications, precipitate manic or hypomanic episodes in bipolar disorder patients, especially if they are not taking lithium or an anticonvulsant.

These agents, due to their better side effect profile, as well as their safety in overdose and easier dose adjustment, have become popular agents. They basically lack anticholinergic side effects, but do cause gastrointestinal symptoms and may interfere with sexual desire or function (e.g., delayed ejaculation, anorgasmia).

Dopamine Reuptake Inhibitors

The dopamine reuptake inhibitor bupropion is a single member of a distinct class. Evidence indicates that bupropion is effective when patients have failed to respond to or are intolerant to the SSRIs. This drug typically must be taken three times a day. This more frequent dosing makes compliance an issue for some patients. The long-term side effects of this drug are minimal and do not include sexual dysfunction, which is common with the SSRIs. It has minimal anticholinergic side effects. If taken in an overdose, the main risk is one of seizures, but it is safer in overdose than the TCAs.

Mixed Norepinephrine/Serotonin Reuptake Inhibitors

The mixed norepinephrine/serotonin reuptake inhibitors include amitriptyline, doxepin, imipramine, trimipramine, and venlafaxine. All of these drugs except venlafaxine are included within the tricyclic or three-ring class. As such, venlafaxine is the safest among this group in overdose situations. Amitriptyline and doxepin are the most sedating of any of these antidepressants. Weight gain is also common with these agents. All of these drugs, save for venlafaxine, have significant anticholinergic side effects which may make longer-term adherence a problem for some individuals.

Venlafaxine is the newest among the combined norepinephrine/serotonin reuptake inhibitor group. Gradual initial dose escalation is required to keep side effects to a minimum. Hypertension spontaneously can occur in 2–4% of individuals taking the drug at 125 mg/day. Higher dosages are associated with a greater incidence of hypertension (over 10% if over 300 mg/day). It is reversible or treatable if the patient needs to continue on the medication. There is evidence that increasing the dose with this drug increases the likelihood of a response and/or the thoroughness of the symptom reduction caused by this agent.

Mixed Action Drugs

The mixed action drugs include amoxapine, nefazodone, trazodone, and clomipramine. Amoxapine has a metabolite which has neuroleptic-like properties. This makes this agent potentially preferable in the treatment of psychotic depression, but the metabolite is associated with akathisia and has the potential of inducing long-term tardive dyskinesia. This agent, therefore, is a second-line treatment.

Nefazodone and trazodone are related structurally but have distinct side effect profiles. Nefazodone is less sedating than trazodone and it is easier, therefore, to get the patients into therapeutic range with nefazo-done. Trazodone has been reported to be associated with priapism in 1 in 6,000 cases. There is no evidence of sexual dysfunction with nefazo-done. There is recent evidence that nefazodone exceeds the efficacy of comparison to tricyclic drugs and/or selective SSRIs in regard to the early reduction in anxiety, improvement in sleep, and the lack of longer-term sexual dysfunction side effects.

Monoamine Oxidase Inhibitors

Although less commonly used because of the necessary dietary precau-tions, the MAOIs are very important in the treatment of bipolar disorder. Some evidence, albeit incomplete, suggests that these drugs may be particularly useful in bipolar disorder because they may be less likely to induce subsequent cycling, or because they are effective when other groups of drugs fail (Himmelhoch, Thase, Mallinger, & Houck, 1991).

Patients taking an MAOI cannot use certain medications, nor can they eat certain foods. The proscribed medications include virtually all cold, cough, or sinus medications; weight-reducing or pep pills; asthma inhalants (except for steroid sprays or Intal); epinephrine in local anes-thesia (such as is used in dental work—the local anesthesia itself is safe); cocaine; amphetamines (speed); other antidepressants (except in special circumstances); Demerol (meperidine); and dextromethorphan (found in many cold and cough preparations, usually labeled as DM). Proscribed foods include cheese (all kinds except cottage cheese and cream cheese); smoked or pickled fish (canned tuna is OK); fermented meats (such as summer sausage, pepperoni, salami); beef liver or chicken liver; yeast/protein extracts (such as Marmite and Bovril spreads); sherry, vermouth, brandy, and red wines (especially chianti—white wine and champagne are OK); fava or broad bean pods (Italian green beans) (the beans themselves are OK, string beans are OK); overripe figs or overripe bananas (young bananas [white pulp] are OK). Foods and beverages to be used in moderation include beer, yogurt, sour cream, canned or powdered soup, avocados, raspberries, sauerkraut, chocolate, and caf-feine.

If these proscriptions are not followed, the blood pressure may increase suddenly, causing headache, nausea, vomiting, and the risk of stroke. Even if a food does not cause a reaction the first several times that a patient eats it, there may be a reaction the next time. Moreover, the amount of proscribed food or medication taken determines the risk of this sudden increase in blood pressure (a hypertensive episode). For instance, four glasses of red wine are more likely to provoke a hypertensive reaction than are two. The headache that signals the onset of a hypertensive episode is severe and pounding, unlike a tension headache. Patients who develop such symptoms should go to an emergency room where their blood pressure can be measured and, if needed, treatment given immediately to normalize it.

Other more common side effects of the MAOIs include postural hypotension, weight gain, sexual dysfunction (anorgasmia, erectile dysfunction, retarded ejaculation), insomnia, energy slumps, stimulation (especially with tranylcypromine; nervousness, irritability, tremor, sweating, tachycardia, palpitations), edema (swelling), and muscle twitching.

Other Antidepressant Medications

Other agents are sometimes used as antidepressants typically in treatment-resistant cases. These agents are not recommended as first-line treatments and those with monoamine-releasing activity have particular risks involved in their use in bipolar disorder. The monoamine-releasing agents include dextroamphetamine, methylphenidate, pemoline and methamphetamine. These agents are virtually never used as solo antidepressants for patients with bipolar disorder.

Other agents used in the treatment of depression may include the serotonin 1A partial agonist buspirone (Buspar) or the benzodiazepine receptor agonist alprazolam (Xanax). Again, these agents are not first-line antidepressants but may be used to augment the effect from other antidepressants, when effect is incomplete symptom remission.

DRUG INTERACTIONS

Since patients with bipolar disorder are often taking multiple medications, the psychopharmacologist must be aware of the potential of drug interactions. Several mechanisms underlie that potential, including protein binding and displacement. For example, one drug may displace another drug from circulating proteins. Protein-bound drugs are not able to enter cells and are, therefore, not active until they are made free or become unbound from the proteins in the bloodstream. Thus, one drug may displace another drug creating an increased level in the displaced level by increasing its bioavailability (ability to enter cells). For example, nefazodone displaces haloperidol from proteins which increases the haloperidol bioavailability and, therefore, the therapeutic and side effects if the dose is not adjusted.

A second mechanism underlying drug interactions is the competition from the same enzyme systems that are involved in the metabolism and breakdown of the drugs. For example, fluoxetine and the tricyclic agents (e.g., amitriptyline, imipramine, desipramine, and nortriptyline, etc.) compete for the same isoenzyme system in the liver. When fluoxetine is used with a TCA in the same patient, the circulating blood levels of the TCA are markedly increased (two- to threefold) as compared to using the TCA alone. Thus, this combination can increase side effects due to the TCA. The solution is to reduce the oral dose of the TCA, often with the assistance of blood levels measurements.

A third kind of drug interaction involves autoinduction, that is, the ability of a drug to induce its own metabolism. This was noted above in the discussion of carbamazepine. Carbamazepine can induce its own metabolism, as well as that of other drugs metabolized by the enzyme system involved in carbamazepine's metabolism. Therefore, over time, the dose of carbamazepine may have to be raised or the dosages of other medications may need to be increased when they are given with carbamazepine.

A fourth method of drug interaction includes the combined effect of two drugs in the central nervous system at the level of the neuron. For example, TCAs and alcohol are more than additive in their ability to cause cognitive impairment. This is because both drugs are active at the level of the neuron in the same regions of the brain, which leads to impaired mental processes if both drugs are used in significant doses.

Table 3.5 lists selected medications that are affected by changes in the enzyme system, the so-called hepatic or liver P_{450} system. It is notable that some of these medications include nonpsychiatric drugs such as antibiotics (e.g., erythromycin) and analgesics (acetaminophen or Tylenol). Patients with bipolar disorder should be carefully instructed with regard to the need to tell all physicians, dentists, and others prescribing medication about the nature of the drugs that they are currently taking. This knowledge will allow practitioners to properly gauge the safety of adding or subtracting an agent, as well as to knowledgeably modify the dose of the drug should it be found to be safe to be prescribed.

CONTINUATION AND MAINTENANCE PHASE TREATMENT

The acute phase treatment of a mood episode ends when the symptomatic episode (depression, mania, hypomania) ends. Some patients, especially those who have experienced a breakthrough of depressive symptoms in the past, may require the antidepressant medication for prolonged periods of time. There is no evidence that the available antidepressant medications have long-term negative side

TABLE 3.5. Selected Medications Affected by Alterations in the Hepatic P_{450} System

Acetaminophen and other analgesics
Amitriptyline, SSRIs, and most other antidepressants
Benzodiazepines
Caffeine, ethanol, and other substances of abuse
Carbamazepine
Codeine, dextromethorphan, and other antitussives
Cyclosporine
Erythromycin, ketoconazole, and other antimicrobials
Lovastatin
Metoprolol and other ß-blockers
Neuroleptics
Nifedipine, ecainide, lidocaine, and other cardiac medications
Omeprazole
Oral contraceptives, estrogens, and other steroids
Tamoxifen
Theophylline
Tolbutamide
Valproate

effects, although they may increase the likelihood of mania or increased cycling in some patients. Many patients with bipolar disorder do not need to use antidepressants after acute phase treatment, however, since lithium or the anticonvulsants alone, or in combination, may prevent depressive symptoms. Alternatively, antidepressants may be used intermittently to treat depressive symptom breakthrough. It is preferable to use the fewest medications possible, since that means fewer side effects, better compliance, lower cost, less inconvenience, and fewer drug interactions.

The objective of pharmacological management of bipolar disorder is the complete removal of all manic and depressive symptoms, not just partial improvement. Complete symptom remission is the objective, because the patient's prognosis (long-term outcome over time) is better if an asymptomatic state can be attained and maintained. Antimanic medications (i.e., lithium, anticonvulsants) and antidepressant medications can usually control episodes of both mania and depression and prevent their return. In many cases, however, patients with bipolar disorder require combinations of medications, such as lithium plus and anticonvulsant or lithium plus an antidepressant, because there is clear evidence of only a partial response to one alone. Sometimes, it is necessary to switch from one medication to another. For example, a patient may begin lithium, but discontinue the lithium and move to an anticonvulsant if the lithium proves ineffective. If some depression remains after the use of lithium or anticonvulsants, an antidepressant is added. For some, hypomanic symptoms remain, calling for a different antimanic medication or a combination of medications.

In summary, the individualization of medication regimens requires substantial collaboration between patient and practitioner, diligent attention to side effects, monitoring of systems, and substantial expertise in pharmacology. Given that a trial-and-error effort to identify the optimal (best benefit, least problems) medication(s) for patients is needed, the importance of this collaboration cannot be underestimated.

ELECTROCONVULSIVE THERAPY

Although electroconvulsive therapy (ECT) is not usually a first-line treatment, it can be extremely important for some patients with bipolar disorder, especially when the manic or depressive episodes do not respond to medication. That is, candidates for ECT usually have had only a partial or no response to various earlier treatments during the manic or depressive episode. ECT is also effective for patients in a mixed (or dysphoric) manic episode.

There is substantial evidence that ECT works. In fact, it is approximately 70–90% effective in manic and severe depressive episodes that have failed to respond to medication treatments. So, while often not a first-line treatment, it can be life saving. ECT is not typically used in the maintenance phase. Patients are placed on medication instead, and doses adjusted as previously described.

CHAPTER SUMMARY

Medications are the mainstay of treatment for bipolar disorder. However, selection of the best medicine or combination of medicines for a particular patient depends on individual responses. Physicians and patients must work together to try out, carefully and diligently, one and sometimes several medications to get the best results. Because of symptom breakthrough, intercurrent illnesses, pregnancy, the use of medicines for general medical conditions, and a variety of other situations, medications need to be carefully adjusted over the months and years of treatment for bipolar disorder. Well-informed patients, knowledgeable about symptoms, side effects, and the general objectives of medication treatment, are essential members of the treatment team. While finding the right medication regimen can be time consuming, the effort almost always pays off in a return to good functioning with minimal side effects. Patients are to be encouraged to ask, learn, and discuss all medication questions they have with the appropriate clinician in a timely manner.

FOUR

Symptom Monitoring:
An Early Warning System

SESSION 5. INDIVIDUAL SYMPTOMS
OF BIPOLAR DISORDER

Purpose of the Session

The purpose of this session is to help patients and their family members to understand how their daily experiences with the symptoms of bipolar illness are common sequelae of the illness shared by thousands of others. In addition, therapists will begin to teach patients and their family members how to distinguish normal mood variations from symptoms.

Goals of the Session

1. Help patients and their family members to begin to identify how their day-to-day experiences may be related to symptoms of bipolar illness.
2. Help patients and their family members begin to differentiate normal mood states from symptoms of depression and mania.

Procedure

1. Elicit feedback on the reading assignment from the previous session. If the homework was not completed, use the compliance intervention (Chapter 5) and add the reading materials to the next homework assignment.
2. Ask patients and their family members how bipolar illness has affected their lives and home environment.
3. Complete the Symptom Summary Worksheet.
4. Assign homework to the patient and any other session participants.

(cont.)

(continued from page 65)

Homework

Provide the session participants with copies of the Symptom Summary Worksheet that was completed during the session. Ask them to add to the list over the next week and return the list for further discussion.

SESSION 6. SYMPTOM MONITORING

Purpose of the Session

To prevent full episodes of depression or mania from recurring, it is essential to identify the early warning signs. Early identification can lead to early intervention and may "head off" a full-blown episode of mania or depression. Early detection requires that the patient and those around him or her be aware of the signs and symptoms of the disorder. Helping the patient and others to identify and label their experiences of bipolar symptoms is the first step toward early intervention. The second step is to regularly monitor key symptoms, such as changes in mood, that indicate a shift into mania or depression. This session will review mood graphing as a method for monitoring symptom fluctuations.

Goals of the Session

1. Introduce the use of Mood Graphs.
2. Design a Mood Graph that best suits the symptom presentation of the patient.

Procedure

1. Review procedure for completing the mood graph. Complete the graph for yesterday and today. Modify the graph design as needed.
2. Assign homework.

Homework

Ask patients and family members that are present to keep graphs of the patients' moods for 1 week. This will help patients and their family members to begin to discriminate between normal and symptomatic mood states.

When a group of young soccer players took the field to warm up for an afternoon game, they heard thunder in the distance. Heeding the early warning of the impending storm, the mother of one young player took her child and left the field before the rain began. The game proceeded, evenly matched and exciting; few noticed the ominous storm clouds getting closer and the crackling lightning now nearer than ever. One by one, the nearby soccer fields emptied as referees decided it was unsafe to proceed. Despite the worsening weather, the last referee refused to stop the game until the rain began to fall in torrents.

For patients with bipolar disorder, their experience is like watching a storm roll in. They must decide whether the storm is coming their way and, if so, when to seek shelter. Some believe that it is necessary to take protective measures at the earliest signs of danger, for example, when their mood begins to shift. Others feel that it is foolish to act until they are certain that there will be a storm. The number and intensity of signs and symptoms of mania or depression required to convince patients that a relapse or recurrence is imminent vary from person to person. Those who have had several manic episodes or severe depressions may seek help more quickly than those whose symptoms have been less severe or less frequent. Perhaps more common in patients with mania than in patients with depression is the false confidence that they can weather the storm. Sometimes individuals who do not heed the warning signs can become immobilized and find themselves standing in the middle of a thunderstorm.

Once the storm (i.e., mania, severe depression) has hit, CBT is minimally effective. Its strength lies in the prevention of relapses or recurrences. By enhancing the prophylactic effects of pharmacotherapy, reducing the stressors that can exacerbate symptoms, and sensitizing patients to early exacerbations of symptoms, it can prevent initial symptoms from evolving into depression and mania.

Monitoring symptoms is a learning process for patients and clinicians. Together they must determine how the symptoms of the patient vary over time, what causes those fluctuations, at what point intervention is most helpful and most necessary, and when they have reached a critical threshold where relapse is imminent. Many with bipolar disorder are not tuned in to their symptoms; others know themselves and their illness so well that they can predict an upcoming relapse. Some act quickly and decisively; some test the limits. Clinicians must discover with each new patient when to trust that the individual can judge the severity and likely course of symptoms, when to get nervous about a recurrence of depression or mania, when to insist on stronger interventions, and when to begin thinking about hospitalization.

The reason to monitor symptoms is to develop an early warning system that signals the need for intervention before it is too late. Although the signs and symptoms of depression, mania, and mixed states are common to many patients with bipolar disorder (see Chapter 2), each person has a unique expression of them. Standardized instruments for assessing the common symptoms of depression and mania are useful, but patients and their therapists or physicians are also likely to find it helpful to design their own method for following the progression of each bipolar disorder patient's unique signs and symptoms. We will review three methods for examining patients' symptoms: Life Charts, Symptom Summary Worksheets, and Mood Graphs. Life Charts produce a global view of an individual's course of bipolar disorder. Symptom summaries focus more closely on symptoms within an episode and Mood Graphs monitor daily fluctuations in symptoms.

LIFE CHARTS

A chart of the course of a patient's illness illustrates the number, sequence, and duration of manic and depressive episodes. The Life Chart can also diagrammatically represent the influence of treatment and significant life events on the course of the illness.

> Ms. Childs, a 37-year-old woman with bipolar disorder, experienced her first episode of depression at age 20 (see Figure 4.1). This episode lasted almost a year and eventually remitted without treatment. After the birth of her son, she had her first manic episode, which was misdiagnosed as a hormonal fluctuation. Her family doctor treated her fall into a severe depression following this brief manic episode with TCAs, and the episode eventually remitted.
>
> Ms. Childs associated her next episode of depression, which occurred at age 26, with job stress. She was once again treated with TCAs, but this time the result was a shift into mania. She was hospitalized, where her physician diagnosed her condition as bipolar disorder and prescribed lithium in combination with a neuroleptic to control auditory hallucinations. After this episode, lithium continued to be helpful in controlling her symptoms when she took it regularly.
>
> When she felt better, she looked at the 20 pounds she had gained while taking lithium and decided to stop taking her medication. A few weeks later, she began to feel even better than she had in the previous months. The good feeling increased so slowly that, at first, it was barely noticeable to her or to others. Feeling more energetic, she was able to do more around the house. She started several cleaning projects that kept her busy well into the early morning hours. Before long, her

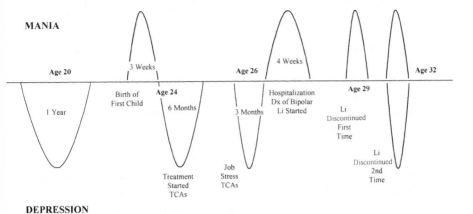

MANIA

DEPRESSION

FIGURE 4.1. Ms. Childs's Life Chart.

symptoms were recognized as a recurrence of mania, and she was hospitalized. She recovered, but unfortunately did not learn from this experience. Several years later, she once again discontinued her lithium against the advice of her psychiatrist and the pattern repeated itself. This time her symptoms evolved into a dysphoric mania.

During the first few therapy sessions, patients and their therapists can work together to construct Life Charts. (The process of constructing a Life Chart can be very educational for the patient, especially when medication noncompliance has predated recurrences of symptoms.) The first step in constructing a Life Chart is to draw a reference line in the middle of the page that represents a euthymic or "normal" state. Many patients report that they have never felt "normal"; therefore, the reference line must represent relative normalcy, that is, relative to the extremes of depression and mania that the person has experienced. For example:

> "Think of a time when you felt a lot better. Maybe you were able to do more, think more clearly. That will represent the middle of the graph. You have had days when you felt more depressed than that, and you have had days when you felt more hyper or manic than that."

The second step is to draw the episodes of depression, mania, and mixed states on the time line. Points below the reference line represent depression; points above the line indicate mania. The greater the distance from the reference line, the more severe the symptoms. The width of each episode on the time line reflects the relative length of the episode. The onset of the illness should be on the far left end of the chart, the patient's current mood state on the far right end. The Life Chart shows the evolution of the illness from its beginning to the present.

In most instances, patients can draw their own Life Charts. Begin by explaining how the chart works. Draw a reference life for them and explain how depressions and manias are depicted. Ask how they are feeling now and mark the far right side of the line as is shown in Figure 4.2. Next, ask when they believe the current symptoms began. Another way to think about it is to ask them to recall when they last felt well, asymptomatic, or "normal." Make a mark on the line, note the approximate date, and ask them to draw how the symptoms evolved from the start point to the present time. The next step is to draw the first episode together. Give the patient a pencil and the chart and ask him or her to draw in the remaining episodes.

If an individual has had numerous episodes of illness, the construction of a Life Chart may be difficult. In other cases, the course of bipolar disorder does not begin with an easily defined, distinct episode of depression or mania. There may have been problems at school, at home, or on the job, or there may have been some difficulty in getting along with others. It is usually easiest to start with the most recent episode and work backward in time. It can also be helpful for the patient to try to recall hospitalizations or emergency room visits and use these events as reference points for episodes.

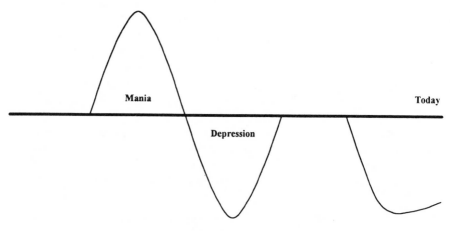

FIGURE 4.2. Life Chart.

Reviewing medical records or talking with family members can also help flesh out the patient's course of illness for a Life Chart.

The next step is to fill in the types and dates of treatments received. The medical record may be particularly helpful in completing this task. Although a clinician may have prescribed medications over distinct periods of time, it is possible and even likely that the patient did not always take them. This part of Life Chart construction provides the clinician with an opportunity to introduce the topic of medication compliance by simply conveying that many people have difficulty taking medications regularly, especially if they are feeling better or are having uncomfortable side effects. Does the patient recall taking medications regularly prior to each episode of illness? When appropriate, write in "stopped medication."

Significant life events should also appear on the life chart so that both patients and therapists can determine whether any life events have precipitated recurrences of depression or mania. Studies of life events in bipolar illness have shown that 45–75% of bipolar disorder patients experience a major life stressor prior to the onset of their first episode of bipolar illness, while 13–56% of patients report experiencing major life events prior to later episodes of depression or mania (e.g., Ambelas, 1979; Glassner et al., 1979).

Some work with major depression (Hammen, Ellicott, Gitlin, & Jamison, 1989) suggests that some people may be particularly sensitive to certain kinds of stressors (e.g., achievement-related stress); as a result, they are more likely to have a recurrence of or relapse into depression when that specific type of stressor occurs.

> When Mrs. Weinstein is angry with her husband, she begins to drink more than usual to "calm her nerves." She knows that mixing her medication with alcohol is dangerous, so "to be safe" she stops taking her medication. Her intoxication loosens her tongue, and she says hurtful things that exacerbate the conflict with her husband. The conflict disrupts her sleep and leaves her feeling lonely and hopeless. She self-medicates the emotional pain with more alcohol. Her situation worsens until she becomes suicidal and is taken to the emergency room. She recovers until the next time she and her husband quarrel. Knowing this about Mrs. Weinstein helps in planning interventions that may prepare her for the next conflict and subsequent pattern of behaviors and symptoms.

Events associated with recurrences of depression and mania include those that are seen as stressful to any individual: divorce or separation, a parent's illness or death, loss of a job or increased job stress, legal problems, and financial stress. Even positive events, such as the birth of a child, a new marriage, a move to another city, and vacations or business trips that cross time zones and disrupt the sleep–wake cycle, can precipitate episodes of depression or mania. Some life events are predictable, often beginning as minor stressors and building over time. It may be possible to plan for these events or to address them when they pose only a small threat to the patient. Other events are sudden, unpredictable, and outside the control of the patient. The Life Chart gives patients and clinicians a larger view of the course of illness, including the influence of treatment and stress. This information can aid treatment planning.

For example, symptom reduction in the past may have been accomplished with use of a specific medication. Therefore, the doctor may want to prescribe that medication again. Another example is if a recurrence of symptoms is associated with an event such as childbirth or loss of employment. If these events are anticipated, the patient and the health care provider can develop a plan for recognition of the symptoms, prevention, or early intervention.

Dr. Robert Post and his colleagues at the National Institute of Mental Health have developed computer software (not yet commercially available) for generating Life Charts. The dates, polarity of episodes, degree of functional impairment, and treatment types are documented as described above. This information is entered into the computer program which generates a chart. Figure 4.3 shows the computer-generated version of the Life Chart illustrated in Figure 4.1.

SYMPTOMS OF DEPRESSION AND MANIA

In addition to the signs and symptoms that constitute the diagnosis of bipolar disorder, patients with this disorder may experience several other symptoms. These roughly fall into three categories: changes in mood, changes in thinking, and changes in behavior.

When depression begins, mood can change from euthymic to neutral, often described by patients as blah, blue, empty, sad, hopeless, and irritable. When depressed, patients describe themselves as impatient, intolerant, edgy, nervous, lost, misunderstood, disinterested, sensitive, angry, or "stuck." Depressed moods are usually very apparent to the person who is suffering, but may not be obvious to others if the individual's internal coping resources compensate for the depression. In contrast, the mood changes in mania are often quite noticeable to others, but may be less apparent to the patient. Mood changes in mania can be uplifting, positive, hopeful, excited, euphoric, "on top of the world," or optimistic. Although the stereotypic manic is happy and carefree, few patients have predictably pleasant manic episodes. Mania can also leave

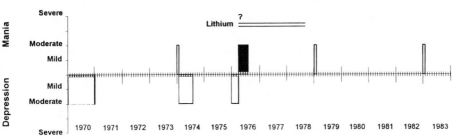

FIGURE 4.3. Computer-generated Life Chart.

people feeling extremely irritable, agitated, anxious, tense, and fearful. For some patients, the pleasant or euphoric mood evolves into irritability as the mania progresses and worsens.

The cognitive changes associated with depression are apparent to others only when verbalized by the patient. In fact, depressed patients are often unaware of their own changes in views or beliefs. The cognitive shifts can be subtle at first (e.g., less optimism and more pessimism). Events in an individual's environment can reinforce and strengthen these changes in perspective.

> Mr. Daniels described how nothing was going right. He was probably not going to get the promotion that he deserved because the boss had been showing more interest in the new guy. Last week, his car started making a strange noise, just when he had almost paid off his car loan. He would probably have to put a lot of money into repairs, and those mechanics cannot be trusted; they are just out for money. The circumstances in Mr. Daniels's life reinforced his pessimism. In his mind, he was just being realistic, and the optimists in the world irritated him.

Depressed people may have negative or distorted perceptions of themselves, the world at large, and the future—the "cognitive triad" as described by Beck (1976; Beck & Rush, 1995). They may misinterpret the words and behaviors of others, jump to conclusions, or take personal offense when one was not intended. When others point out these negative cognitions, depressed individuals may react in a defensive, embarrassed, or angry manner: "I'm not being overly sensitive; you're just inconsiderate."

The cognitive changes observed in mania are qualitatively different from depression. There are two types: changes in the content of thoughts and changes in the thinking process. Patients in the early stages of mania not only may have increased confidence, optimism, and interest, but also may be more suspicious of others in their environment. These cognitive shifts can evolve into grandiose and/or persecutory delusions. A concomitant of the content changes are process changes, such as racing thoughts, distractibility, impaired judgment, and auditory and visual hallucinations. Although the grandiosity may be pleasant, the process changes are usually unpleasant.

> Ms. Clark knew that she was becoming manic. Her thinking was confused. She talked about having difficulty in concentrating on the television and listening to the radio. The sounds and movements around her were magnified and distorted. She longed for quiet, solitude, and freedom from all the stimuli in her environment.

Observers can usually identify the behavioral symptoms of depression and mania, particularly when the observers have seen the patient in both states. Depression is usually characterized by a reduction in psychomotor activity. Unless able to compensate, depressed persons may neglect their daily responsibilities (e.g., household chores), cease to engage in their usual hobbies, and withdraw from others. They may continue to work or care for children, but they often prefer to be left alone. They may actually begin to move more slowly and talk more slowly than usual. Other physical symptoms of depression manifested in behavior are sleep changes, altered eating habits, decreased sex drive, and low energy.

In striking contrast is the increased activity associated with mania. Patients in the early stages of mania or hypomania often exhibit more ideas and interests than actual changes in activity. As mania progresses, their physical activity may increase. Restlessness or agitation may become evident in pacing, walking long distances, and seeking out activity. Many patients in a manic episode may have a strong drive to be more socially or sexually active. They may start new tasks that they never complete. Every new opportunity seems like a good idea that is worth their time, energy, and money. The concomitant impairment in social judgment facilitates the activity, because patients cannot always rely on their reasoning to inhibit inappropriate actions.

DIFFERENTIATING NORMAL
FROM ABNORMAL MOODS

Everyone has fluctuations in mood in reaction to factors in the environment such as stress, good news, disappointments, or internal events such as humor, hormone shifts, fatigue, worry, and affection. In fact, within a single day it is not unusual for a person to experience several different mood states. Because it is normal for people to react emotionally to both internal (e.g., recollections, fears) and external (e.g., football, television commercials) stimuli, patients with bipolar disorder will have "normal" mood shifts and "abnormal" or symptomatic mood shifts. The challenge for clinicians, patients, and their family members is to differentiate the two.

Normal mood fluctuations are transient and/or tied to specific stimulus events. When the stimulus event has passed, the mood slowly returns to normal. Some stressful events, like divorce, will have an enduring impact and are not considered abnormal. The stresses involved are not discrete events that end when the person goes to sleep; each day may present new problems or powerful reminders of the old. Other events (e.g., death in the family) may be discrete, but the emotional reaction may persist for some time. As a general rule, once a stressor has ceased, a person's mood should begin to improve. A persistent or gradual worsening of mood rather than improvement may indicate that the initial reaction may be evolving into a clinically significant depression.

The mood state alone may not provide enough information to determine whether a reaction is normal or abnormal. The concomitant cognitive, behavioral, and physiological changes may be more informative. To distinguish normal from abnormal mood shifts, the patient and the clinician need a reference point against which to gauge symptomatic changes.

SYMPTOM SUMMARY WORKSHEET

While the Life Chart provides a global view of a person's course of illness, the Symptom Summary Worksheet focuses more closely on the specific symptoms that occur during episodes of depression and mania (see Figure 4.4). As shown in Table 4.1, the Symptom Summary Worksheet is one way of beginning to differentiate normal from abnormal mood states and symptoms. The worksheet summarizes the major symptoms of depression and mania for a given patient and contrasts those symptoms with the person's normal or euthymic state. This provides the patient and the clinician with guidelines against which to compare mood and symptom fluctuations. If some of the symptoms listed on the worksheet under depression or mania accompany mood fluctuations, these are more than "normal" reactions to stressors and should be monitored closely. Table 4.2 is a Symptom Summary Worksheet for a 48-year-old man with a history of bipolar disorder.

To begin the symptom summary, the clinician may ask patients to describe what they are like when in a "normal," nonsymptomatic state.

TABLE 4.1. Symptom Summary Worksheet

Name of patient: _____   Date: _____

Normal	Depression	Mania
_____	_____	_____
_____	_____	_____
_____	_____	_____
_____	_____	_____
_____	_____	_____
_____	_____	_____
_____	_____	_____
_____	_____	_____
_____	_____	_____
_____	_____	_____
_____	_____	_____
_____	_____	_____
_____	_____	_____
_____	_____	_____
_____	_____	_____
_____	_____	_____
_____	_____	_____
_____	_____	_____

TABLE 4.2. Sample Symptom Summary Worksheet

Name of patient: ___Mr. Smith_____   Date: ___Today_____

Normal	Depression	Mania
6–8 hrs. of sleep	don't want to get up	need 5 hrs. sleep
more introverted	18 hrs. in bed/day	poor concentration
pleasant	suicidal thoughts	"Mr. Wonderful"
people enjoy being	desperation	look for challenging
around me	worthless	things to do
can converse with others	hopeless	I'm brilliant
I think I'm all right	no energy	ambitious
confident	no motivation	very creative
	not hungry	want to be with people
	read more/in bed	increased sexual
	bleak	appetite
	no future	spend money/use
	no interest in people,	credit cards
	don't care	judgment impaired
	don't answer phone	above reproach
	want to destroy myself	euphoric, excited
		talkative, change topics
		not paying attention
		my ideas are more im-
		portant than others'

This can be difficult at first, especially if patients have been symptomatic more often than not in the past few years. Probing for a description of their personality, style, typical behavior, likes and dislikes, temperament, sense of humor, and daily habits and routines can help. A running list of these descriptors can be kept on the Symptom Summary Worksheet in the column labeled "Normal." Input from family members and friends can be particularly useful for this exercise, because they can often recall what the patient was like before the illness began.

Separately for episodes of depression and episodes of mania, the patient lists the symptoms that he or she most commonly experiences. If uncertain, the clinician can review the symptoms identified at the time of a past diagnostic evaluation. For each symptom, the clinician asks how it differs in the other states. For example, if insomnia is a symptom of depression, the clinician may ask how the person's sleep habits are different when hypomanic or manic and when euthymic. Each symptom is listed in the appropriate column on the worksheet. (The symptoms of hypomania are added to the mania column of the worksheet.) If symptoms of both depression and mania commonly occur within a single episode, the clinician marks on the summary worksheet that the symptoms in two columns occur simultaneously. Probing questions that help patients to recall symptoms include the following:

- How does your life change when depressed or when manic?
- How, if at all, does your view of yourself, others, and the future change when depressed, when manic, and when feeling fine?

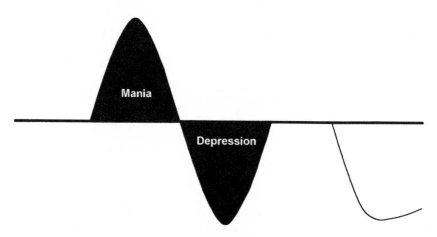

FIGURE 4.4. Focus of Symptom Summary Worksheet.

- What do other people notice during symptomatic times?
- What kinds of comments do you hear from others?

The responses to each of these questions can be included on the Symptom Summary Worksheet. Table 4.3 summarizes the steps for completion of the Symptom Summary Worksheet.

When completed, the worksheet provides a fairly detailed description of the patient in depressed, manic, and asymptomatic states. A copy of the Symptom Summary Worksheet is given to the patient and another copy kept in the chart for reference. If family members or friends are participating in the session, it may be helpful to provide them with a copy of the worksheet as well. More information can be added as it becomes available.

Like the Life Chart, the Symptom Summary Worksheet allows the clinician and the patient to look for larger patterns of symptoms across the history of the illness. With prevention of relapses and recurrences of depression and mania as the goal, this information provides a reference point against which the patient can check fluctuations in symptoms. When these fluctuations seem transient and minimally distressing, the patient can learn to note them, but not worry. When they persist and begin to resemble the descriptions of depression and/or mania on the Symptom Summary Worksheet, it is time to intervene to circumvent a relapse or recurrence.

The Symptom Summary Worksheet is particularly helpful when a patient, his or her family members, or the clinician suspect that the symptoms may be worsening. In the following example, this patient was concerned about feeling too good.

TABLE 4.3. Differentiating Normal from Pathological Mood States

1. Review the rationale for symptom detection with the patient and his or her significant others.

2. Ask patient and significant others to describe what the patient is like when in a "normal," nonsymptomatic state. Probe for a description of the patient's personality.

3. Review of manic and depressive symptoms.

    a. For episodes of depression and mania separately, ask the patient to list the symptoms he or she most commonly experiences. Add this to the Symptom Summary Worksheet.

    b. Ask for specific information regarding the course, duration, and severity of the symptoms.

    c. What do other people notice about the patient during symptomatic times?

    d. What kinds of comments does the patient hear from others?

    e. How does the patient's life change when manic?

PATIENT: Do you think I'm getting manic? I feel so up. I just got a new job, but I'm not sure that I should be so happy.

THERAPIST: Mania for you is usually more than just a happy feeling. What else is happening that has you concerned?

PATIENT: I'm not sure. I am looking forward to all the things I'm going to do with all the extra money I'm going to make. Is that crazy?

THERAPIST: Not necessarily. Let's look at this objectively by going over the symptoms of mania you listed on your Symptom Summary Worksheet.

The therapist and patient review each item on the worksheet. The patient had good mood and more optimism, but nothing else. They agreed that the patient will watch her symptoms closely for a week and check in with the therapist to discuss any changes.

The Symptom Summary Worksheet is particularly helpful in settling family disputes when a problem or event is being attributed to the patient's illness.

MRS. CERLINSKY: You are on my case again. There you go; you're irritable and edgy. That's how you get when you're sick. Have you been taking your medicine?

MR. CERLINSKY: I am not irritable, you just make me angry. Every time I catch you blowing money on those ungrateful kids you turn it around and blame me and my illness.

MRS. CERLINSKY: I am not. And besides, those sneakers were on sale and the kids have been wanting them for months. It's the least we can do after all you've put them through.

MR. CERLINSKY: There you go again. The same old line. You are making me sick.

Mr. Cerlinsky sees his doctor later that week and replays the argument. He's still angry with his wife. He and his doctor had agreed long ago that when Mrs. Cerlinsky complained about his irritability she would be given the benefit of the doubt. Mr. Cerlinsky and his doctor carefully reviewed the Symptom Summary Worksheet. Along with irritability, Mr. Cerlinsky was also having trouble sleeping and some difficulty with concentration on the job. These were his hallmark symptoms of the onset of depression. It was early October, his most vulnerable time of year. Mr. Cerlinsky refocused his energy away from his wife and onto himself and the prevention of a full episode of depression.

Equally as often, the observations of family members are misattributions to the patient's illness. A review of the Symptom Summary Worksheet, especially in the presence of the accusing family member, can help to end the conflict. If inconclusive, symptoms can be monitored more closely until both the patient and his or her therapist are certain that the symptoms are under control. When in doubt, check it out.

MOOD GRAPHS

Mood Graphs can be used to narrow the focus from the broad groupings of symptoms during typical episodes to daily changes in mood, cognition, and behavior. It is this level of monitoring that is required to identify subsyndromal symptoms that precede episodes of mania and depression. The Mood Graph can be used to rate affective changes such as sadness or euphoria, but is most helpful when used to track symptoms that are the earliest signs of symptom worsening for a given individual. Some people are most sensitive to changes in their outlook on life (more optimistic or pessimistic) or their views of themselves (more confident or more self-critical). Others notice changes in energy (increased or decreased) or activity (more active or more socially withdrawn). The Symptom Summary Worksheet can help the clinician and patient decide which symptoms will be most useful to monitor.

The anchor row in the middle of the graph shown in Figure 4.5 represents euthymia. The points above the anchor row, from 0 to +5, represent levels of mania; the highest points on the graph indicate manic episodes. The points below the anchor row, from 0 to –5, represent levels of depression, with the lowest points indicating major depressive episodes. Normal variations in mood vary from –1 to +1. Ratings of +2 to –2 alert patients to begin monitoring their symptoms a little more closely. A score of –3 or +3 indicates that it is time to intervene to keep the symptoms from worsening. For example, at a rating of +3 or –3, it is time to call the doctor if the patient does not have an appointment scheduled within the next few days.

This simple Mood Graph may be sufficient for some patients. However, it is better to tailor a Mood Graph to the special needs of each patient. For example, those who have several shifts in mood during a day may need a mood graph designed for separate ratings at different times of the day (e.g., morning, afternoon, and evening). Information about the circumstances surrounding mood shifts can be noted on the graph. This information can help clinicians to design interventions that prevent worsening of moods. For example, patients may find that their mood shifts when they leave home and go to work, when their children return from school, when they see their spouses, or when they are hungry. These

Name of patient: _____   For week of: _____

Completed by: _____   Relationship to patient: _____

MOOD GRAPH

	Day 1	Day 2	Day 3	Day 4	Day 5	Day 6	Day 7
Date:							

Manic

+5	•	•	•	•	•	•	•
+4	•	•	•	•	•	•	•
+3 Time to Intervene	•	•	•	•	•	•	•
+2 Monitor Closely	•	•	•	•	•	•	•
+1	•	•	•	•	•	•	•
0 Normal	•	•	•	•	•	•	•
−1	•	•	•	•	•	•	•
−2 Monitor Closely	•	•	•	•	•	•	•
−3 Time to Intervene	•	•	•	•	•	•	•
−4	•	•	•	•	•	•	•
−5	•	•	•	•	•	•	•

Depressed

FIGURE 4.5. Mood Graph.

mood shifts do not necessarily require a pharmacological intervention, but may be addressed with CBT techniques.

> Mrs. Williams does not notice when her mood changes, but she does notice that her activity level varies greatly and is usually an indicator that she is "getting sick." "I don't know what's wrong with me. I'm doing fine, working at a normal pace, and suddenly I just want to sit in front of the television and do nothing. I stay that way for days and just get worse and worse. There are other days when I am full of energy and want to clean the house, go shopping, and visit the neighbors. I work at the office a lot more than I should. I get so wound up. What's wrong with me?"

It is also possible to monitor activity fluctuations on a Mood Graph. The Symptom Summary Worksheet helps in defining anchor points for activity levels on the graph. For example, a rating of +3 may be appropriate if the patient becomes more active and sleeps less by at least an hour (i.e., two symptoms in the mania column of the worksheet).

Patients who are sensitive to their cognitive shifts in mania and depression may prefer to monitor changes in thinking.

> Mr. Gibson becomes increasingly suspicious when he is shifting into mania. He starts to question the intentions of his family, and he hears strange noises that suggest malicious behavior in his neighbors and friends. He begins to read things into the words of others, takes offense easily, and feels that the world is against him. His therapist shows appropriate empathy for his discomfort, but also points out to him that he typically has these kinds of thoughts when he is becoming manic. Mr. Gibson's Life Chart and Symptom Summary Worksheet support this point.

It is possible to process these types of cognitive distortions when the distortions are somewhat mild and the patient can still use logical reasoning. When the cognitive changes have evolved into paranoid delusions, however, cognitive restructuring can be more difficult. (See Scott, Byers, & Turkington, 1993, for cognitive restructuring techniques for delusional thinking.)

Patients can combine the monitoring of affective, behavioral, and cognitive shifts on the same graph by using the letters *A*, *B*, and *C*, respectively, at each rating time. This method works well with patients who experience depressive and manic symptoms simultaneously. In these patients, the clinician does not look for polarity shifts, but rather for any symptom changes greater than +2 or −2 on the graph.

The amount of alcohol consumed, money spent, and medications needed can also be monitored on a graph. Similarly, symptom shifts, such as sleep changes, can be tracked. Because the selection of symptoms to be monitored depends on the special symptom presentations of the patient, it is wise to work with each patient in developing a personalized monitoring system. The clinician should encourage each patient to be creative in developing a graph that will provide as much useful information as possible.

FEEDBACK FROM OTHERS

Unlike the onset of depression, which patients can generally recognize, the onset of hypomania or mania may be apparent to others before the patient has noticed any changes. Subtle symptomatic changes in mood, behavior (e.g., psychomotor speed), and speech (e.g., rate and content) are cues that others can communicate to the patient. The input of family members and friends is not always welcome, however. There may be tension in the family because of negative past experiences associated with the episodes of illness. For example, the anxiety, guilt, and paranoia that can accompany depression or mania may leave patients hypersensitive to the comments and perceived criticisms of others. It is also not unusual for the bipolar disorder patient to become the family scapegoat, inaccurately blamed for every family problem. In such families, patients are likely to reject without consideration even accurate feedback from family members.

The issue of giving feedback without angering a patient is a common problem in therapy with the families of bipolar patients. Family members may have useful observations to share but may not have the skill to present them in a nonaccusatory fashion. They often ask, "What should I do if I see that he is spending too much money?" "Should I tell her to bathe if I notice that she hasn't in a while?" "How can I ask if he has taken his medication without starting a fight?" When these questions come up, we turn the question to the patients, "Is feedback from family members ever useful?" "How would you like them to communicate their observations?" "How can they be helpful and not hurtful?" Patients most frequently reply that the information is useful and is least offensive when communicated as a show of caring or concern. For example, "I'm worried about you today. You've been alone in your room for a long time. Is there anything I can do to help?" In exchange for the show of concern, the patient must agree at least to consider the input and examine his or her Mood Graphs and Symptom Summary Worksheets to determine if, in fact, symptoms are beginning to develop. The effectiveness of symptom monitoring, after all, depends on the patient's ability to recognize symptom fluctuations and act before symptoms are out of control.

CHAPTER SUMMARY

The strength of CBT is in the prevention of recurrences of depression and mania. To be maximally effective, symptom fluctuations must be identified early in their course of development. If clinicians and patients can identify the prodromal symptoms of depression and mania, these symptoms can be monitored regularly.

Methods used for symptom detection are Life Charts, the Symptom Summary Worksheet, and Mood Graphs. Life Charts depict an individual's history of bipolar disorder including episodes of illness, treatments received, and significant life events. Life Charts can reveal patterns of episodes (e.g., depression always following mania) as well as the influence of stressful events and therapeutic interventions on the frequency and duration of episodes. The Symptom Summary Worksheet lists the typical symptoms experienced during periods of depression and mania as they contrast with euthymia. This worksheet has several uses, but is most commonly used as a reference sheet for self-assessment of symptoms, very much like structured rating scales.

Mood Graphs are used to monitor mood fluctuations or symptoms from the worksheet that present earliest in the course of depression or mania. Selection of a target for monitoring is dependent on patient preference. Mood Graphs can be stylized for multiple daily ratings or for tracking of several symptoms simultaneously (e.g., mood and activity level).

Making the assessment of symptoms more objective can help eliminate the guesswork that occurs for patients and family members. It takes the observations of others and gives them structure so that the accusatory process is greatly reduced. For patients who live with other family members, the Symptom Summary Worksheet is a powerful educational tool. It can help to evaluate misattributions of behaviors and family problems to the patient's illness. Patients report feeling a greater sense of control when they are able to monitor the occurrence of cognitive, affective, and behavioral changes and intervene early, before they lose the capacity for self-evaluation.

FIVE

Encouraging Adherence to Treatment

SESSION 7. TREATMENT COMPLIANCE

Purpose of the Session

In this session, the therapist will introduce the idea that it is common for patients on a long-term course of prophylactic medication to have difficulty in fully complying with the prescribed treatment. Various factors can interfere with the patient's ability to follow through. This inevitable part of medication treatment should be expected and planned for by patients and clinicians. Increasing patients' comfort with the discussion of adherence problems will allow patients and therapists to assess and resolve any current or anticipated problems with adherence to the prescribed treatment plan.

Goals of the Session

1. Introduce the CBT treatment compliance model.
2. Assess for current or potential obstacles to following the treatment plan.
3. Develop a plan of action for addressing these obstacles.

Procedure

1. Invite questions regarding the mood graphing assignment from last session. If the Mood Graph was not completed, proceed with the compliance intervention. Have patients try to retrospectively complete the Mood Graph for the previous week. Assign the graph again as the next homework assignment.

(cont.)

(continued from page 86)

2. Introduce the CBT model of adherence.
3. Assess under what circumstances patients are most likely and least likely to follow their treatment plans explicitly. What are the outcomes?
4. Ask patients to describe their current treatment plans. Assess patients' attitudes and beliefs about their diagnoses and treatment plans. Identify any misconceptions about either their diagnoses or treatments and address any misconceptions with information and/or cognitive restructuring techniques (see Chapter 6).
5. Assess current level of medication compliance. Ask patients how they are taking their medications. Compare prescribed plan to actual behavior. Assess for difficulties with the plans and negotiate changes with patients to accommodate their schedules and lifestyles. Seek approval from their designated psychiatrists, if needed.
6. Assess for and resolve any current or anticipated obstacles to treatment using the problem-solving model. If patients deny having any current or anticipated difficulties, review problems encountered in the past, choose one, and proceed with the intervention.
7. Provide patients with the homework materials for this week.

Homework
1. Implement plan to overcome obstacles to adherence.
2. Ask patients to keep a Mood Graph for the next week.

Nonadherence to pharmacotherapy accounts for a large percentage of recurrences of depression and mania in patients with bipolar disorder. Compliance is not an all-or-none phenomenon. Patients cannot be classified into discrete groups of compliers and noncompliers. Data show that it is difficult to predict a priori which patients will have more difficulty adhering to treatment. The goal of CBT is to enhance compliance in all patients, prevent compliance problems when possible, and, if not, identify and remove the obstacles that interfere with compliance.

WHY ALL THE FUSS ABOUT COMPLIANCE?

Up to 46% of those taking lithium fail to take their medication as prescribed (Basco & Rush, 1995). In a survey of patients for whom lithium had been prescribed, 90% of patients who had not yet discontinued taking the medication reported that they had considered doing so (Jamison, Gerner, & Goodwin, 1979). Because it lowers the amount of lithium in the body below a therapeutically useful level, inconsistency in taking medications can render this medication as ineffective as discontinuing lithium altogether.

The picture is similar for antidepressant medications. Even in clinical research settings where patients receive considerable attention, 38–60% of patients being treated with antidepressant medications stop taking their medication prematurely, usually against medical advice (Jacob et al., 1984; Overall, Donachie, & Faillace, 1987; Park & Lipman, 1964; Pugh, 1983). In general practice settings, up to 68% of patients have shown themselves to be noncompliant with antidepressant treatment regimens (Johnson, 1981). The efficacy of medications in preventing relapse and/or recurrences of mania and depression, even in patients with bipolar disorder who take their medications conscientiously, is not 100%. Inconsistent use of these medications further compromises the effectiveness of pharmacotherapy.

WHAT IS NONCOMPLIANCE?

"I don't understand. When you are sick, you take medicine. When you are well, you stop. I had pneumonia once. I took medicine. I got better. The doctor told me I didn't need any more medicine. I was cured. So why do they make such a big deal about taking lithium when I feel fine? I don't see the point. It makes me feel sluggish, dull, bored. So why should I take it?"

Mr. Jeffries was a 36-year-old musician who had been hospitalized and given lithium for mania on four occasions over a 15-year period. He saw no reason for taking lithium when he was feeling well, however, so he had stopped taking it soon after each discharge from the hospital.

The story was always the same. Mr. Jeffries would feel fine for a period of time and saw no need for the continued use of lithium. He considered each episode of mania to be an independent event that would have occurred with or without medication. As far as Mr. Jeffries was concerned, he needed medicine when he had a recurrence of mania, just as he might need medicine for a recurrence of the flu.

As many studies on medication compliance have shown (Marston, 1970), patients often discontinue treatment when acute symptoms and pain remit, even when they receive instructions to complete a longer course. In the prophylactic treatment of chronic conditions such as hypertension, diabetes, and bipolar disorder, patients may discontinue or reduce their effort in following treatment recommendations when they are feeling better, especially if there is some discomfort associated with treatment. When euthymic, some patients with bipolar disorder find that the side effects of medications are intolerable. Compliance appears to be greater if the intervention is brief, minimally uncomfortable or inconvenient, or if the individual believes that the beneficial effects greatly outweigh these discomforts.

IS IT RESISTANCE?

Mr. Jeffries's beliefs about treatment precluded prophylactic treatment. His psychiatrist interpreted the noncompliance with lithium treatment as evidence of Mr. Jeffries's denial that he had a chronic psychiatric illness. The psychiatrist believed that, when Mr. Jeffries stopped taking his medicine, in spite of advice to the contrary, he was acting out his anger toward the physician who was attempting to confront the patient's denial. The therapeutic relationship was tense. Mr. Jeffries missed several appointments. The psychiatrist had difficulty in demonstrating any genuine compassion or empathy for this patient, whose noncompliance greatly irritated him.

The traditional view equates noncompliance with resistance. Although they may interpret such behavior as a manifestation of an underlying psychic process within the patient, many clinicians still feel angry when patients fail to follow their prescribed treatment regimens. This is especially true when noncompliance leads to relapse or recurrence of illness. Health care providers may give lip service to the underlying psychic processes that impede treatment, but they are as likely to communicate blame as they are to communicate empathy. A clinician will usually not say "I told you so!" to the noncompliant patient who has sought emergency care for a new episode of mania or severe depression; however, frustration naturally follows when patients persist in being noncompliant after being warned of the potential consequences.

The conceptualization of noncompliance as resistance offers few treatment options. Clinicians can attempt to interpret the noncompliance and work through the emotions attached to the behavior, but such an approach may take considerable time and may not improve adherence in the long run. The cognitive-behavioral view defines noncompliance differently. Specifically, noncompliance is defined as a discrepancy between the practitioner's instructions and the patient's behavior that results from a failure in the development of the treatment plan. It is assumed that every patient is capable of achieving a certain degree of compliance to treatment; however, obstacles can arise that interfere with even the best treatment plans. In Mr. Jeffries's case, for example, his misconception of the recurrent nature of bipolar disorder, his misunderstanding of maintenance treatment, the strained therapeutic alliance, and the side effects that he experienced when taking lithium all interfered with his ability or willingness to take his medications regularly. Resolution of the compliance problem consists of identification (or anticipation) and reduction of the various obstacles to compliance. In Mr. Jeffries's case, this would mean addressing his misconceptions with education (see Chapter 1) and cognitive restructuring (see Chapter 6), mending the therapeutic alliance (see below), and attempting to reduce or control the side effects of the medication (see Chapter 3).

TYPES OF NONCOMPLIANCE

Patients' actions and physicians' prescriptions can diverge in several ways. The greatest deviation is for a patient either to refuse treatment altogether or to discontinue treatment prematurely (i.e., against the physician's advice). Attrition from treatment does not always mean discontinuation of medication. In fact, seeking more acceptable treatment elsewhere could suggest that the person is a discriminating consumer. However, most patients who drop out of treatment are no longer following the prescribed treatment plan. Most patients follow their treatment plans to the best of their abilities most of the time, but intermittently make errors in the dosage, timing, or regularity of medication.

Errors of dosage include taking too many or too few pills. Most problems with compliance involve missing some doses of medication.

> Ms. Nelson, for example, was to take medications three times a day for a total of 21 dosings per week. With some effort, she could usually remember to take 16 or 17 doses per week. She believed that her medications were helpful and would ultimately keep her well. She would just forget from time to time to take her medication. Her doctor told her that if she were uncertain about whether or not she had taken her medicine, it was best not to take any than to risk overdosing.

At times patients deviate from their treatment plans by taking more medication than prescribed. Some take the medications of their friends or family members in conjunction with or instead of their own. Occasionally, a patient intentionally takes an overdose of medication, but this should not be defined as a compliance problem. Errors of timing are common. Some patients take medications earlier or later than instructed, such as every 4 hours rather than every 6 hours. Some medications are to be taken in conjunction with food, others on an empty stomach. Missing these key events are errors of timing. Using recreational drugs or alcohol to control symptoms can be considered treatment noncompliance, particularly when abstaining from these substances is a stated treatment goal.

MEASUREMENT OF COMPLIANCE

The simplest way to assess compliance is to ask patients if they have taken all their medication, if they have missed any doses, and if they have taken them at the correct times of day. Questionnaires can also be helpful because they provide a standard format for measuring self-perceived, self-reported compliance and make it possible for clinicians to compare the compliance scores of a given patient over time or the scores of several patients. Although they are simple, self-reports can be inaccurate because of memory deficits, recall bias, or deliberate distortion.

In scientific investigations and in some clinic settings, health care providers use "pill counts" to measure patient compliance. After dispensing a number of pills that may match or exceed the amount needed until the next visit, a clinician instructs the patient to return any unused pills at the following visit. The clinician then counts the remaining pills and compares the total to the number previously dispensed. Discrepancies are considered evidence of poor compliance. Pill counts are considerably more complex, but tend to be more accurate, than self-reports. When they compared self-reports of compliance and pill counts in the same patients, Park and Lipman (1964) found that 40% of the patients' self-reports did not match the results of the pill counts. They also found that minor discrepancies tended to occur more frequently than major deviations in compliance.

A more commonly used method for assessing treatment compliance is to measure the plasma concentrations or blood level of medications. A higher than expected ratio of prescribed dose to plasma drug level may suggest poor compliance. A comparison of dose to plasma level ratios in a given individual over time allows for individual variations in metabolism and avoids invalid accusations of poor compliance when the ratio in one patient is different from those observed in other patients. Changes in the ratio within an individual may be more likely to indicate poor compliance, provided that the timing of doses and blood sampling remains constant.

Although measuring medication blood levels appears to be a more accurate method than self-reports, the consistency with which blood levels reflect the dose ingested may vary with the type of medication (Hollister, 1982). This suggests that, with some medications, it may be necessary to rely on alternative methods for monitoring compliance.

Plasma concentrations of lithium may be fairly reliable indicators of patient compliance, assuming consistency in timing of doses and blood sampling. This method, however, is not foolproof.

> Mr. Yamaguchi has been taking lithium for bipolar disorder over several years. He revealed that, if he has missed doses, he can take his medication very consistently for a few days just before his blood lithium level measurement and his test will show a level in the therapeutic range.

To avoid the possibility that such behavior might obscure actual compliance levels, Schwarcz and Silbergeld (1983) conducted unannounced spot-check plasma lithium level measurements on 26 lithium clinic patients. They found that 42% ($n = 11$) of their patients had lithium levels outside the therapeutic range. The 11 patients received counseling about compliance and more than half subsequently improved in their adherence to the treatment regimen.

The degree to which patients actively participate in treatment also indicates the level of their compliance. Appointment attendance, tardiness to sessions, level of involvement in the treatment sessions, and completion of homework assignments between sessions are all indicators of general compliance to treatment.

In clinical practice, the best method for assessment of compliance is an open and nonjudgmental discussion with patients. We discuss below the methods for establishing a therapeutic environment where compliance can be discussed openly. This does not mean that assessment of medication blood levels is unnecessary. On the contrary, it is often critical to pharmacological management of patients. We do not believe, however, that it is the best way to monitor compliance.

PREDICTION OF COMPLIANCE

The most consistent finding in studies comparing the diagnostic characteristics of patients with mood disorders who comply with and complete treatment and those who do not is that those with greater psychopathology have more difficulty following treatment instructions (Aagaard & Vestergaard, 1990; Danion et al., 1987; Jacob et al., 1984; Overall et al., 1987; Persons, Burns, & Perloff, 1988; Rabin, Kaslow, & Rehm, 1985). For example, those patients with personality disorders or substance abuse problems are less likely to adhere to treatment.

Compliance does not appear to be consistently related to the length or polarity of the index episode, age of onset of the illness (Aagaard & Vestergaard, 1990; Connelly et al., 1982; Danion, Neureuther, Krieger-Finance, Imbs, & Singer, 1987; Frank, Prien, Kupfer, & Alberts, 1985; Jacob et al., 1984; Simons, Levine, Lustman, & Murphy, 1984), number of previous episodes of illness, or interepisode recovery (Aagaard & Vestergaard, 1990; Frank et al., 1985). Just as all patients are capable of compliance, it is fair to say that all patients are capable of noncompliance.

CBT COMPLIANCE MODEL

Although we assume that everyone is capable of some degree of treatment compliance, obstacles often arise that interfere with the person's ability to fully follow the health care provider's recommendations (Meichenbaum & Turk, 1988). The CBT approach to compliance focuses on maximizing the chance of adherence by minimizing the obstacles that interfere with the treatment plan. Table 5.1 lists some of the more common obstacles to adherence.

> Mrs. Denton believed that the prophylactic treatment plan for her bipolar disorder was reasonable, but, when she was busy, she forgot to take her pills. She had never admitted this to her physician, because she knew that this admission would not be well received. No discussion of the issue also meant no opportunity for creative problem solving, however. Thus, the obstacles to Mrs. Denton's adherence to treatment were forgetfulness and an inability to discuss this problem with the clinician.

The clinician can introduce the CBT model of compliance to patients as follows:

> "Mrs. Denton, there are a lot of things that can keep people from following through with treatment plans, even when they think the intervention will be helpful. For example, I think exercising regularly would be good for me, but things keep interfering with my exercise schedule. So I don't always follow the plan my doctor prescribed,

even though I know it is important. Have you found this to be true for you?"

Ask about patients' experiences with missing doses of medications, stopping medications altogether, and missing appointments; the circumstances under which they detoured from treatment; and any ensuing consequences, then try to reconceptualize the experiences in terms of the CBT model.

"So you think that taking medication is a good idea but what gets in the way is that when you are busy with other things, you sometimes forget to take your medicines. Let's think about what we can do to help you remember during busy times and what to do when you forget and actually miss doses altogether."

MAXIMIZING TREATMENT ADHERENCE

Adherence to treatment is not an all-or-nothing phenomenon in most cases. That is, it is not a matter of taking or not taking medication,

TABLE 5.1. Common Obstacles to Adherence

1. Intrapersonal variables.
   a. Remission in symptoms and seeing no need for further treatment.
   b. Decrease in energy, enthusiasm, creativity, and/or productivity.
   c. Denial that they have a chronic illness/stigma associated with bipolar illness.
   d. Depressive relapse.
2. Treatment variables.
   a. Side effects of medication.
   b. Medication schedule does not conform to patient's personal schedule.
3. Social system variables.
   a. Psychosocial stressors.
   b. Competing medical advice.
   c. Discouragement from family and friends.
4. Interpersonal variables.
   a. Poor rapport with the therapist and/or psychiatrist.
   b. Busy, uncomfortable, or otherwise unpleasant clinic environment.
5. Cognitive variables.
   a. Patient does not like the idea of having to depend on drugs.
   b. Patient thinks he or she should be able to handle mood swings on his or her own.
   c. Patient misattributes symptoms of bipolar illness to another source.

but more likely an issue of consistency. The interventions in this chapter for enhancing compliance to treatment do not aim for achievement of full and total compliance (i.e., each pill taken exactly at the right times each day, or each homework assignment executed exactly as instructed each time), although, of course, this is preferable. Instead, the emphasis here is on improvement, optimization, or maximization of adherence for a given individual. Perfection is not a reasonable goal, because if perfection is not obtained, the likely interpretation is that the patient has failed. This type of categorical or black-and-white thinking sets patients up for failure when applied to issues of compliance. The message to patients should be that it is important to do the best they can to take this medication regularly, to figure out what interferes with their good intentions and remove or compensate for these obstacles as much as possible.

Developing the Therapeutic Alliance

The effective treatment of patients with bipolar disorder requires long-term therapeutic relationships based on trust. Clinicians are often stabilizing forces in the lives of these patients. Unfortunately, those with bipolar disorder may have had negative past experiences in seeking help from health care providers. They may be suspicious of a clinician's treatment recommendations, such as hospitalization, especially if their symptoms include paranoia or severe anxiety. Therefore, in order to establish rapport, clinicians may have to convince patients through both words and actions that they are trustworthy.

> Ms. Schmidt and her psychologist have been working together for 3 years. Initially, Ms. Schmidt had been very reluctant to get involved with the therapist, because she had several "weird" experiences with other therapists in the past. She knew that she needed help, however. After Ms. Schmidt told her therapist about the experiences with other clinicians, the psychologist took special care to develop the relationship without pushing her. They found a way to talk about relationship issues, such as Ms. Schmidt's feelings of abandonment when the therapist went out of town. The resulting trust facilitated the patient's examination of difficult personal issues that in the past had hindered her ability to comply with treatment.

In traditional physician–patient relationships, patients are expected to follow their physicians' instructions without question or complaint. In contrast, the CBT approach encourages patients to be informed consumers, which means asking questions, giving opinions, and feeling comfortable in disagreeing with clinicians. Active involvement in treatment helps patients to become invested in getting better. In a collaborative health care relationship, both parties are able to discuss the negative and the positive aspects of the treatment process. Although the physician may ultimately "know best," patients' experiences with their own illnesses and treatments may give them insights that can be valuable in treatment planning. Moreover, the physician's demonstration of respect for patients' ideas models and further facilitates collaboration.

The interactions that patients have with other medical personnel can also influence their feelings and attitudes about treatment and, ultimately, their level of compliance. If the office is busy, if the receptionist or nurse appears distant or unfriendly, or if the patient must wait a long time before being seen, he or she may develop negative attitudes toward the provider or toward the health care establishment in general. Such attitudes can reduce the patient's willingness to cooperate with treatment.

Similarly, the demeanor of the health care provider can have an impact on the patient's adherence to treatment.

Dr. Stanley was an excellent psychiatrist, well trained and greatly respected for his work. "My dear woman," he explained, "you are suffering from a breakthrough of depression. It is probably a good idea to run some routine tests to rule out any organic contributor to this recent exacerbation of symptoms. If everything checks out, as I imagine it will, we will continue with the current regimen—perhaps with the addition of one of the newer medications, such as valproic acid. Not to worry. Just trust me, and you'll do fine. See me in 2 weeks."

Mrs. Jenkins left the office and joined her husband in the waiting area. "What did the doctor say?" her husband asked. "He wants to do some tests, because he thinks there is something wrong with me. If I don't get better, he's going to experiment on me with a new drug called 'something acid.' He said he wants to see me in 2 weeks, but the receptionist says he doesn't have an appointment available for another month." Mrs. Jenkins was scared. She did not completely understand why Dr. Stanley wanted to run some tests, as he had never done so before. The mention of a new medicine with a name like "acid" was especially frightening. She had not asked for details because she was embarrassed to admit her ignorance. Obviously, the doctor thought that she should be able to understand what he was saying or he would not have said it. He had also implied that he was going to take good care of her, but she later found that he could not see her as he suggested.

Mrs. Jenkins knew that she was fortunate to have such a well-known psychiatrist as her doctor. She knew that she was one of a few patients that he saw, out of the goodness of his heart, at a reduced fee. She could not complain for fear of appearing ungrateful; she could not ask questions for fear of appearing ignorant. Furthermore, she could not demand to be seen sooner, because she was "lucky to be seen at all."

Dr. Stanley was a kindhearted and well-intentioned clinician. His manner demonstrated that he was comfortable with psychiatric jargon. He also verbalized his thinking about treatment decisions and was accustomed to working with bright, articulate, and well-read patients. He believed that his authoritative approach provided his patients with a sense of security and a feeling that they were in the hands of a master healer. What Dr. Stanley had forgotten was that not all patients are the same. Some find the authoritative stance comforting, and, in fact, respond well to ("need") strong limit setting and direct commands. Mrs. Jenkins was not one of those people, however, and the well-intentioned psychiatrist failed to notice.

Attending to the therapeutic alliance means that clinicians must look beyond the content of each visit or session and attend to the interpersonal process and social context of treatment. As Mrs. Jenkins's experience shows, this requires the clinician to respond to each client's individual, unique needs. To do so, clinicians must evaluate their own performance with each person they treat. Attention to nonverbal cues, such as facial expressions, and solicitation of questions about the treatment plan are two ways to evaluate the patient's concerns or needs. Some sample questions are "Does this plan sound OK to you?" "Does this make sense?" "Do you think we are getting at the main problem?" Another method is to ask the patient to paraphrase the doctor's assessment and treatment plan. Listen for misinterpretations and provide corrective feedback.

DESIGNING THE "RIGHT" TREATMENT

The success of a treatment plan depends largely on its acceptability to the patient. The simplest way to determine the patient's response is to review the diagnosis and treatment with the patient and ask his or her opinion: "Does this diagnosis make sense?" "Do you think it describes what you have been experiencing?" "Do you think this treatment plan will work?" As the patient responds, the clinician listens for underlying beliefs or attitudes about treatment.

It is not unusual for patients to feel apprehensive about treatment. If they have lingering concerns, they might agree to follow treatment recommendations while in the office, but do not follow through at home. Inquiring about patients' feelings and concerns gives health care providers opportunities to address these issues before they interfere with treatment. Simple questions (e.g., "How long will I have to take the medication?") may suggest some concern about addiction, dependence, or expense of treatment. Nonverbal behaviors can also provide clues to underlying concerns. Looks of confusion, skepticism, or other facial expressions may suggest that they are troubled or are not paying attention. Verbalizing these observations (e.g., "You look confused") can open the door for discussion.

Although patients' fears or beliefs about treatment may seem illogical or absurd, it is better to validate their underlying concerns than to negate or dismiss them. If patients say, "I feel like a drug addict when I have to take medication every day," inquire about their concerns and convey understanding of this perspective. For example, clinicians may ask, "What do you think will happen if you keep taking this medication?" A less effective strategy is to invalidate their concerns. "Don't be silly. These are prescribed mediations, not street drugs. They won't make you high and they won't cause addiction."

To be able to adhere to treatment, people must understand (1) the rationale for treatment, (2) the purpose of the intervention, (3) the outcome expected if the intervention is successful, and (4) their specific responsibilities. A person who does not understand the importance or purpose of the treatment has no reason to comply with it. Table 5.2 lists some questions from patients that practitioners should address when beginning or changing a treatment regimen. Patients do not always realize that they need this type of information or that they have the right to ask these questions. Clinicians can help their patients to be knowledgeable consumers by encouraging them to ask questions and to be as active in treatment planning as they are expected to be in the execution of the regimen.

The degree to which patients feel that they have the necessary resources to carry out an intervention also affects compliance. Resources can include money to buy medication or to pay for office visits, transportation to the clinic, the ability to remember to take multiple daily doses, and tolerance for side effects, as well as encouragement and assistance from others. Lack of resources is a common obstacle to adherence for

TABLE 5.2. Questions for My Doctor

1. What is my diagnosis?
2. What does the diagnosis mean?
3. Why do I need medication?
4. How will each medication help me?
5. How will I know if it is working?
6. What should I do if I have side effects?
7. What should I do if I miss a dose of medication?
8. Does it matter what time of day I take my medication?

people who are unable to work because of their illness. Assistance from financial case workers, social workers, and families can be particularly helpful in reducing this treatment obstacle.

ESTABLISHING A FORUM FOR A DISCUSSION OF COMPLIANCE PROBLEMS

Mrs. Valdez did not take her medication regularly. With all the things that she had on her mind, she often forgot. She had been relatively free of symptoms, but knew that it was impossible to predict how much longer she would feel good before the pain of depression or the chaos of mania could come crashing down on her. Periodically, she vowed to become more diligent about taking her medication. Mrs. Valdez did not always tell her therapist, Dr. Mendez, the whole story. "Oh yes, Doctor, I'm still taking my lithium, and I'm feeling great. No problems with symptoms. I think I'm home free for a while." Mrs. Valdez had come to like her doctor and to care what he thought of her. Dr. Mendez would be disappointed if he knew that Mrs. Valdez had not been adhering to her medication regimen. "He would just worry about me," she thought. "I'll be OK." Although Mrs. Valdez felt comfortable in talking with Dr. Mendez about most things, she believed that her failure to take her medication as prescribed would upset him. She feared his disapproval, rejection, and withdrawal of support. Thus, she withheld the information about her missed doses.

To avoid such problems, it is important to establish a precedent of discussing compliance issues at the outset of treatment. However, clinicians must first come to accept the fact that patients are not always going to follow directions, even if they are clearly explained, are in the best interest of patients, and will greatly help their condition. Second, it is important to introduce the idea that full compliance can be difficult to achieve even when a person has the best intentions. For example, the clinician might say,

"As we have discussed, this medication will be most helpful to you if you take it regularly. What I would like to do as an ongoing part of our sessions is to anticipate times when it is difficult for you to take your medicines consistently, such as when you are busy and forget to take them. This will give us a chance to develop a plan that helps you to be more consistent with medicines or to talk about making changes when either of us thinks a change is needed. Does this idea make sense to you? To accomplish this, you and I have to be comfortable talking about the times you don't take your medicines."

Some clinicians are concerned that this type of discussion about compliance may inadvertently invite noncompliance from patients by implying that it is acceptable. This is much like the concern that inquiring about suicidal ideation may actually suggest suicide to patients. This theory has not been formally tested, but experience suggests that it has no basis in fact. To avoid such a situation, the message to patients must be that nonadherence to treatment is common, but carries consequences for their well-being.

> After Mr. Silver complained about his medication's side effects, his internist suggested that he call his psychiatrist to ask about discontinuing the medication. Mr. Silver was feeling better, and he and his internist were concerned about the weight that he had gained since he had been taking lithium. Although patients typically discontinue medication without first seeking consultation, Mr. Silver called his psychiatrist for permission. The psychiatrist had made it a practice to discuss medication compliance with all patients, and this precedent, which was set during treatment, made Mr. Silver feel comfortable discussing the medication change before any action was taken.

If more than one clinician is treating a patient (e.g., a psychiatrist and a psychotherapist), it is best if each is aware of the other's treatment plan. In this way, they can work together to monitor patients' progress and to determine if noncompliance is a problem. It is not necessary to begin each visit with an interrogation: "Have you taken your medication this week? Are you sure you haven't missed a dose? Show me your medicine bottle and let me see for myself." A less accusatory approach is best. For example, "Have you had any problems in taking your medication this week?" If there is no indication that compliance has been a problem, there is no reason to continue the discussion. If the clinician has evidence that the patient has not been taking the medication (e.g., laboratory results that indicate a low plasma medication level), it is best to tell the patient directly that the laboratory findings were outside the therapeutic window, which usually suggests that the patient has missed some doses of medication. The clinician can normalize the problem by reminding the patient that many people find it difficult to adhere to treatment over a long period of time.

NEGOTIATING TREATMENT GOALS

During the acute phase of mania or depression, the primary goal is to achieve a remission of symptoms. As treatment progresses and symptoms begin to ameliorate, other issues may become targets for therapeutic intervention. If patients are unemployed, for example, employment may become a treatment goal. Involving patients in setting their own treatment goals helps to maximize compliance and can strengthen the therapeutic alliance. Well-defined goals keep the therapy focused and provide a structure with which to assess progress regularly. Following are a few helpful hints for defining preliminary treatment goals:

1. Encourage the patient to set his or her own treatment goals. Taking medication consistently will usually be a treatment goal.
2. Keep goals simple.
3. Set small, easily achievable goals at first and increase the complexity or difficulty after the patient has had some success with the preliminary goals.
4. Make each step in the process of achieving a larger goal (e.g., finding a job) a subgoal (e.g., looking in the want ads).
5. Define each goal in sufficient detail so that (a) both the patient and the clinician understand what is to be undertaken and (b) attainment of the goal can be easily identified and/or verified.

REDUCING OBSTACLES TO ADHERENCE

Once rapport has been established and a treatment plan has been agreed upon, identify the potential obstacles to treatment compliance and develop strategies to reduce or eliminate each obstacle. After introducing each intervention, whether it is taking medication or carrying out some other activity, the clinician asks the patient, "What could keep you from following through with this part of the treatment plan?" The clinician then writes down the obstacles identified for later reference.

Clinicians can also help patients to anticipate obstacles to treatment adherence by asking about what has interfered with treatment in the past.

> Ms. Weller remembered that the last time she was on medication for depression her mother had been fearful that she would become addicted and had pressured her to stop taking the antidepressant. Her mother believed that Ms. Weller was a strong woman who could pull herself out of her depression without having to depend on medication. Ms. Weller's father had been an alcoholic for most of his life, and her mother was fearful that the children could become similarly addicted. Therefore, her mother's beliefs about medications potentially interfered with Ms. Weller's treatment. This would be listed as a potential obstacle to adherence.

To anticipate potential obstacles to adherence, it is sometimes helpful to have patients picture the usual circumstances under which they take their medicines or execute a homework assignment. What are their typical activities during the time that they generally take their medication? Where are they likely to be? Are there any other factors in their environments that may be relevant (e.g., being alone vs. with others, proximity to medication, mealtime)?

> Ms. Weller often had dinner with her mother. Under her new medication regimen, she was to take some of her medication at dinnertime. Although she kept her medication for the day in a plastic container in her purse, she sometimes put off taking it until after dinner, when her mother was not around. When Ms. Weller delayed taking her medication, however, she often forgot it altogether until it was time for the next dose. The patient and her therapist worked out a plan for those times when Ms. Weller dined with her mother. They changed the way that Ms. Weller took her medication and tried to resolve her mother's fears of medication addiction by educating her mother about bipolar disorder.

Identifying the obstacles to adherence can be the most difficult step in the CBT approach to improved compliance. Obstacles may not be obvious or easily definable. In their book *Facilitating Treatment Adherence* Meichenbaum and Turk (1988) provide a more complete listing of potential obstacles to adherence. It is often necessary to use a trial-and-error method by working through initial obstacles and having patients monitor the circumstances that accompany noncompliance. Resolution of obstacles to adherence becomes the immediate goal of treatment.

Once obstacles have been defined, the following problem-solving steps can help to reduce or work around each obstacle to adherence:

1. Identify and describe the problem (obstacle) in operational terms. Assist the patient in defining the specific nature of the problem (e.g., the patient forgets to take the evening dose of lithium).
2. Brainstorm with the patient on possible solutions to the problem without evaluating the feasibility of the solutions. Let the patient take the lead in generating solutions. Add solutions as needed. Encourage creativity in problem solving by asking for or introducing humorous and/or unreasonable solutions (e.g., "you could tape the evening dose of lithium to the back of your hand each morning"). Write down the options on a sheet of paper or blackboard.
3. Evaluate the potential efficacy of these solutions in addressing the obstacle to adherence.

4. Choose the solution that is most acceptable to the patient and that has the highest potential for success.
5. After implementing the plan, evaluate the effectiveness of the intervention and repeat steps 2 through 5, if necessary.

Once obstacles have been identified, the treatment plan can be adapted to minimize them. For example, the frequency with which medications are taken can be adjusted to accommodate schedules, or the complexity of the treatment regimen can sometimes be reduced. When the treatment plan is definite, it is often helpful to punctuate with a written plan. A document that summarizes how and when medications are to be taken and how to address obstacles to compliance when they occur can guide both the patient and the clinician (see Figure 5.1).

Intrapersonal Obstacles to Adherence

Among the intrapersonal obstacles to treatment compliance are symptoms, mood, beliefs, attitudes, and fears. The severity of symptoms is an intrapersonal variable that can determine a patient's eagerness to engage in or remain in treatment. Patients with easily noticeable symptoms who

---

I, _____ patient name _____, **plan to follow the treatment plans listed below.**

1. Take 300 mg of lithium three times each day (morning, noon, and evening).
2. Take 20 mg of Prozac each morning.
3. See my doctor once every 6 weeks.
4. Call my doctor if I begin to feel more depressed or if I have trouble with the medication.

I anticipate these problems in following my treatment plan.

1. Pressure from my mom to stop taking medication.
2. Forgetting the evening dose.
3. I might not have a ride to my next appointment.

To overcome these obstacles, I plan to do the following:

1. Give my mom a pamphlet on medications for bipolar disorder and invite her to go with me to the next DMDA support group meeting.
2. Consider bringing my mom to my next doctor's appointment.
3. Put a note next to my clock on the night stand reminding me to take my evening medications.
4. Ask my mom for a ride to my next appointment. Find out the bus route from my apartment to the clinic.

FIGURE 5.1. A sample treatment plan.

desire immediate relief of discomfort are more likely to comply with treatment. If the symptoms are less noticeable and the side effects are uncomfortable, full compliance becomes more doubtful. Some symptoms of bipolar disorder, such as mental confusion, racing thoughts, poor concentration, or memory impairment, may make it difficult for patients to understand fully, recall, or organize themselves well enough to follow through with treatment.

A simple intervention that helps patients stay on track with their medications is to use divided pill containers. They are relatively inexpensive and come in sizes that range from single daily doses up to four times/day with the days of the week labeled on the lid of the containers. Another advantage of divided pill containers is that they can help to reduce the conflict patients sometimes have with their family members over whether or not the former are taking their medications. While not a foolproof method, if patients agree to leave their containers in an accessible place, family members can look at the clear plastic pill containers rather than confront patients when they suspect noncompliance.

Symptoms of depression or mania can also affect compliance. When depressed, patients may find it difficult to motivate themselves to seek treatment, may be too tired to get up and take medication, or may not be interested in attempting a homework assignment. Feelings of hopelessness may accompany a belief that treatment is useless, so why bother? If hypomanic or euthymic, bipolar disorder patients may see no need for further medication.

This is a time when family and friends can be particularly helpful in encouraging medication compliance or help seeking. Family members often ask whether or not they should "push" their depressed relatives to get out of bed, shower and dress, take medication, or see their doctor. The answer is "yes, but gently." The recurrent nature of bipolar disorder does allow for some opportunities to plan ahead to the next episode of illness. When euthymic, patients and their family members can discuss what each should do when depression or mania recurs. For example, Mr. Benito has begun to recover from his depression. He met with his doctor and his parents before leaving the hospital.

DOCTOR: You seem to be doing much better.

MR. BENITO: Yes, Doctor, I am. I didn't think I would make it this time.

FATHER: Neither did we. We were so frightened that we would come home from work one day and find him dead from an overdose or something.

MOTHER: He didn't want to go to the hospital. He didn't take his medication. He didn't want help.

DOCTOR: You started to get depressed 6 months ago, but it seemed manageable to you. Is that right?

MR. BENITO: That's right. I was able to work up until about a month ago.

DOCTOR: I know you were initially reluctant to call me or to come to the hospital. Do you feel OK about your experience here?

MR. BENITO: It's OK. I feel better, but I would rather be home.

DOCTOR: I think if we had been able to catch this episode of depression earlier, we probably could have treated you as an outpatient. If you begin to get depressed again, I wonder what we could do to get you treated more quickly.

MOTHER: I tried to get him to call you, but he refused. That's why I gave up on arguing with him and called you myself.

FATHER: We could see this coming. It was just like the last time.

DOCTOR: What did you see?

FATHER: He kept to himself. Wasn't hungry. He just sat in his room and listened to the radio. We could hear the radio sometimes at 2:00 or 3:00 in the morning. We knew he wasn't sleeping. We thought that maybe he wasn't taking his medicine.

MOTHER: He was tired. He would sleep in and be late for work and then he just stopped going to work. They called but what could we tell them? We just said he was sick and they assumed he had that flu that was going around.

DOCTOR: What can your parents do next time, if there is a next time, to motivate you to stay on your medicines and to get help?

MR. BENITO: Be supportive.

MOTHER: We are supportive.

MR. BENITO: You nag me every time I look a little tired. If I don't want to eat, you get upset. You always think I'm getting sick when I'm usually just fine.

DOCTOR: But you are not always "just fine." Like this time, it wasn't just work stress that made you look tired or stop eating.

MR. BENITO: Sometimes it is serious. I just get tired of the nagging.

DOCTOR: What can they say when they are worried about you that would not sound like nagging?

MR. BENITO: (*He pauses.*) They can just say that "I'm worried about you, are you OK?" And if I say yes, they need to drop it.

MOTHER: That's what I do.

MR. BENITO: No, Mom, you don't believe me so you ask again and again until I get angry. Then you get worried that I'm irritable.

DOCTOR: Perhaps there's a solution that would get you the help you need without antagonizing you. If your parents agree to ask and then drop it when you say that you are fine, would you be willing to do a couple things?

MR. BENITO: Like what?

DOCTOR: Take their concerns seriously and ask yourself if you are beginning to have the symptoms of getting sick, depressed. If it is not depression, you will not have all the symptoms at the same time.

MR. BENITO: OK. What else?

DOCTOR: When you are uncertain or when you believe you may be having a return of symptoms, call me so we can do something about it before you become incapacitated. Another thing, before you stop taking your medicines altogether, call me so I know what's going on and so we can discuss your plans.

MR. BENITO: I'm willing if they're willing.

FATHER: We'll try, but we get nervous. We want to make sure he's OK.

DOCTOR: Let's give this plan a try. If it doesn't work, we'll get creative and come up with a better plan. (*to parents*) Here is a list of symptoms of depression. If you are worried, look at the list and ask yourself if he has several symptoms at the same time. If not, it is probably nothing to be concerned about. Everyone feels down or tired from time to time, even your son.

Another type of intrapersonal obstacle to treatment compliance is misconceptions about illness and treatment. For example:

- "You only take medications when you're ill, not when you are feeling better."
- "If you take medications too long, you may become immune to them. Then, when you really need them, they won't work anymore."
- "How will I know if I still need medication if I keep taking it?"
- "When I take the medication, I feel like a pill popper. I'll become dependent on medication if I take it."
- "I resent being controlled by drugs."
- "If my depression is biological, then there is nothing that can be done about it."

The thinking errors that are typical of depressed patients can also interfere with treatment adherence. For example, *selective attention* to the negative aspects of treatment, such as potential side effects or the probability of poor response, may provide patients with more reasons not to take medications than to feel confident about their efficacy. *Overgeneralization* of prior experiences can also be a problem: "Well, I tried medication for this once, and it didn't help me. I don't see why I should take it again." *Personalizing* the bad experiences of others can also influence patients: "My mom took that, and it didn't do her any good," or "My aunt took that medication, and she had a heart attack." *Should* statements (e.g., "I shouldn't need to depend on medication" or "I shouldn't be getting sick") also keep many patients from seeking or following through with treatment.

For some patients, the continued use of medication is an uncomfortable reminder that they are different, that they are plagued with a chronic illness, and that this illness may compromise their futures. Omitting the medication eliminates the reminder. In several surveys of patients who take lithium (Jamison et al., 1979; Johnson, 1973, 1974; Simons et al., 1984; Vestergaard & Amidsen, 1983), one of the most common reasons that patients gave for discontinuing medication was their dislike of relying on medications to control their mood. In these cases, the obstacle to adherence is the meaning attached to taking medication. Resolution of the problem requires an examination of this special meaning, evaluation of its validity, and a redefinition of "taking medications" that is acceptable to patients and, thus, makes it comfortable for them to comply with medication treatment.

PATIENT: I hate taking these pills.

THERAPIST: What do you hate about it?

PATIENT: They make me thirsty. I've gained all this weight. I hate having to excuse myself so I can go in the bathroom and take my pills. It's not fair.

THERAPIST: What's not fair?

PATIENT: (*with tears in his eyes*) This stupid illness. Having to be thinking about it all the time. Not being able to do the things normal people do.

THERAPIST: What kinds of things?

PATIENT: Everything!

THERAPIST: Help me understand what you mean by "everything."

PATIENT: Life. My life isn't normal. I'm not normal and I never will be.

THERAPIST: You're right. You have an illness that makes you different from most people. Having to take medicines everyday is part of it. Are there some specific things you would like to do that you feel your illness is keeping you from doing?

PATIENT: Well, uh, I can't stay out all night with my friends like I used to. I can't drink. I'll never be able to fly planes, live free, or just have fun without worrying that I may be having too much fun, you know, losing control.

THERAPIST: Are you saying that having bipolar disorder and taking medicines is like losing your freedom?"

PATIENT: Yeah, like I'm a prisoner, restricted. My wings have been clipped.

THERAPIST: Do you always feel this way?"

PATIENT: No. Most of the time I can deal with it pretty well. It's when the guys come over to watch the game and then want to go party. I have to act like my own mother and say (*sarcastically*), "No, boys. Charlie needs to stay home and count his pills."

THERAPIST: Are those the times when you stop taking your medication?

PATIENT: Yeah. I guess. But I start feeling bad after a while and I have to start taking them again.

THERAPIST: When you stop taking the pills, do you feel like you have more freedom?

PATIENT: No, not really.

THERAPIST: Then how does it [not taking pills] help you?

PATIENT: It doesn't. I'm just mad.

THERAPIST: If it is not helpful, maybe there is something else you can do when you feel like you have lost your freedom that would make you feel better.

PATIENT: Like what?

THERAPIST: Well, it sounds like you have come up with two solutions so far—total freedom, which means no medications and no illness, or total restriction, which means no fun. I wonder if there is any room for compromise?

PATIENT: I guess I could go party but come home before I turn into a pumpkin, or maybe it's more like a werewolf. (*Chuckles.*)

THERAPIST: You may be on to something. Maybe we can figure out a way for you to keep your freedom and still maintain your health. Does that sound like a good plan? This way when you begin to feel restricted, you have choices of action other than stopping your medications. What do you think?

PATIENT: I'll try.

In this example, the patient and therapist can remove the cognitive obstacle to medication adherence by dealing with the patient's feelings of restriction in a more effective way.

Where appropriate, clinicians may address patients' misconceptions about medication by providing them with information. Several studies have demonstrated the effectiveness of patient education in changing patients' attitudes toward the illness (Cohen, 1983; Peet & Harvey, 1991; Seltzer et al., 1980; Van Gent & Zwart, 1991), teaching social strategies for coping with symptoms (van Gent & Zwart, 1991), and improving compliance (Altamura & Mauri, 1985; Seltzer et al., 1980; Van Gent & Zwart, 1991; Youssel, 1983). In general practice, it is best to provide verbal information to the patient and to recommend supplemental reading on the subject. A list of recommended educational materials can be found in the Appendix. Informational videotapes are available to supplement readings or verbal instruction. Patients can view these videotapes in the waiting area or in private viewing rooms, if space allows.

As it is with other obstacles to compliance, prevention is the key to overcoming intrapersonal obstacles. When beginning treatment, clinicians can inquire about the patients' past experiences with treatment, medication, psychotherapy, and health care providers. Do patients have any concerns about beginning treatment again? Do patients have any concerns about the therapist? Have patients ever had difficulty adhering to treatment? Taking time to discuss this potential difficulty early in the course of treatment provides an opportunity to reduce these obstacles before they cause problems.

Social Obstacles to Adherence

Family and friends can encourage patients to seek treatment, can provide physical care when needed, and can help patients cope with stress. Family members and friends whose beliefs about treatment are contrary to those of clinicians can negatively influence treatment adherence, however. In particular, if friends or relatives have had or have heard of others having bad experiences with medication, they may discourage patients from taking medications. Moreover, family members who believe that patients should be able to "snap out of it" alone may frown upon seeking help from others. The feedback they receive can include:

- "My husband thinks psychiatry is a bunch of baloney."
- "My mom said I just need a vacation away from the kids."
- "After my roommate saw that special on television about medications, she said that, with all the risks involved, I was better off depressed."
- "My dad said only wimps take those pills."

In these cases, it can be helpful to meet with patients and their significant others to discuss these issues and provide all participants with an opportunity to voice their concerns. If patients are willing, it can be beneficial to invite family members to attend some treatment sessions, to call when they have concerns, and to become active in the treatment process. It is helpful to relabel their skepticism about the therapy and the therapist as a sign that they are interested in the patients' well-being. It is particularly important for clinicians to control their level of defensiveness and try to model open-mindedness and respect for others' opinions.

Competing medical advice is one of the most powerful social obstacles to compliance. The source of the advice can be other health care providers, television news or talk shows, newspapers, magazine articles, or the *Physicians' Desk Reference* (PDR; 1995):

> "When I lived in California, my therapist said I had psychological problems which stem from my dysfunctional family. He said I needed long-term psychotherapy, not medication. My family doctor says that you can get hooked on those drugs, so he never let me have them."

Clinicians take a big risk if they try to discount the words of other clinicians with whom patients may be allied. Dismissal of the other clinicians' advice forces the patient into the awkward position of having to choose which clinician to believe. A strategically safer position is to assume that, given the information available at the time, the recommendations may have been valid or that patients may have incorrectly recalled the views of other clinicians. Before openly disagreeing with another clinician, therapists should demonstrate an attempt to understand the competing advice. For example, the therapist may ask patients what they think about the competing advice. If they are uncertain which treatment approach is best for them, the therapist can discuss it further, refer them to readings on the subject, and/or suggest that they get another opinion.

If published materials are the source of competing medical advice, take time to discuss these materials with patients. The descriptions of potential side effects of medications listed in the PDR, for example, frequently frighten both patients and family members. It is useful to discuss with patients the probability of such problems, to weigh these effects against the potential beneficial effects of treatment, and to develop a plan for assessment of their occurrence and intervention, if necessary.

Stressors as Obstacles to Adherence

Psychosocial stressors, such as marital problems, financial strains, or unemployment, can interfere with treatment in three ways. First, people who are preoccupied with problems of daily living can forget to take medications, to complete homework assignments, or even to keep appointments. Second, stressors consume time that might otherwise be set aside for treatment-related activities (e.g., going to a support group meeting). Third, stressors exacerbate symptoms. For example, stress can keep people awake at night. The lack of sleep can, in turn, cause fatigue, lethargy, decreased motivation, or even bring on a manic episode.

> Mrs. McNelly had a lot on her mind. Her company had been sold, and she was afraid of losing her job soon. It had been difficult for her to find this job, and she worried that she might not be so lucky the next time. Mrs. McNelly's bipolar disorder had incapacitated her for lengthy periods of time in the past 8 years. Her employment record was full of holes that were difficult to explain to potential employers. She lay awake at night thinking about these problems. When she finally fell asleep, she was restless. In the morning, she was tired and easily fatigued. Mrs. McNelly knew that, without sleep, she would begin to experience the symptoms of mania before too long. Although she might be taking her medication as prescribed, it was not sufficient to prevent a breakthrough of symptoms if her sleeplessness persisted. If she recognized the emergence of symptoms, she could choose to intervene with pharmacological agents to improve her sleep, with problem-solving methods to cope with her stressors, or with behavioral techniques to facilitate sleep.

The appropriate interventions for reducing the psychosocial stressors that interfere with treatment vary according to the type of stressor. A structured problem-solving approach may be effective for problems that are under the patient's control (Chapters 10 and 11). Interpersonal problems, such as marital or family conflict, child behavior problems, or getting along with friends, may require conjoint counseling for patients and these significant others (Chapters 10 and 11). For psychosocial stressors such as unemployment, medical problems, indebtedness, or school problems for children, it may be useful to enlist the help of social service agencies. Until a stressor can be removed effectively, a compensatory plan is needed to deal with symptoms (e.g., sleeplessness) and treatment obstacles (e.g., forgetfulness).

Treatment-Related Obstacles to Adherence

Factors within the treatment regimen that make it difficult for patients to comply include complex combinations or dosages of medicines that are difficult to remember, side effects, and dosing schedules that are inconsistent with the individual's personal schedule.

> Mrs. Henry was to take her medication first thing in the morning, around lunchtime, and before bedtime. She was a late sleeper, however, and inevitably missed her morning dose. She often stayed up to watch the late movies on television and delayed taking her medication on these evenings because they made her sleepy. Sometimes, she would fall asleep during a movie before she had taken her bedtime dose of medication.

In most cases, tailoring the treatment regimen to patients' schedules and lifestyles prevents treatment-related obstacles to adherence. In practice, it may be necessary to match dosing schedules to patients' daily routines. For example, reducing the number of daily doses needed by using single-dose sustained-release formulations simplifies regimens and decreases the likelihood that patients will miss doses. The use of sustained-release lithium preparations has several advantages. Studies have shown that sustained-release formulations produce a steady serum lithium concentration more easily and reliably (Arancibia, Flores, & Pezoa, 1990; Caldwell, Westlake, Schriver, & Bumbier, 1981; Wallis, Miller, & McFadyen, 1989). There appear to be no significant differences in the total lithium bioavailability of sustained-release versus standard lithium carbonate preparations (Caldwell et al., 1981; Cooper, Simpson, Lee, & Bergner, 1978). Moreover, although somewhat controversial, there seem to be no significant differences in the side-effect profiles of the sustained-release and standard lithium formulations (Lyskowski & Nasrailah, 1981).

For antidepressants, the literature on using a once daily versus multiple dose regimen has concluded that, for many patients, single (generally nighttime) doses of antidepressants are as effective as a multiple dose regimen. Specifically, patients achieve comparable medication blood levels on the two dosing regimens and patients report similar levels of treatment response. When differences do exist, it is generally in favor of the single dose regimen. It is suggested that this is due to decreased reporting of side effects with a nighttime only dose as side effects generally occur during the first few hours after ingestion while the patient is asleep. Single dose schedules as opposed to multiple dose schedules are less complicated and therefore may improve patient compliance to treatment.

In tailoring a medication regimen to patients' needs, it is helpful to consider the patient's daily activities.

> Mr. Sanders experienced a worsening of manic symptoms at the end of the day. His fast-paced and high-pressured job stimulated him. By evening, he had difficulty unwinding, turning off his thoughts about the day, and falling asleep. Because the evening activation had led to sleeplessness and eventually mania in the past, Mr. Sanders's doctor had tailored his medication regimen to this variation in symptoms. In addition, the doctor allowed Mr. Sanders to have a small amount of extra medication to help him sleep when needed. Although the general philosophy is to minimize the number of medications prescribed, in this case, flexibility in this responsible patient helps to prevent mania.

If a regimen requires multiple daily doses of more than one medication, the dosing times can be difficult to remember for some patients. If the medication is purely prophylactic, there are no symptoms to cue individuals to take it. In this case, it can be helpful to pair pill taking with another regularly occurring event such as eating a meal, brushing one's teeth, or having a cup of coffee in the morning. Some pocket-size pill containers have alarms built into them as reminders. With time, pill taking can become part of the daily routine just like dressing or eating.

RESPONSIBILITY FOR ADHERENCE TO TREATMENT

Achieving a high level of treatment compliance requires collaboration between mental health care professionals, patients, and significant others in patients' social system. Health care providers must facilitate the development of collaborative relationships by explaining to patients and their families, first, what is meant by collaboration and, second, how each can contribute to treatment.

Clinicians' Responsibilities

The primary responsibility of clinicians is to ensure that the patient receives quality care. It is also their responsibility to inform patients of their diagnosis and the specific plans for treatment including what the patient can expect from medications or other interventions and what he or she can expect from the clinician. Table 5.3 summarizes clinicians' responsibilities for enhancing compliance.

TABLE 5.3. Clinicians' Responsibilities

---

1. Educate patients about:
   a. the diagnosis and treatment options
   b. the rationale behind treatment decisions
   c. explicit treatment instructions, including dosage, timing, and any other critical information
   d. the possible effects of medications
   e. the estimated length of treatment
   f. the estimated length of time in treatment before an amelioration of symptoms should be expected
   g. patient rights and responsibilities
   h. what assistance can be expected from the clinician
   i. maintaining confidentiality
2. Communicate with the patient in a direct and noncondescending manner.
3. Tailor the medication regimen to fit the patient's schedule and lifestyle. Inquire about eating and sleeping habits and how they might affect timing of dosages.
4. Provide a clear explanation of the treatment regimen. Provide explicit information regarding time course of expected benefits and side effects. Provide written instructions rather than relying solely on the patient's memory.
5. To assure continuity of care:
   a. Specify a contact person if other than the primary clinician andprovide the patient and his or her family members with a means of contacting this clinician.
   b. Limit the number of clinicians responsible for the care of the patient and his or her family.
   c. Be certain that the patient meets all relevant staff members.

It is especially helpful for clinicians to meet patients' immediate family members (if the patient permits), provide them with clinic telephone numbers, and give them instructions for handling psychiatric emergencies. The clinician shares the responsibility with the family members to keep the lines of communication open. Family members should be encouraged to call with any questions or concerns.

Patients' Responsibilities

Table 5.4 summarizes patients' responsibilities for enhancing compliance. In addition to taking medications as prescribed, patients are responsible for completing homework assignments and for scheduling and attending appointments. If they cannot keep an appointment, they are responsible for calling in advance to cancel and reschedule.

Patients are also responsible for voicing concerns and asking ques-

TABLE 5.4. Patients' Responsibilities

---

1. Take medication.
2. Attend appointments.
3. Complete homework assignments.
4. Call ahead when unable to attend appointment.
5. Ask questions when unclear about the information presented or what is expected of him or her.
6. Voice concerns.
7. Be honest about symptoms and compliance.
8. Talk to doctor before making any medication changes.

---

tions when they do not understand what their clinicians are saying. If they want to change treatment plans, it is their responsibility to inform clinicians so that there is opportunity for discussion before any action is taken. Furthermore, patients' are responsible to report accurately and honestly on their progress or lack thereof, the degree to which they have been able to follow the treatment recommendations, and any problems that they have encountered.

Family Members' Responsibilities

Not all bipolar disorder patients have close family members who want to be involved in their care. Most patients, however, have regular contact with one or more individuals who can assist in their treatment. It is the responsibility of these family members to learn about the illness and the prescribed treatments; they can read material on this subject, talk with patients' health care providers, attend educational seminars, or get involved in support groups. If family members have questions or concerns about treatment, it is their responsibility to meet with health care providers to address these issues directly. Family members should not interfere with treatment by discouraging patients from following their clinicians' recommendations. If they disagree with the clinicians' treatment decisions, it is their responsibility to discuss these concerns with the patients and the clinicians, or to gain information from other sources.

Family members also have the responsibility to protect patients from self-harm. If patients imply or directly report suicidal ideation, family members must convince patients to see their health care provider, have their condition evaluated in an emergency room, or call the authorities if they refuse treatment. It is the responsibility of the family members to know how to reach clinicians or other health care professionals at all times. Although following the treatment regimen is ultimately the respon-

TABLE 5.5. Family Members' Responsibilities

---
1. Detect symptoms.
2. Encourage and support the patient.
3. Learn about the illness and prescribed treatment.
4. Voice concerns about treatment to the health care provider if the patient permits.
5. Do not interfere with treatment.
6. Protect patients from self-harm.
7. Know how to reach clinicians.
8. Attend some treatment sessions.
9. Help patients with transportation to doctors' appointments when necessary.

---

sibility of the patient, family members can help by encouraging patients to take their medications, by being supportive, and by providing transportation to and attending some treatment sessions. Table 5.5 summarizes the family's responsibilities.

CHAPTER SUMMARY

Nonadherence to treatment is common to all pharmacological interventions, but is most troublesome with chronic or prophylactic medication regimens. While this problem is common, it often goes unaddressed. This chapter provides a model for conceptualizing and discussing compliance with treatment as a regular part of each visit with a clinician. A nonpunitive, collaborative approach to enhancement of treatment adherence is presented.

In CBT, noncompliance is defined as a behavior rather than as resistance. Medication compliance, in particular, is a behavior or complex set of behaviors that make it possible for patients to receive the maximum benefit from pharmacotherapy. Everyone is capable of some degree of compliance. However, many things can interfere with even the best treatment plans. These obstacles to adherence include intrapersonal (e.g., symptoms, fear), interpersonal (e.g., patient–clinician relationship), social (e.g., competing advice), and treatment (e.g., complexity, side effects, cost) factors. The goal of CBT for compliance is to identify these obstacles and use problem solving, cognitive restructuring, or education to eliminate or reduce their influence on compliance.

The patient, therapist, and the patient's family members share the responsibility for ensuring compliance. The clinician's role includes (1) attention to establishment and maintenance of the therapeutic alliance; (2) design of the "right" treatment, that is, one tailored to the symptoms, lifestyle, and preferences of his or her patients; (3) creating a trusting environment where compliance problems can be discussed in a nonjudgmental manner; (4) negotiating treatment goals with patients; and (5) educating patients about their illness and treatment options.

Patients have the responsibility to participate in treatment as they have agreed and to ask questions when uncertain or concerned about treatment.

SIX

Cognitive Changes in Depressive Episodes

SESSION 8. BIASED THINKING

Purpose of the Session

The intention of this session is to lay the groundwork for the teaching of cognitive-behavioral techniques for coping with depressive and hypomanic symptoms. Although pharmacotherapy may control the majority of symptoms of bipolar illness most of the time, it is not uncommon for patients to experience breakthroughs of symptoms while on medication. Equipping them with some cognitive-behavioral techniques provides additional coping strategies when medication alone is not enough.

Goals of the Session

1. Introduce the concepts of negatively and positively biased thinking.
2. Emphasize how biased thinking can influence the interpretation of events and subsequent actions.
3. Help patients to begin to associate mood shifts with events, thinking patterns, and behavior.

Procedure

1. Assess treatment compliance.
2. Review the compliance assignment from last session. Did patients encounter any of the obstacles to compliance that were anticipated and planned for at the last session? If yes, was the intervention helpful? If not helpful, what interfered? Use the compliance intervention and revise the plan to address these obstacles.

(cont.)

(continued from page 118)

3. Review the Mood Graph for the past week. Discuss any variations from the normal range including the circumstances under which the mood shift occurred.
4. Biased thinking. Define "mood shifts" and "negative automatic thoughts." Review the association between events, mood shifts, and automatic thoughts. Provide examples of negative and positive mood shifts and concomitant shifts in cognitions (e.g., views or outlook). Ask patients to provide several examples of such occurrences and list them on the Summary of Positively and Negatively Biased Thoughts.
5. Provide patients with the reading materials for this week.

Recommended Reading
Beck and Greenberg (1974). *Coping with Depression.*

SESSION 9. COGNITIVE CHANGES IN DEPRESSION

Purpose of the Session
The purpose of the session is to begin to train patients to monitor their thinking for negatively biased thoughts and to identify thinking errors when they occur. Identification of negative automatic thoughts can cue patients to monitor their symptoms more closely or to use one of the cognitive interventions for negative automatic thoughts that will be covered in the next session.

Goals of the Session
1. Review the concept of negatively biased thoughts.
2. Teach patients to monitor thoughts and to identify negative automatic thoughts.
3. Teach patients to identify thinking errors.

Procedure
1. Assess treatment compliance.
2. Review the homework assigned in the last session.
3. Review the concept of negatively biased thinking (refer to the Summary of Positively and Negatively Biased Thoughts from Session 8). Try to elicit an example of a mood shift that might have occurred in the last week and any accompanying automatic thoughts.
4. Use an Automatic Thought Record as a guide for teaching patients to identify their negative automatic thoughts.

(cont.)

(continued from page 119)

5. Define "thinking error." Provide patients with the list of common thinking errors. Refer back to the Automatic Thought Record or the Biased Thoughts Summary and note any examples of thinking errors.
6. Provide patients with the homework materials for the next week.

Homework

1. Keep an Automatic Thought Record for the next week.
2. Assign the task of looking for thinking errors on the Biased Thoughts Summary if there was not sufficient time to complete it during the session.

SESSION 10. LOGICAL ANALYSIS OF NEGATIVE AUTOMATIC THOUGHTS

Purpose of the Session

The purpose of this session is to teach patients two cognitive therapy techniques for combating negative automatic thoughts and reducing the intensity of associated mood shifts—generating evidence for/evidence against the thought and generating explanations for events.

Goals of the Session

1. Teach patients the "evidence for/evidence against" technique to evaluate the validity of negative automatic thoughts.
2. Teach patients to generate alternative explanations for events as a means of combating negative automatic thoughts.

Procedure

1. Assess treatment compliance.
2. Review patients' Automatic Thought Record homework. Evaluate how well patients understood the procedure, clarify any confusion, and reinforce the association between events, thoughts, and feelings. If patients did not complete their assignment, ask them to fill in a diary sheet for how they are feeling now for use in the skills training exercise of this session.
3. Evidence for/evidence against. Give a rationale for evaluating the validity of negative automatic thoughts. Provide patients with the Logical Analysis of Automatic Thoughts worksheet for use in this exercise. Walk them through the proce-

(cont.)

(continued from page 119)

dure using the automatic thoughts generated in the Automatic Thought Record homework assignment from the last session.
4. Alternative explanations. Provide a rationale for this intervention. Use the third column of the Logical Analysis of Automatic Thoughts worksheet to generate alternative explanations for the event in question. Ask patients to choose the explanation that seems most likely. Generate evidence for/evidence against the alternative explanation if necessary.
5. Have the patient rerate the intensity of the emotion associated with and belief in the original automatic thought. Help the patient to review the process from the initial negative automatic thought through the logical analysis and summary. Reinforce the logic of this exercise and its purpose.
6. Provide patients with homework materials for the week.

Homework
Provide an Automatic Thought Record and a Logical Analysis of Automatic Thoughts worksheet. Ask patients to try using the two cognitive interventions during the next week.

"I can't do anything right. No matter how hard I try, I always seem to fail. I'm so stupid—ugly and stupid. I need to lose weight, and I can't even do that right. If I can't change my weight, how am I supposed to be able to change my life? 'Get a new job,' they say. Yeah . . . , who's going to hire me? I'm so pathetic. They'll look at my pathetic little resume and laugh. It's never going to change. It's hopeless. I'm hopeless. I wish I were dead."

One of the hallmarks of depression is a negatively biased view of self, the world, and the future (Beck, 1976; Beck & Rush, 1995). The negative thinking of depressed individuals can take on several forms. For example, these individuals may be very pessimistic. In their view, options may be closed, change is probably impossible, and the future looks bleak. The encouragement of others is not only useless, but can seem patronizing and irritating.

"What is there to be optimistic about? The air is poisoned with pollution. It isn't safe to walk the streets. Everything you eat gives you cancer. People don't care about anything but themselves. So what, if the sun is shining. It will probably give me skin cancer." Although this bias in thinking is not uncommon among healthy adults, it is a more pervasive problem for those with depression.

An inability to take in and process positive information is also characteristic of the negative cognitive bias of depressed persons. They may overlook positive events or experiences, but readily recall negative events, even minor ones. They often discount small accomplishments while magnifying small errors in importance.

> Ms. Silverberg, a young administrative assistant, overlooks the positive employee evaluation she received last month, the thank you cards from the executives she assists, and the larger than expected pay raise she received. Instead, she tells her therapist about the report that did not get out in time, the long-distance telephone call she accidentally disconnected, the dirty look the boss gave her as he walked out of his office, and all the work she has failed to complete as quickly as she would have liked.

The perceptual bias of depressed persons can lead them to make faulty negative interpretations of events or the behaviors of others. That is, they may jump to conclusions without sufficient evidence to support their assumptions.

- When Mr. Dressler's parents offered to help him get back on his feet, he rejected their assistance. He said, "They just feel sorry for me. I hate it when people feel sorry for me."
- Ms. Hernandez heard her coworkers' offers of help as implications that she was not competent, not able to handle things on her own, "losing it."
- When her roommate went to the movies without inviting her, Ms. Wu saw it as inconsiderate, rejecting, and proof that she was looking for a new roommate.
- Mrs. Portello was convinced that her husband did not love her anymore. He had not complimented her on her meatloaf and had gone to bed without kissing her good night. "My marriage is over."

As Beck et al. (1979) noted, several common cognitive distortions (or thinking errors) are associated with depression:

1. Arbitrary inference: jumping to conclusions without sufficient data to back up the conclusion
2. Selective abstraction: viewing or evaluating things out of context, ignoring important details, or distorting contrary information

3. Overgeneralization: assuming that one particular event or a series of isolated events indicates a global and persistent negative pattern
4. Magnification or minimization: exaggerating the actual significance or intensity of a negative event, or reducing the actual significance or meaningfulness of a positive event
5. Personalization: assuming that events are related to oneself when no evidence supports this claim
6. Absolutistic/dichotomous thinking: viewing situations in terms of extremes (e.g., good or bad, black or white, success or failure)

Thoughts and feelings are inextricably linked. Thoughts elicit feelings, and feelings elicit thoughts. The negatively biased thoughts of depressed patients inevitably give rise to negative shifts in mood. For example, Mrs. Portello's thoughts about her marriage left her feeling sad, fearful, and angry. Self-criticism for actions taken or not taken can result in feelings of guilt. Patients who have pessimistic outlooks for their future or who are unsure of their capabilities may feel anxious or frightened. It is not necessary to determine whether thoughts precede or follow emotional changes. To understand and work with depressed patients, it is necessary only to recognize the co-occurrence of thoughts and feelings.

Events in a person's life can precipitate thoughts and emotions, both negative and positive (see Figure 6.1). For example, criticism from an employer can lead an individual to doubt his or her own competence, to fear being fired, and to believe that others view him or her negatively. As a result, the individual feels sad, fearful, and embarrassed. One patient who received some minor criticism from her employer became so fearful of losing her job that she resigned before her employer had the opportunity to fire her. In this case, the emotional and cognitive changes led to a behavioral response, perhaps one that was too hasty.

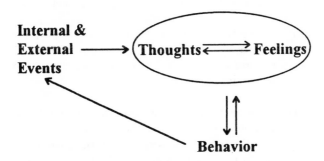

FIGURE 6.1. Cognitive model of depression.

Precipitating events can be large or small, subtle or obvious, internal or external. The actual nature of the event is not as important as the meaning that the individual attaches to it.

> Mr. Portello may not have complimented his wife on her meatloaf because he was preoccupied with problems at work. For Mrs. Portello, however, his oversight meant that her husband did not care about her anymore, was ungrateful, and was not giving her credit for her efforts. She was sad, angry, and very worried about the future of her marriage.

Some precipitating events can be internal. For example, physical symptoms, such as heart palpitations or headaches, can elicit anxious thoughts about a physical illness or self-critical thoughts about the person's inability to cope. Internal precipitating events also include thoughts or conclusions drawn after thinking about other events or situations.

> Mr. Fontain was thinking about the talk that he had with his brother Jim yesterday. It occurred to him that his brother could have misinterpreted what he was trying to say and could be angry with him. Perhaps that explained why his brother seemed to be in a hurry to leave. If Jim told other family members about it, no one would want to talk to Mr. Fontain. He began to feel anxious.
>   Anticipating that his brother and other family members would be angry with him, Mr. Fontain tried to avoid them and behaved defensively when they called. This behavior created tension in the family. This could be considered a self-fulfilling prophecy. Because Mr. Fontain mistakenly thought that everyone was angry with him, he behaved in a manner that offended the others and evoked their anger.

It can be difficult to determine the specific sequence of shifts in affect, behavior, and cognition or of the events that appear at times to precipitate the sequence. For each circumstance, it is likely to be different.

> Being in a sad mood influenced Ms. Marin's actions at work and at home. Her isolating behavior led to negative reactions from others. This made Ms. Marin feel worse and elicited a string of self-critical thoughts. In response, she withdrew further.

To intervene successfully, it is not necessary to identify the specific sequence of contributory events, but rather to intervene somewhere in the cycle to prevent the further exacerbation of negative moods, behaviors, and thoughts. Instructing patients to feel happier, less anxious, less frustrated, or less guilty is unlikely to change their emotions. Patients' cognitions, however, may be more amenable to change. Identifying distorted cognitions gives patients the opportunity to examine the validity of their negative beliefs or assumptions more closely and to modify invalid or inaccurate thoughts. If successful, this approach reduces the intense negative emotion associated with the distorted cognitions.

IDENTIFYING NEGATIVE AUTOMATIC THOUGHTS

One of the first steps in combating the negative emotions, actions, and thinking of persons who are experiencing depression is to identify the thoughts associated with the negative mood state. These thoughts are called negative automatic thoughts, because they occur automatically and rapidly, sometimes outside of conscious awareness. Frequently, they come in a string; that is, one negative cognition leads to another and another until the patient is overwhelmed.

It can be helpful to introduce the concept of negative cognitions by first sensitizing the patients to the occurrence of their own negative automatic thoughts. Many people will immediately recognize their own automatic thoughts, particularly if they are prominent during depression. For others, the clinician will have to work harder to help the patient to identify examples. To begin teaching people to identify their negative automatic thoughts, it is usually easier to begin with mood or affect shifts. Affect and cognition tend to shift closely in time. Therefore, the clinician may instruct patients to watch for shifts in their mood and to take note of the thoughts running through their mind at the time that the mood shift occurs. Although the shift in mood does not necessarily occur before the onset of the negative cognition, a change in mood is often more easily identified than is a change in thinking.

Some patients may find it difficult to identify the flow of cognitions that occur with a mood shift. A sequence of thoughts may flood a patient's mind more rapidly than he or she can verbalize. Sometimes, negative automatic thoughts consist more of general impressions and visual images than specific words.

Ms. Tanaka had to give a talk before a group of her company's executives. Her boss was to be in the audience, as was Roberta, a coworker whom Ms. Tanaka believed would love to see her look bad in front of the Board. As Ms. Tanaka prepared for her talk, she envisioned herself forgetting her speech, dropping her materials, and crying in frustration. She pictured Roberta whispering into the boss's ear and the two of them laughing hysterically. She developed a sick feeling in her stomach and saw herself in the unemployment line. Ms. Tanaka's images were powerful and frightening. She could not identify specific thoughts, but she could summarize the pictures as images of failure and humiliation.

If patients think in pictures not sentences, they can describe the images in some detail until they are able to identify the theme, belief, or underlying concern. To elicit thoughts, ask the person to imagine him- or herself in the stressful situation and describe the picture he or she sees in as much detail as possible. Who is present? What are they doing or saying? What is the emotional tone of the image? How is the patient feeling? What does he or she think will go wrong? What are the consequences?

To introduce the concept of biased thinking, ask patients if they have noticed any changes in attitude or view when depressed, upset, stressed, or bothered. If yes, what type of changes have been noted? If no, prompt the patient for changes in his or her view of self, life in general, others, or the future (e.g., How does your future look when you are depressed?). Listen for negatively biased thinking, thinking errors, and negative assumptions. List the negative thoughts on the Summary of Positively and Negatively Biased Thoughts (a.k.a. the Biased Thoughts Summary; see Figure 6.2) and label them for the patient as examples of negatively biased thoughts. Explain further the relationship between depression and negatively biased thinking using the examples on the Biased Thoughts Summary. Help the patient to contrast those thoughts with his or her view when asymptomatic. (This exercise will also be discussed in Chapter 7 on cognitive changes in mania.)

Once patients appears to understand how feeling depressed can influence the way in which people construe the world or themselves, move on to help them examine the environmental precipitants of mood shifts and negative thinking. To do so, ask patients to imagine the kinds of situations or experiences that might elicit negative thoughts. If possible, generate a list of situational precipitants for each of the negatively biased thoughts listed on the Biased Thoughts Summary. It is not necessary to identify specific or real events that led to the thoughts, but rather an example of the types of experiences that would typically elicit negative thoughts. In this part of the exercise, you are merely trying to get the patient to associate negative thoughts with events or experiences. Add these events to the corresponding negative thoughts listed on the worksheet and explain to patients how events can precipitate a mood shift and subsequent negatively biased thoughts.

The final component of this introduction is to begin to examine how the negative thoughts and feelings experienced in response to a stressful event might influence the actions of the individual. Ask patients to identify how they might behave when feeling bad and thinking in a negative way. This is best accomplished by referring to the Biased Thoughts Summary and precipitating events and asking patients to recall or imagine how they might have acted (or failed to act) in response to those situations. Add these behavioral consequences to the worksheet in the appropriate column and explain the connection between events, mood, thoughts, and behavior. Ask patients whether these behaviors have caused problems for them in the past.

MONITORING NEGATIVE AUTOMATIC THOUGHTS

In order to analyze the validity of any negative automatic thoughts associated with mood shifts, the patient must be able to identify mood shifts, the events that precipitated them, and the associated automatic thoughts. One method traditionally used to monitor the occurrence of negative automatic thoughts is a patient diary. There are many forms and

Name of patient: _____   Date: _____

Completed by: _____

Event	Mood	Thoughts	Actions
_____	_____	_____	_____
_____	_____	_____	_____
_____	_____	_____	_____
_____	_____	_____	_____
_____	_____	_____	_____
_____	_____	_____	_____
_____	_____	_____	_____
_____	_____	_____	_____
_____	_____	_____	_____
_____	_____	_____	_____

Note: You will be referring back to this sheet in future sessions. Keep a copy in the patient's chart for future reference.

FIGURE 6.2. Summary of Positively and Negatively Biased Thoughts.

names for the thought diary, the most common of which is the triple-column Daily Record of Dysfunctional Thoughts (DRDT). This form has been designed by cognitive therapists to meet the specific needs of their patient populations. We present two versions. The first (Figure 6.3) was developed for patients whose difficulties with concentration and memory made homework assignments of record keeping very difficult. This simplified form walks patients through the steps of recording affective and cognitive shifts associated with events in their life. We have found it especially useful in the early phase of therapy when the cognitive model is introduced.

We have also designed a more comprehensive Automatic Thought Record tailored after the DRDT. This Automatic Thought Record, as shown in Figure 6.4, expands the DRDT by allowing the patient to rate again the intensity of thoughts and emotions after CBT interventions have been used. The following are instructions for completing the Automatic Thought Record:

1. When a mood shift occurs, note the date in the first column of the Automatic Thought Record.

2. In the second column, describe the circumstances under which the mood shift occurred. Only a few words are necessary as a reminder of the stimulus for the mood shift.

3. Indicate in the third column the types of emotions that occurred (e.g., sadness, anger, anxiety). If several emotions are experienced simultaneously, list each separately. Use a 0–100% scale to rate the approximate intensity of these emotions as they were experienced at the time of the event (Time 1). In this scale, 0% is the absence of that emotion and 100% is the greatest intensity of that emotion ever experienced.

4. Rerate the intensity that these same emotions are felt at the time that the form is completed (Time 2).

5. Leave blank the third column. This is for rating the intensity of emotion (Time 3) after a CBT intervention has been tried.

6. In the "Automatic Thoughts" column, list the thoughts that were associated with each emotion experienced. To identify these thoughts, it is helpful for the clinician to ask what it was about the event that made the patient feel each of the emotions; for example, "What was it about your mother's criticism that made you feel guilty?" "What was it about that situation that made you angry?" "What made you feel like crying?" Using the same 0–100% scale, where 0% means a total lack of belief and 100% means absolute certainty, rate the intensity with which the automatic thought was believed at the time of the event (Time 1).

7. Rerate the intensity with which the automatic thought is believed at the time the form is completed (Time 2).

1. How am I feeling right now?

_____ _____ %

_____ _____ %

_____ _____ %

2. How strong are these feelings?

0%	50%	100%
Hardly notice	Somewhat strong	Very strong

Write in the number (%) next to each emotion in question 1.

3. What happened that upset me?

_____

_____

_____

_____

_____

4. What am I thinking? What bothers me most about this event?

_____ _____ %

_____ _____ %

_____ _____ %

0%	50%	100%
Not at all	Somewhat strongly	Very strongly

How strongly do I believe this thought? Write in the number (%) next to each thought in question 4.

5. How did I react to this event?

_____

_____

_____

_____

FIGURE 6.3. Simplified Automatic Thought Record.

Date	Event	Feeling	Intensity (0–100%)			Automatic Thoughts	% Believed (0–100%)		
			Time 1	Time 2	Time 3		Time 1	Time 2	Time 3

FIGURE 6.4. Automatic Thought Record.

130

8. Leave blank the third column for rerating the intensity of the belief (Time 3) until after a CBT intervention has been tried.

An assessment of the intensity of the emotion experienced and the intensity of belief in each of the negative automatic thoughts provides a baseline against which to compare any changes that cognitive restructuring subsequently produces. Because patients often complete the Automatic Thought Record long after the precipitating events, the intensity of the emotion and belief may have changed. If so, it suggests that some intervening event (either internal or external) caused that change. Therefore, the record includes three columns to rate intensity (1) at the time of the event, (2) at the time that the form is completed, and (3) after an intervention with CBT. If the intensity changed—increased or decreased—determining the reason for the change may be helpful in identifying existing strategies for coping with strong emotional shifts.

For example, if an event that elicited anxiety occurred (e.g., worker receives a memo that the boss is calling a meeting), there is usually a cognitive response ("Oh no! This isn't good"). With time, however, the person could have ruminated over the event and heightened the emotional reaction by contemplating the catastrophic potential of the event ("I bet the company is going under and we'll all lose our jobs"). Others could reconsider the same event and minimize the catastrophic feeling of the initial reaction ("It's probably about that memo that went out last week"), putting it into perspective, thereby decreasing the intensity of the emotion. In either case, it is helpful for the therapist to know what cognitive process occurred that created the change. Processes that decrease emotion can be operationally defined and applied to new events that arouse negative emotions. Processes that increase emotion will give clues about when and how to intervene.

Ms. Belinda was furious (100%) when she found out that someone had broken her favorite cup. By the time she filled out the Automatic Thought Record, she was only 65% angry. When asked about the change, she reported, "I didn't have all of the details at first, and I imagined the worst. After asking a few questions, I was still angry, but I felt like I was back in control." Ms. Belinda believed that she had overreacted initially. In working with her in CBT, the therapist helped Ms. Belinda to extend her own natural cognitive intervention to further reduce the intensity of the emotion.

When Ms. Winchester visited her parents on the occasion of their 40th wedding anniversary, she had not been home in 3 years and was anxious to see her family and friends. Just before that time, she had begun treatment for depression. Not only was she taking medication, but also she was receiving cognitive therapy from her psychiatrist. She had been learning how her emotional state affected her view of things and how, together, they influenced her ability to handle herself in difficult situations.

Ms. Winchester had always done well in school and, with considerable effort, had recently advanced several steps along her career path. For her sister, Edith, things had always come easy. Edith was her parents' "shining star." She was beautiful, brilliant, and successful. In the past, when Ms. Winchester had tried to tell her parents about her job as an accountant, they had interrupted her with news about Edith's latest achievements. Ms. Winchester was going to be assertive this time. She was going to make her parents listen to her. She was going to make them proud this time.

At the anniversary party, many relatives asked Ms. Winchester about her new job and her family. When it came time to talk with her parents, she was nervous, but she was determined to get the attention that she needed. As she began to talk about her promotion at work, her mother interrupted to ask if she had heard that her sister had also just been promoted. Ms. Winchester was furious and heartbroken at the same time. A stream of angry and hurtful thoughts flooded her mind. "They don't care. They don't love me, and they never have. I hate them. I hate her. It doesn't matter how hard I try, I'll never be successful. I may as well stop trying." Ms. Winchester knew she was going to cry. She left the room without explanation. The entries that she subsequently made in her Automatic Thought Record are shown in Figure 6.5.

Date	Event	Emotion	Thought
June 1	Mother interrupted	Anger (85%)	I hate them. I hate her. (25%)
		Frustration (100%)	It doesn't matter how hard I try, I'll never be successful. I may as well stop trying. (85%)
		Sadness (90%)	They don't care. They don't love me, and they never have. (50%)

FIGURE 6.5. Ms. Winchester's Automatic Thought Record.

An intervention to evaluate the validity of the negative automatic thoughts listed generally follows completion of the Automatic Thought Record. Practice in thought monitoring for any extended period of time without teaching a cognitive restructuring intervention will not be useful to patients, but will merely draw their attention to their negative mood shifts and their negative thoughts.

EVALUATING THE VALIDITY
OF NEGATIVE AUTOMATIC THOUGHTS

Often, the automatic thoughts associated with negative shifts in mood are partially or completely invalid or inaccurate. Because the negative bias in automatic thoughts generally elicits or exacerbates a patient's shift in mood, one of the goals of CBT is to teach patients how to evaluate the validity of their own negative automatic thoughts. One technique is to collect and examine the evidence that supports the validity of their thoughts and the evidence that contradicts or refutes the validity of their thoughts. This technique helps patients to focus on the facts that support their view instead of the "gut-level" feelings that can influence their thinking. This is more effective than trying to change peoples' views by dismissing them (e.g., "Don't worry about it"), discounting their validity (e.g., "Oh, that's ridiculous"), or otherwise attempting to convince others that their views are false (e.g., "You don't really believe that, do you?" "Don't think that way").

The first step in the process is to refer to the Automatic Thought Record and select the automatic thought associated with the greatest amount of emotion or the one that troubles the patient the most. The Logical Analysis of Automatic Thoughts worksheet shown in Figure 6.6 can be used for this exercise. After providing a rationale for this intervention, ask patients to list all the facts that support or validate the automatic thought (evidence for) and all the facts that refute or invalidate the thought (evidence against). It is usually more difficult for people to generate evidence against negative automatic thoughts because their idea "feels right" and they may never have considered the possibility that their first impressions could be wrong. In this exercise, the clinician does not lead the patient by suggesting evidence against the negative thought. Instead, the clinician may pose facilitating questions, such as:

"Is there anything else that makes you think this idea is true/false?"
"Does anyone say or do things to you that make you think this idea is true/false?"
"Have you had any experiences that suggest this idea is true/false?"

Automatic Thought:		
What Evidence Do You Have That This Idea Is True?	What Evidence Do You Have That This Idea Is False?	What Is Another Possible Explanation for the Event? What Might Someone Else Think in This Situation?

After examining the evidence for and against the automatic thought, rerate the intensity of the emotion and belief in the column labeled Time 3.

FIGURE 6.6. Logical Analysis of Automatic Thoughts.

By not attempting to refute any of the evidence for or against the negative automatic thought, even if it seems silly or illogical, the clinician tries to provide a neutral response.

Only when the two columns of evidence have been completed is there an attempt to evaluate the quality of the evidence. The patient weighs the evidence for and against the negative automatic thought and draws a conclusion about its validity. An informal review of the two columns may be sufficient, but it is important to remember that the column with the greatest number of entries is not necessarily the one that is more accurate or the one that carries the most weight. Some pieces of evidence may carry less weight than others or may have a greater influence on the conclusion drawn. A more formal method for analyzing the evidence for and against a negative automatic thought is to examine the evidence lists and assign a weight to each item. For example, those pieces of evidence that weigh heavily on a patient's evaluation may be assigned three stars, whereas those that have less bearing on a patient's conclusion may be assigned one or two stars.

Ms. Winchester's conversation with her mother stimulated her negative automatic thoughts. The thought that she believed most strongly was the one associated with feelings of frustration: "It doesn't matter how hard I try; I'll never be successful." She believed that thought with 85% certainty at the time

As evidence for the negative automatic thought, Ms. Winchester listed the following (*** very important; ** moderately important; * important):

1. My parents are only interested in my sister.
2. I have been struggling to get ahead all my life. School was a struggle. Raising my kids was a struggle. Getting a job was a struggle.***
3. I have failed many times in my life.***
4. My parents seem disinterested in my accomplishments.
5. I never seem to get the jobs I really want.**
6. People brag about my sister, but I never hear them brag about me.**

As evidence against the negative automatic thought, Ms. Winchester listed:

1. I graduated from college, even though it took 2 years longer than planned.**
2. I recently got a promotion.***
3. I am overcoming my depression.
4. My husband is very proud of me.*
5. My children are healthy and usually happy.**

There are three possible outcomes in the evaluation of a negative automatic thought. First, the individual may conclude that his or her negative automatic thought was false. In this case, the clinician encourages the patient to replace the negative automatic thought with a more valid statement. For example, if the negative automatic thought was, "I can't do anything right" and this was found to be incorrect, a more valid statement may be, "I do some things well, but there are other things I'm not very good at, such as keeping the house clean."

Second, the patient and the therapist may conclude that the negative automatic thought is true. If the clinician believes that there is some validity to a patient's negative evaluation (e.g., "I ruined my marriage"), it is not helpful to attempt to revise or replace the negative automatic thought with a more positive thought (e.g., "This frees me up to find someone better"). Instead, the content of the negative automatic thought can become a specific target for change in CBT—for example, mending the relationship, coping with the separation. Third, the patient may find that the evidence for or against the negative automatic thought is inconclusive. These steps are summarized in Table 6.1.

> When Ms. Winchester weighed the evidence for and against her negative automatic thought, she decided that her original thought was only partially correct. She had been successful in the areas of family and career. Not like her sister, but on her own scale, she was successful. She modified her negative automatic thoughts as follows: "I have worked hard and have been somewhat successful. I have not been successful in getting my parents to give me as much attention as they have given my sister."
>
> Since there was some validity to Ms. Winchester's view and she continued to experience considerable frustration when she encountered

TABLE 6.1. Negative Automatic Thoughts

1. Choose an automatic thought to evaluate. Choose one listed in the Automatic Thought Record for the week or select one from the Summary of Positively and Negatively Biased Thoughts worksheet. A thought or belief associated with a significant amount of negative emotion should be selected and listed at the top of the Logical Analysis of Automatic Thoughts worksheet.

2. Explain that the task is to first generate evidence to support and refute the automatic thought and then to objectively review the evidence. Ask the patient to list all evidence supporting and refuting the automatic thought in the appropriate columns.

3. After examining the evidence for and against the thought, the patient may conclude that the thought is invalid, that the evidence is inconclusive, or that the thought is indeed valid. Use your clinical judgment and decide what intervention(s) should be implemented given the results of the logical analysis. Some suggestions are:
   a. Invalid thoughts: Revise the original automatic thought to make it more accurate.
   b. Valid thoughts: Ask the patient what the consequences are given that the negative thought is valid and what the probability is of these consequences occurring. If the probability is high and the consequences are significant, take a problem-solving approach to generate a plan for decreasing the probability of negative consequences.
   c. Inclusive evidence: Find out what kind of evidence would be needed to confirm or disconfirm the thought. Generate a plan for accumulating more evidence.

situations like the one at the party, she focused her attention on developing a plan to solve the underlying problem. Her plan included talking with her parents about what it was like to grow up in the shadow of her sister Edith and how it made her feel when they bragged about Edith, but showed little interest in her more modest achievements.

If it is unclear whether the automatic thought is true or false, more information is necessary to complete the evaluation. An experiment can be set up to gather more data.

Mrs. Delgado was a new member of a support group for patients with bipolar disorder. She had the feeling that the people in her group did not like her. She was not certain why, but she often felt that they were giving her the cold shoulder. When Mrs. Delgado and her therapist evaluated the evidence supporting and refuting this notion, the results were inconclusive. Some group members seemed to be interested in what she had to say, but she was rarely invited to join the group for coffee after the meeting and was not called by other group members between meetings. Mrs. Delgado and her therapist agreed that more information was needed.

Although Mrs. Delgado believed that she needed direct feedback from another group member, just thinking about this made her very anxious. "What if they tell me I'm a jerk and they don't want me in the group?" After some discussion, she agreed that she needed to know what others thought of her. Bad news would become goals for improvement. Good news would disconfirm her negative automatic thought.

Mrs. Delgado decided to talk with Joe, the group member whom she trusted the most and who seemed capable of being honest with her. At the next group meeting, she asked Joe if he thought that the other group members liked her. He told Mrs. Delgado that he liked her, as did others, but that she was sometimes hard to approach. She seemed to get her feelings easily hurt, and others were afraid of offending her. Joe's explanation helped Mrs. Delgado to understand why it was difficult for her to determine how others felt about her. She and her therapist focused their energy on Mrs. Delgado's sensitivity to perceived criticism and the use of CBT techniques to evaluate those feelings when they occurred.

GAINING EMOTIONAL DISTANCE

Taking a different perspective on an event that stimulated a mood shift or negative automatic thoughts often allows patients to look at a situation more objectively and, thus, to draw more objective conclusions. In order to accomplish this, clinicians may ask patients to evaluate the situation as if it were happening to someone else, such as a friend, relative, or even a stranger. This method allows patients to examine a stimulus problem without the emotion that may be distorting their perceptions, as they are less likely to make the same negative interpretations of situations from the perspective of others that they make from their own perspective.

> When Mrs. Turner and her husband entered the room to begin their therapy session, she was furious. Her hands were shaking, and her eyes had already begun to well up with tears. Mr. Turner knew his wife was angry, but did not understand why. The holiday times, which are generally stressful, had gone particularly well. Their son had come to visit. There had been no conflict. Mrs. Turner had tried to stay calm, but her quiet fury soon gave way to tears and angry words: "You aren't trying. You won't talk to me. You won't kiss me. You don't care. I'm not going to try either. If you want this marriage to work, you will have to come to me. I'm not coming to you."
>
> Mrs. Turner described how a series of small events in which her husband failed to meet her needs had led to her anger. When she needed to be left alone, he tried to hug her. When she needed a hug, he kept his distance. The fact that she turned down his offers to help did not mean that she wanted him to stop offering. Mr. Turner looked lost. He reported feeling hopeless about their future. The therapist acknowledged how hurtful it can be when others seem to be letting you down when you need them the most. She also discussed how frustrating it can be when every attempt to improve the marriage seems to make matters worse.
>
> After the couple had aired their feelings, the therapist asked Mrs. Turner to imagine that she was hearing this story from an acquaintance. What if her friend complained that her husband kissed her at the wrong time and did not persist in his offers to help? "Imagine that your friend insisted that this was evidence that her husband did not care about her anymore." When asked to think of any other possible explanations for the husband's behavior, Mrs. Turner immediately thought of her friend Doris. Mrs. Turner explained that Doris sometimes gets upset with her husband Larry about situations like this. Although Larry is a great guy and really does try to be a good husband, Doris is apt to see Larry's benign actions as intentionally malicious when she is upset about other things. On these occasions, Mrs. Turner would advise Doris to calm down and "give the guy a break." When looking at the situation from Doris's perspective, Mrs. Turner could see that Doris expected her husband to read her mind and to know what she wanted and when she wanted it.

When the less personal perspective generated is different from the individual's initial assessment of the problem, the clinician may ask him or her to examine and explain the discrepancy. For example, the clinician may ask, "How is it that, when you focused on your experience with your husband, you concluded that he doesn't care, but when you looked at it from a friend's perspective, it seemed to be the wife's fault as much as the husband's? How is your situation different from your friend's? How might you apply this new observation to your own situation?" The goal of this technique is for logic to override emotional reasoning.

> Mrs. Turner admitted to being upset about the slowness of the progress that she and her husband were making in therapy, the fact that the holidays had not turned out as she had hoped, and also her breakthrough of depressive symptoms. She was able to see herself in Doris, however, and acknowledged that she may have attributed too much blame to her husband.

Another means of gaining emotional distance is to let some time pass so that the intensity of the emotion can decrease before any conclusions are drawn about the event. This is similar to counting to ten before speaking.

ALTERNATIVE EXPLANATIONS

Like taking another individual's perspective, exploring alternative explanations for events listed in the Automatic Thought Record can elicit additional, more objective evaluations of these events. These are sometimes referred to as rational responses. In this intervention, the clinician asks patients to generate alternative explanations for their own behavior and experiences (see Table 6.2). For example, if the negative automatic thought is "I am incompetent," the list of alternative explanations may include "I'm not very good at this task," "I didn't have time," "Someone

TABLE 6.2. Alternative Explanations

---

1. Provide a rationale for using this intervention to combat negative automatic thoughts.

2. Continue with the same example used in the evidence for/evidence against exercise or choose another negative automatic thought that may seem more appropriate for this intervention.

3. Use the third column of the Logical Analysis of Automatic Thoughts worksheet to generate alternative explanations for the event in question. Ask the patient to choose the explanation that seems most likely. Generate evidence for/evidence against the alternative explanation if necessary.

---

tried to make it difficult for me," "I was having a bad day," "I had too much on my mind," or "I've never been trained to do this particular task." When the lists are complete, the patient examines and evaluates the listed items. After eliminating unlikely explanations, the patient considers the remainder to determine if any apply to the circumstance under evaluation. The patient can then choose the alternative explanation for the event that is most appropriate.

The final step is to gather evidence to determine the validity of that alternative explanation. Some clinicians prefer to use the evidence for/evidence against technique; others ask the patient to monitor new experiences to determine if the alternative explanation is correct. For example, if an alternative explanation for "incompetence" is a lack of skill in a specific area, the patient can evaluate his or her competence and skill in executing a similar task on the next attempt. If further examination shows this alternative explanation to be valid, it can become a treatment goal for the patient (e.g., to gain more training in that particular work-related area).

PREDICTION OF NEGATIVE AUTOMATIC THOUGHTS

After learning to identify, evaluate, and restructure negative automatic thoughts, the patient needs to learn to predict their occurrence before they become a problem. It is helpful first to identify situations that typically elicit emotion and negative thinking.

> "That's easy," said Mr. Randolph. "Every time I have to pay bills, I feel horrible and start thinking about what a rut I'm in and how incompetent I am. Every month, like clockwork."

In many patients' lives, there are typical situations that are emotionally troublesome. Such situations may predictably elicit anxiety, anger, sadness, or guilt. Rather than waiting for these events to elicit emotions and negative automatic thoughts, patients can reflect on past experiences and analyze their depressogenic cognitions in a more dispassionate manner. This reanalysis of negative automatic thoughts provides patients with alternative responses to their automatic thoughts.

CHAPTER SUMMARY

Emotional responses to internal and external events are mediated by one's perceptions and interpretations of these events. In depression, the interpretations of events that are associated with negative emotions such as sadness, anxiety, anger, or guilt are stereotypically distorted. These distortions represent faulty information processing that systematically bias the evaluation of stimuli in a way that emphasizes the negative aspects and overlooks the positive. The subsequent behavioral responses can exacerbate problems because they are based on incorrect or incomplete information. Some examples of cognitive distortion include pessimism and drawing conclusions prematurely based on insufficient information.

The goal of CBT is to identify thoughts associated with significant changes in mood. Once isolated, these thoughts can be evaluated objectively to determine their validity. Invalid negative thoughts are modified to increase their accuracy, thereby reducing the intensity of the feelings associated with the cognitive distortion. If the negative thought is valid, the content becomes a goal for therapy. If the evaluation of the cognitive distortion is inconclusive, a means for gathering additional information to do the evaluation is devised.

Automatic Thought Records allow patients to document their emotional reactions and immediate negative automatic thoughts following stressful events. The validity of these negative thoughts can be tested by objectively examining the evidence that supports and refutes the thoughts, by gaining emotional distance from the stimulus events, and by generating and evaluating alternative explanations for events.

Guided discovery is the best method for closely examining the distorted cognitions of depressed persons. When patients are guided to evaluate their own thoughts and draw their own conclusions they will be more convinced of their reinterpretation than if it was handed to them by therapists as reframes or interpretations. This method takes time to get to what may seem obvious for the clinician. Remember that the power of these interventions is not in their conclusions, but in the process of discovery.

SEVEN

Cognitive Changes in Mania

SESSION 11. COGNITIVE CHANGES IN MANIA

Purpose of the Session

The purpose of the session is to begin to train patients to monitor their thinking for "positively biased" or irritable thoughts that might signal the onset of mania and to intervene with methods that contain and organize cognitive symptoms. When patients find their thinking marked with increased interest in taking on a greater number of activities, increased self-confidence, or grandiosity, or that their thinking is more scattered or disorganized, they can use these thoughts as cues to begin monitoring these changes, which may herald a manic or hypomanic episode, more closely, and to intervene appropriately.

The cognitive changes associated with the onset of hypomania and mania are often subtle early in the course of the episode. In teaching patients to monitor these thoughts, consider the evolution of mania as symptoms become clinically noteworthy.

Goals of the Session

1. Review the types of thoughts that may serve as indicators of the onset of mania.
2. Train patients to identify positive mood shifts and associated hypomanic and manic thoughts.
3. Practice the application of cognitive restructuring methods to cognitions that may be distorted by hypomania.
4. Teach methods for evaluating plans before taking action.

(cont.)

(continued from page 142)

Procedure

1. Assess treatment compliance.
2. Review the Logical Analysis of Automatic Thoughts homework from last session.
3. Review the positively biased thoughts that are associated with the onset of hypomania or mania. Ask patients for personal examples of their thoughts when hypomanic or manic.
4. Use the Automatic Thought Record as a guide for teaching patients to identify their positively biased thoughts.
5. Discuss how and when to monitor thoughts that may herald mania. Apply a cognitive restructuring technique to evaluate biased thoughts and modify accordingly. Discuss when to notify their psychiatrists of these cognitive changes.
6. Teach advantages/disadvantages technique and goal setting.
7. Assign homework.

Homework

Ask the patient to keep a Mood Graph for the next week. When the patient's mood falls outside normal limits ask the patient to complete an Automatic Thought Record. Emphasize monitoring positive changes in mood for this homework assignment.

For many, but not all, people with bipolar disorder, the onset of mania or hypomania can be a pleasant experience. Their mood improves considerably; they feel energized, excited, and optimistic. For others, mania and hypomania begin with irritability and agitation. Feelings of dysphoria and euphoria can also alternate rapidly in some people who are entering a manic episode. In mixed episodes, quick changes can occur between good humor and extreme irritability. Patients who experience these dysphoric or "mixed" manic episodes report that they are unable to predict their moods from hour to hour during these episodes. They notice both racing thoughts and intermittent feelings of severe sadness.

The dysphoria may or may not be associated with an increased speed or rate of speech. Patients may experience extreme fatigue and desire to rest but be unable to put their minds at rest or to disengage from a variety of activities. They have the uncomfortable, unpleasant experience of being driven to engage in more and more activities, while feeling more and more miserable.

Manic, hypomanic, or mixed episodes usually emerge over a period of days to a week. The nature and severity of the symptomatology (particularly in manic episodes) may preclude effective intervention by the patient alone. For some people, there is a typical sequence of symptom progression to a manic or hypomanic state, beginning with one symptom (e.g., insomnia) and progressing to others (e.g., increased sexual interest, feelings of euphoria). Changes in thinking patterns, cognitive processing, or preoccupation with certain ideas can be part of this progression. Some are aware of these cognitive changes and can say, "Here I go again. I always start thinking that way when I'm getting manic." This recognition can be a critical step in taking appropriate and early action to control symptoms.

Family members or others close to patients can help them to recognize when manic or hypomanic symptoms are returning. Family members can often recognize the onset of hypomanic symptoms in patients before the patients are aware of their own changes in mood or actions. If family members are supportive and helpful, rather than critical, patients can rely on their observations to help determine whether symptom progressions are consistent with the development of a manic or hypomanic episode and whether further intervention is needed.

While this sounds simple, there is often considerable tension between the patient and other family members surrounding the emergence of manic symptoms. For the person who has been depressed for some time, a shift out of the depression can be mistaken for hypomania by others.

PATIENT: I feel really good today. It's been a while since I've felt like doing anything. I think I'll go out for a while.

MOTHER: Now be careful, you know how you can get.

PATIENT: There you go again. I'm not getting sick. I'm finally having a good day, and all you can do is try to spoil it for me. You never change.

The cognitive changes of hypomania can be subtle at first and easily mistaken for "having a good day." When uncertain, the symptom monitoring or mood graphing exercises described in Chapter 4 can be helpful. The therapist can facilitate the use of symptom monitoring by meeting with patients and their family members to first discuss when and how to monitor symptoms and how to provide feedback and handle disagreements.

COGNITIVE SYMPTOMS
OF MANIA AND HYPOMANIA

The cognitive changes associated with mania or hypomania include changes in the way information is processed, changes in view or attitude, changes in perceptions of people or other stimuli, and changes in amount and quality of new ideas. These changes should signal to patients and therapists that an episode of mania is imminent and that aggressive action should be taken to forestall a full episode of mania. This chapter focuses on containing the cognitive symptoms to attempt to slow the progression into mania and to use cognitive changes as a cue to seek professional help to evaluate current pharmacological treatments. The intervention based on the outcome of this evaluation can be to correct problems with noncompliance to pharmacotherapy (see Chapter 5), increase or add medications to the regimen, and/or modify patients' activities and behaviors (e.g., reduce stimulation and increase sleep—see Chapter 9) in an attempt to control symptoms.

This chapter reviews some of the most common cognitive changes in mania and methods for evaluating and taking control over cognitive distortions. These methods should be used in combination with the behavioral interventions for mania and with evaluation and possible modifications in pharmacotherapy.

Increased Optimism and Grandiosity

The most common cognitive symptom of mania or hypomania is the development of an unusually positive view of self, the future, and the world at large. When becoming manic, people often find themselves experiencing an increased sense of self-confidence and well-being. This might include an overestimation of their abilities, an irrepressible optimism that causes them to view the world as particularly helpful or beneficial, or an underestimation of the negative consequences of their behavior. For some, this self-confidence may progress to a sense of inappropriate grandiosity that, in severe cases, can be delusional.

When entering a manic or hypomanic episode, patients often develop a wealth of new ideas and plans. The world seems full of possibilities just waiting for the right person with the intelligence and drive to make them happen. For example, when entering into a manic episode, they may begin to think of new business ventures that they view as virtually guaranteed of success. Often, some of these ideas may, in fact, be ingenious and potentially successful. Unfortunately, during mania a person's ability to distinguish between good ideas and grandiose delusions is compromised. The natural intelligence, creativity, and adventurousness of some people with bipolar disorder can sometimes lead to financial successes. However, during manic episodes, as activity increases and the need for sleep decreases, the ability to concentrate and follow through with plans declines. This, coupled with impaired judgment (inability to distinguish good from poor ideas) and an increased drive to action with little or no planning, can cause even the best ideas to fail.

In addition, when entering a manic or hypomanic episode people may fail to note, evaluate, or take into account the potential negative consequences of their behavior. They experience an intense sense of or a need to rush to activity without carefully considering the pros and cons associated with various options or choices. Also, their sense of irrepressible optimism may be such that, if they even consider the potential negative consequences of an activity or event, they dismiss these consequences summarily.

Another cognitive distortion that often accompanies grandiosity is the perception of having special powers, particularly in the realm of creativity or interpersonal transactions (e.g., conducting business deals, sexual seductions). This perception can be reinforced as individuals also begin to personalize certain events in their lives, attributing unrelated occurrences to their own special powers. For example, when manic or hypomanic, a person riding in a cab down a busy thoroughfare may feel able to predict changes in stoplights or actually able to control the stoplights during the drive. When the light turns green just as the cab arrives at the intersection, the person may believe that he or she caused it to change. When experiencing these symptoms, the hypomanic or manic individual may selectively attend to environmental events that appear to confirm these presumed special powers, but ignore evidence to the contrary. Thus, these individuals have a tendency to magnify the positive and overlook negative feedback from others and from environmental events. When the grandiosity reaches psychotic levels, these patients may be convinced of their ability to prophesy or to control the future.

Upon hearing about these feelings of being exceptional, family members or friends will tend to disagree or suggest alternative explanations for these seemingly mystical events. If others fail to validate their inflated sense of self-esteem, patients may attribute this attitude to hostile or malevolent intent. In some cases, the manic individuals may begin to view those around them as obstructing or interfering with their grandiose plans or failing to recognize their special abilities. Some believe that others are jealous of these "special gifts."

Cognitive interventions are likely only to be effective before delusional thinking begins—that is, when patients are able to reason through their ideas, to look objectively at and evaluate their thought processes. Questioning optimistic thoughts or new plans is a delicate process for therapists, because there is a risk of insulting or invalidating patients. When raising the possibility that these potentially positive but unrealistic ideas are actually symptoms of illness, therapists are, in fact, also questioning their patients' reasoning abilities. For those who have suffered particularly severe depressions, this questioning can feel like therapists are trying to take away their chances at some well-deserved happiness. Resentment and bitterness can follow. Therapists can often minimize this reaction by being sensitive to patients' feelings and by acknowledging how their concern might be viewed as criticism or suspiciousness. The groundwork for this intervention should be laid when teaching patients about symptom recognition and monitoring, especially when euthymic. Discuss with patients early in the treatment process that the therapist's job is to help the patient recognize and monitor symptoms and that that responsibility will sometimes mean being concerned when patients' moods become too elevated. In addition, when possible, teach the method for evaluating the validity of automatic thoughts as outlined in Chapter 6 even before the person becomes hypomanic, so that there is familiarity with the method before it is needed to remediate grandiose thoughts.

Mr. Michaels, a 40-year-old systems analyst, came bouncing into his session with a great new idea for a business. He had spent the three-day weekend at a seminar about a new cable television station that broadcasted "infomercials" 24 hours a day. The business was a variation on a pyramid program where each investor found five new investors and so on with each layer profiting from those that he or she brought into the program.

MR. MICHAELS: (*talking a little faster than usual*) I could get in on the ground floor for a mere $25,000 with a chance to make millions. This is my opportunity to make it big.

THERAPIST: You sound very excited about this. What would happen to your computer job?

MR. MICHAELS: I wouldn't need it. In a matter of weeks I would be making more than that lousy job could ever pay me.

THERAPIST: And the $25,000?

MR. MICHAELS: I've got it in my retirement account. That's another reason to quit. I can get access to my money that the company has been hoarding all these years.

THERAPIST: (*silent and looking concerned*)

MR. MICHAELS: I know what you're thinking. I'm not manic. I feel fine. I'm sleeping. I'm not arguing with people. I'm being totally responsible. You're just like my wife, always negative, no vision.

THERAPIST: What does your wife think about this change?

MR. MICHAELS: I haven't told her yet. You know how she gets. She panics before I have a chance to explain.

THERAPIST: I have to be honest with you. I *am* concerned. You do seem a little more hyper than usual today. You hired me to help you. Part of my job is to watch for subtle changes that could signal the onset of hypomania. I know I must sound like a wet blanket to you. I just want you to be in total control of your decisions, especially big ones like this. In the past, when your ideas were influenced by mania, how did things turn out?

MR. MICHAELS: (*sounding disgusted*) You know how they turned out. There was that rug deal, but I was ripped off by that jerk. And the landscaping thing would have worked out, but my neighbors have no imagination. The camera business, well, that was bad, but we've recovered. We're back on our feet. I always come through one way or another.

THERAPIST: Do you have any symptoms of hypomania? Will you humor me enough to review your Symptom Summary Worksheet?

MR. MICHAELS: Yeah, all right. If it will make you happy. (Therapist hands him the Symptom Summary Worksheet completed several months ago.) I can concentrate just fine. My outlook is more positive than usual, but I had been depressed for a while. My sex drive has returned. I'm sleeping 5 or 6 hours, but that's all I really need. No one should need 8 hours. I am more optimistic about the future. I don't have racing thoughts. I'm not paranoid. I'm not argumentative with my wife or my boss, although he really did get on my nerves today. I'm not dressing weird. I haven't bought anything that I couldn't afford.

THERAPIST: You are talking a little faster than usual, and you don't usually criticize me.

MR. MICHAELS: (*sarcastically*) I'm sorry if I hurt your feelings. OK, OK, I admit it, I'm excited, so I'm a little hyped up. But I am under control. This really is my opportunity to make it big.

THERAPIST: You may be right. I can see your enthusiasm. I know that you do not want to go through the pain of another manic episode or see your family suffer financially. So let's take the usual precautions. Agreed?

MR. MICHAELS: Agreed.

THERAPIST: You have taken the first step by reviewing your symptoms. You have a few symptoms. Let's watch them for a few days and see how it goes. Do you need a new Mood Graph? I have some blanks. Call me in a couple of days and let me know how you are feeling. Have you changed the way you take your medication?

MR. MICHAELS: Not really. I haven't needed the sleeping meds. I can fall asleep just fine. I had stomach flu last week. That sometimes throws off my lithium levels. I know, I'll get it checked today.

THERAPIST: Let's look more closely at your business idea. You said you believe that this is your chance to make it big.

MR. MICHAELS: That's right.

THERAPIST: Let's examine the evidence for and against that idea.

MR. MICHAELS: What idea?

THERAPIST: That this is your chance to make it big.

MR. MICHAELS: OK. The evidence for is that the financial projections show how profit can be made. Something like this was done before and produced similar profits.

THERAPIST: Is there any way to verify these facts?

MR. MICHAELS: You think they would lie?

THERAPIST: Has anyone ever lied to you to get your money?

MR. MICHAELS: Yes, but this is different.

THERAPIST: Any other evidence to support the notion that this is your chance to make it big?

MR. MICHAELS: There were testimonials of other people who invested and did well. I saw a videotaped presentation of the things that would be aired on this station, and they looked legitimate. My horoscope this week said that opportunity was around the corner. The chairman of the promotions groups is named Michael. How's that for a cosmic link?

THERAPIST: Any evidence that this is not your chance to make it big?

MR. MICHAELS: Not that I can think of.

THERAPIST: It is usually harder to think of evidence against an idea that you are really sold on. Take your time. Is there anything from your past business ventures that might suggest evidence against this idea?

MR. MICHAELS: My great ideas haven't always worked out. I've been lied to before by people wanting to make money off of me. This is a new and small company. When I'm feeling good, I am more gullible, especially when it comes to money making ideas. I guess I do have some symptoms of hypomania. OK, you win.

THERAPIST: I win?

MR. MICHAELS: This might be another great idea. I'll wait a week and rethink it. Maybe I'll try to verify some of their information about this new company. It couldn't hurt. The only thing I lose by waiting is . . . money.

THERAPIST: Do you gain anything by waiting?

MR. MICHAELS: If this is a bad idea, I save my money, my job, and probably my marriage.

THERAPIST: What other precautions do you need to make?

MR. MICHAELS: I need to check my lithium level and watch my sleep. I need to cut the caffeine for a while and monitor my symptoms. I don't want to get sick.

Another strategy for evaluating grandiose ideas is to examine the advantages and disadvantages of both engaging in and not engaging in the new project. This procedure is described in Chapter 10.

Paranoia

Paranoid thinking early in the evolution of mania or hypomania may manifest as suspiciousness of others, particularly those who have had negative interactions with the patient in the past. The suspiciousness is often based on very real events and a history of bad feelings between the patient and the target of his or her paranoia. Selective attention to confirmatory data—that is, evidence that the paranoid thoughts are valid—may reinforce the paranoid thinking. The patient's interactions with the target will likely be tense because the patient's suspiciousness will affect his or her behaviors and affect. The targets will, in turn, likely react in some way to the patient's suspiciousness or tense demeanor. This reaction can be read by the patient as further evidence that his or her paranoia is valid.

It is not unusual for paranoid thinking to evolve with or soon after grandiosity begins.

> Ms. Hirsh felt certain that her upstairs neighbor had it in for her. It seemed like every night this week, as soon as she had laid down and was drifting off to sleep, that woman in the second floor apartment would drop something on the floor just above Ms. Hirsh's head. That was all it took to keep her awake for hours. She laid there, angry, thinking of all the ways she'd love to get even with that woman upstairs.
>
> Ms. Hirsh got out her therapy notebook and looked for the tab she had labeled "When I get upset." Ms. Hirsh and her therapist had designed an Automatic Thought Record for times when Ms. Hirsh was angry. She filled out the top of the form (see Figure 7.1). She was angry with an intensity of 80%. The event was her neighbor dropping what sounded like a cannonball right above her bed. Her automatic thoughts were that the woman upstairs had done it on purpose just to irritate her. They share a parking area in front of the apartment and Ms. Hirsh had gotten home first all week and had gotten the best space. The neighbor was probably mad at her about that. Ms. Hirsh was sure that the neighbor knew her usual bedtime because the television and lights would go out. It wouldn't be that hard to estimate how much time it took for Ms. Hirsh to fall asleep and then make an irritating noise to disturb her sleep. The more she thought about it, the angrier she became. Ms. Hirsh made a few notes on her Automatic Thought Record and asked herself the question on the form—"What bothers me most about this event?" After some thought, Ms. Hirsh wrote, "She is doing it on purpose just to upset me." "How strongly do I believe this?" "About 80%."
>
> Ms. Hirsh listed the evidence she had that this idea was true and the evidence she had that the idea was not true. This is presented in Figure 7.1. She also filled out the section on what other people would

When I Get Upset

1. How am I feeling right how? ___*Angry*___

2. How strong is this emotion right now? ___*80%*___

3. What event triggered this emotion? ___*The woman upstairs woke me up with a loud noise.*___

4. What bothers me most about this event? ___*She is doing it on purpose just to upset me. She's probably mad because I got the good parking space.*___

5. How strongly do I believe this? ___*About 80%.*___

6. What evidence do I have that the idea in 4 above is true? ___*A loud sound has woken me up three or four times this week. The neighbor upstairs has never been very friendly toward me. She said, "You got the good space again" when she got out of her car after me. I can hear noise coming from the upstairs apartment when I wake up. It sounds like people laughing.*___

7. What evidence do I have that this idea is not true? ___*The walls are thin in our apartment building. It is hard to know where sounds come from. She has always seemed like a nice person. When I apologized about the parking space she said it was no problem. She has a little kid upstairs that makes noise with his toys. I have been more edgy lately and more sensitive to noise.*___

8. What would someone else think who was in my situation? ___*She may not be aware that the noise bothers me downstairs. I may be reading too much into her comment about the parking. I am more irritable that usual. I need to watch myself. It could have been her child making the noise.*___

9. What is my conclusion? (Rerate 4 then rerate 2) ___*I may be jumping to conclusions about her intentionally bothering me. I need to calm down. Anger is 20%. Belief in idea is 10%.*___

10. What is my plan for tomorrow? ___*Begin monitoring my symptoms more closely. Make time to talk to the neighbor about the noise and the parking space. Let her know how sound travels. Ask her if the parking space is a problem and figure out a plan to share it.*___

FIGURE 7.1. Mr. Hirsh's Automatic Thought Record.

think in this same situation. When she was through she wrote down her conclusion and her plan for dealing with this the next day and rerated her anger. It had dropped to 20%. She recognized that she had been quite edgy these past few days and that the woman upstairs probably had more to do with her kids and husband than to take the time to irritate her at bedtime. She knew that she needed to do what she could to control her mood and to get enough sleep.

This use of the cognitive restructuring method described in Chapter 6 may be effective if individuals are still able to logically and objectively evaluate their thinking distortions. They must be able to step back from their emotions and ideas of the moment and to look at the problem from a more dispassionate perspective. The plan for tomorrow gives the person something constructive to focus on and reduces rumination.

Increased Fluency of Ideas

The increased mental activity in mania and hypomania often includes the generation of a flood of new ideas and interests. Individuals with hypomanic symptoms often overestimate how much can be accomplished in a given day and underestimate the time it takes to complete tasks. Even as they engage in activities their mental activity continues and distracts them from their tasks. A common complaint of people once recovered from manic episodes is that they began many activities but finished few or none. If depression followed mania, the uncompleted projects found throughout the house contributed to feeling overwhelmed and discouraged.

The activity driven by the hypomania is itself stimulating, thereby fueling the emergence of mania. The goal is to contain activity by organizing ideas and setting limits. The goal setting exercise presented in Chapter 9 helps patients to organize their thoughts and set priorities. The graded task assignment intervention described in Chapter 8 can be used to limit activity. The list of ideas, plans, and interests are reduced to a daily or weekly activity plan. Higher priority activities for the week are put on the A list, lower priority tasks on the B list. If hypomanic, patients will try to put too many activities on the lists. Planning for the week's activities must include time for usual home, work, and social responsibilities. The items on the A and B lists are added to patients' schedules. To contain activity, patients must complete the A list items before going on to the B list items. An inability to suppress urges to skip ahead or add more activities is an indication that symptoms are worsening and that pharmacological interventions should be more aggressively applied.

Mrs. Chen's Goal Setting Worksheet included 52 items. She complained of not being able to get things done, interruptions, distractions, and feelings of anxiety mixed with excitement. Her A list was negotiated after considerable discussion. She was somewhat tangential in her thinking, so negotiating the list took some time. Tangentiality coupled with her distractibility led to many started, but few completed, tasks. The A list included three things she wanted to do this week. Two had been started the previous week, but not completed. The third item was to take time for herself to relax, meditate, or listen to music. This had always helped to slow her down when she was agitated or anxious. Mrs. Chen's B list had 2 items, one was to evaluate the quality of her work on the A list items and make adjustments if needed. She took pride in her work, but would omit important details when hypomanic.

The key to success in this type of intervention is completion of tasks before beginning new ones. The Goal Setting Worksheet can be used as a continuous log of new ideas so that the person does not have to worry about forgetting creative ideas.

Perceptual Changes

Some patients in a manic or hypomanic episode may note early in the episode that they are experiencing perceptual changes. They may report a heightened awareness of or sensitivity to colors, smells, sounds, or touch. For example, the leaves on the trees appear far more intensely green than usual or the colors on the television set or in a magazine advertisement appear brighter than usual. These perceptual changes can be used as cues to monitor symptoms more closely and make any behavioral changes necessary to normalize sleep and contain activity. Cognitive interventions are not generally applied to these perceptual changes unless they are associated with specific distortions in thinking.

Thinking Errors in Mania

Social judgment can be impaired in hypomania and is usually quite impaired during manic episodes. In describing past manic episodes, people with bipolar disorder often recall a decreased sense of self-awareness with regard to their interactions with others. They may say or do things that are unusual for them under asymptomatic circumstances. They may either fail to notice the impact of their words or actions on others or may misinterpret their impact on others. "I don't know what I was thinking" is a common appraisal of their actions in retrospect.

Some thinking errors are common to many people with bipolar

disorder, particularly early on in the development of hypomania or mania. Many of these thinking errors, briefly described below, are related to their interactions with others.

1. *"They want me."* Increased sexual interest is another symptom of mania or hypomania. It can be manifested in greater frequency of sexual thoughts, increased sexual activity, and sexual activities uncharacteristic of the person when in a nonsymptomatic state (e.g., visiting prostitutes, engaging in "one-night stands" with strangers). Often, these inappropriate or unusual sexual impulses or activities are those that place patients' health or current relationships at risk.

This increased sexual interest/desire sets the stage for patients to jump to conclusions about the sexual interests of others. They may selectively attend to verbal or nonverbal cues that they interpret as indications of the sexual feelings and desires of others. This personalization of cues leads them to conclude that others to whom they are sexually attracted are also attracted to them.

2. *"They are moving too slowly."* The increased speed of thought, speech, and actions, as well as internal agitation or anxiety, leaves the affected individuals feeling that others are moving too slowly. As a result, they may become impatient or irritated with others. For example, patients may honk at other drivers who appear to be driving too slowly; pace around the doctor's waiting room; or call their bosses, subordinates, or care givers too frequently, insisting on immediate responses.

3. *"It's best to go straight to the top."* When hypomanic or manic, some patients tend to prematurely move up the chain of command when dealing with other individuals. For example, a patient may call a hospital administrator when a nurse could have answered the question or call the company president when a salesperson would most appropriately respond to the issue. Going to the top sometimes means going public. For example, a person might pursue the media in an attempt to heighten public awareness of what is perceived as not simply a personal problem, but a "system" problem.

4. *"A little humor never hurt."* Early in a manic or hypomanic episode, there may be an increased use of humor, often in a sarcastic manner. The person's naturally quick wit, verbal fluency, and delight in being the center of attention encourages the use of humor to amuse others. As social judgment becomes impaired during a hypomanic or manic episode, however, humor often becomes biting, critical, or otherwise inappropriate to the social circumstances.

5. *"They love my ideas."* Another positive cognitive distortion in affected individuals is the tendency for them to overvalue even minor cues that others have noted positive aspects of themselves or their ideas.

For example, if another person indicates that the manic or hypomanic patient's ideas regarding revisions in business plans or other endeavors are not really appropriate or acceptable—but does so gently and tactfully—the patient may see only the tactful aspects of the discussion and infer from them an acceptance or endorsement of the ideas.

6. *"Everyone is a drag."* Often, the lack of positive confirmation of the affected persons' new ideas is viewed as lack of care, dullness of wit, or the outright stupidity or lack of creativity in others. Those most likely to be cast in this light are people that know the patient well, since they are often the first to identify this type of expansive, rapid thinking as unrealistic, inappropriate, or even as a herald to a more severe hypomanic or manic episode.

7. *"I don't need my medicine."* It is very common, especially early in the course of the illness, for patients to equate feeling very good with having attained a cure of their illness—meaning, since they are well, they don't need their usual medicine. This view is reinforced when they reduce or stop their mood stabilizer (e.g., lithium) and they soon feel even better (i.e., inappropriately euphoric). To counter this danger, it is useful to explain to patients when beginning medication, and to reiterate when they are euthymic, that their medicines are needed on both good and bad days, and that rapid shifting of medications without professional assistance is as dangerous as a person with diabetes arbitrarily deciding whether and how much insulin to use.

8. *"I know best."* Early in the development of mania or hypomania, patients often experience an increased sense of conviction/intuition, probably due to highly positive (euphoric) emotions that seem to uniformly confirm any and all thoughts. These highly confirming feelings lead patients to distrust others, to avoid critical appraisal of their ideas, and to argue unnecessarily, inappropriately, and usually unsuccessfully with others with greater knowledge, experience, or authority (including the therapist). In essence, the patient thinks, "I'm OK" or "I'm great" and the rest of you are wrong.

In these states, patients may also make inappropriate demands on subordinates and colleagues, who in turn react and resist, causing the patient to become increasingly irritable. Recognition of this pattern/attitude when euthymic can assist the patient and the therapist to identify the pattern early in the development of a new mood episode.

9. *"Live today. Tomorrow will be even better."* A positive glow is given to current and future events when euphoria begins. Patients are likely to believe that they cannot lose, no matter what (i.e., disregard the potential negative consequences of their behavior). This conviction may lead, in some, to gambling, sexual indiscretions, or a lapse in their usual moral behavior (e.g., cheating in business or marital relationships). The

euphoric feelings color and, thereby, override the usual cues for caution, diligence, loyalty, and morality. If not delusional, some patients can be induced to see this pattern and to reappraise it.

Distractibility, Racing Thoughts, and Disorganized Thinking

As symptoms of mania worsen, thinking becomes more disorganized and more difficult for patients to control with cognitive or behavioral techniques. The increased mental activity shows in their speech and actions. When easily distracted, it is difficult for persons to focus their concentration. They will incorporate environmental stimuli unrelated to the topic at hand into their thinking and speech. It may appear that they are jumping from topic to topic or not making sense.

Speed of thinking may increase during a hypomanic or manic episode. Patients describe their thoughts as racing through their head, sometimes more rapidly than can be spoken. Some patients say that they can follow several trains of thought simultaneously. As one patient put it, "It's like watching several television programs simultaneously and understanding all of them."

The increased speed of thinking can sometimes be controlled by decreasing the amount of environmental or mental stimuli. For example, formal relaxation techniques can be used or the physical environment can be modified (e.g., going for a walk, disconnecting telephones, spending time alone, lowering the volume on music or television). This reduction of external noise can reduce internal noise. Self-talk to "slow down" works for some people. Others slow the process by forcing themselves to write down their ideas.

When experiencing racing thoughts and agitation, some people try to control their symptoms through consumption of alcohol, illicit drugs, or by taking additional amounts of their prescription medications, particularly anxiolytics. It is essential that patients avoid increasing their ingestion of alcohol or substances of abuse, particularly at the onset of or during a manic or hypomanic episode. These substances, while sometimes providing temporary relief, may further disrupt their sleep cycle, can precipitate an episode, can increase the severity of manic or hypomanic symptoms, and can prolong episodes and alter levels of prescribed medications. These patients may notice a decreased ability to synthesize information into organized groups. That is, they cannot pull details together to form a complete picture of a particular problem or task. Their thinking becomes muddled. Because they jump from topic to topic without completing full thoughts, others may see this as distractibility. Often unaware of their inability to synthesize and detail fully each of their thoughts, the patients become enamored of the number and types of thoughts that they are having.

Thinking may become so disorganized that logic, information provided by others, and the patient's own experience no longer carry any significant weight in making judgments or evaluating ideas. This shift from logic to a more primitive mode of thinking may evolve into a delusional psychotic state rather quickly. If there is a breakdown in thinking and patients notice the breakdown, they may become dysphoric and are often unable to function. Disorganized thinking usually precludes cognitive interventions because concentration and mental organization is needed. Some patients are aware of their inability to synthesize ideas and are eager to try methods that help impose structure on their thinking. Any of the cognitive restructuring methods described in this chapter or in Chapter 6 can be used to control disorganized thinking. Generally, however, the severity of this symptom requires a pharmacological intervention.

CHAPTER SUMMARY

The onset of hypomania or mania is marked by changes in mood, thought, and behavior. The cognitive symptoms include changes in view or perspective of oneself, others, and the future, often more optimistic or grandiose. There can be changes in the speed of thought and volume of ideas, with thoughts often racing more quickly than can be spoken.

Paranoia, delusions, and hallucinations accompany more severe episodes of mania. The CBT approach to managing the cognitive changes associated with mania or hypomania include (1) early detection of subtle cognitive changes to allow for early intervention, (2) evaluation of dysfunctional beliefs or ideas such as suspiciousness or grandiose ideas, and (3) organization of ideas or plans in an attempt to limit self-stimulating activities. Several of the cognitive and behavioral strategies used in depression are used with manic cognitions—specifically, the evaluation of potentially distorted cognitions and goal setting. Goal setting is used in mania to limit rather than increase activity, as with depression.

Some people with bipolar disorder resent others' suspiciousness of their "good moods." They may be particularly sensitive to family members' or therapists' suggestions that their positive mood, new ideas, or increased self-confidence are, in fact, signs of illness. Therapists can help patients and family members figure out ways of communicating concern and taking appropriate preventive actions without offending patients.

EIGHT

Behavioral Changes and Problems in Depressive Episodes

SESSION 12. BEHAVIORAL ASPECTS OF DEPRESSION

Purpose of the Session

The purpose of this session is to teach patients two cognitive-behavioral skills for coping with common behavioral consequences of depression. These are graded task assignment (GTA) and increasing mastery and pleasure.

Goals of the Session

1. Review common behavioral problems associated with depression (e.g., feeling overloaded and overwhelmed, lethargy cycle).
2. Teach patients two CBT strategies for coping with these problems (i.e., GTA, increasing mastery and pleasure).

Procedure

1. Assess treatment compliance
2. Review the Mood Graph and Automatic Thought Records for the past week and discuss any variations from the normal range including the circumstances under which mood shifts occurred.
3. Review the concept of being overwhelmed and overloaded and provide a rationale for the GTA intervention. Ask patients about times when they may have felt overwhelmed or overloaded. Find out how patients have coped with this type of problem in the past.

(cont.)

(continued from page 158)

4. Describe the procedure for GTA. Choose tasks that patients are having difficulty in completing and apply the GTA exercise.
5. Introduce the importance of experiencing a sense of mastery and pleasure and its role in depression. Assess level of pleasure in the patients' lives at present. If clinically indicated, construct homework assignments aimed at increasing pleasure during the next week.
6. Describe the lethargy cycle. Ask patients to describe their experiences with lethargy. Explain the use of increased mastery and pleasure and GTA to break the cycle. If patients are currently in a lethargy cycle, develop a plan for breaking the cycle and assign this as homework.

Homework
1. Attempt the first step in the GTA if a current problem was identified. Review patients' progress in the next session and continue to assign parts of the task as clinically indicated. Fade out your involvement in monitoring the patients' progress and prompting them to continue as clinically indicated.
2. Assign an intervention to increase mastery and pleasure or to break a lethargy cycle if clinically indicated. Follow up on these assignments. Continue to assign these interventions as long as clinically useful.

Many of the symptoms of depression are accompanied by changes in behavior. For example, insomnia leaves people tired and easily fatigued, making it difficult for them to maintain normal levels of activity. A loss of interest, desire, motivation, or energy to engage in routine or even pleasurable activities is common. In addition, when depressed, people find it difficult to make simple decisions, such as what to do, what to eat, or what to wear. When faced with what seems like endless choices and little drive or energy, the response is often to do nothing. With an avoidance of work-related tasks or chores and social activities, the depressed person has only limited opportunities to experience the feelings of pleasure or accomplishment that can help to combat depression.

Lethargy, decreased interest and motivation, inertia, and indecisiveness can have not only emotional but practical consequences. While immobilized by depression, a person may execute projects poorly, fail to complete them, or neglect them altogether. Uncompleted household tasks can cause tension or conflict between family members, and a decline in performance can threaten job security. Some people are able to maintain their usual job performance, but have no energy to spare for family and recreational activities. Work, responsibilities, and problems soon dominate life. Without play, there is no diversion from daily demands or no opportunities to experience things that might brighten the individual's mood. Contact with others who might provide emotional support decreases, leaving the person to cope all alone.

LETHARGY CYCLE

When Mrs. Nelson looked at the mess in her kitchen, the piles of unwashed laundry, and the dust all over her furniture, she criticized herself and felt guilty for having no energy or motivation to clean her house. She was overwhelmed by the volume of tasks awaiting her. Just being in these unkempt rooms made her feel anxious inside, like she wanted to run away from it all. She retreated to her small room to watch television. Her focus on the screen blocked out the images of her house closing in on her. Mrs. Nelson also felt sad and lonely because she had not talked with or seen her friends in several weeks. They had called and left messages about going out to the movies or to lunch, but she had not been able to motivate herself to return their calls. It took too much energy to act cheerful on the phone. Mrs. Nelson worried about the long-term consequences of her depression, particularly her lack of motivation. She knew that her husband was trying to be patient, but he would eventually reach his limit. Who knew what would happen then? Maybe he would leave. Who could blame him? Her guilt, loneliness, and anxiety seemed to deepen each day. It was like she was stuck in mud up to her hips. She saw no escape.

When depression induces lethargy, the accumulation of uncompleted tasks can be overwhelming. A sense of ineffectiveness validates feelings of guilt and hopelessness. Others can misinterpret depressed persons' inertia as laziness or selfishness and accuse them of using the illness to avoid responsibilities. This criticism feeds self-doubt and a sense of failure and worsens the depression. Although the inertia of depression is often mislabeled by patients as a character flaw, the real culprits are low energy and decreased interest.

Generally speaking, the more severe the depression, the lower the patient's energy level. With considerable effort, patients can often carry out some, or even all, of their daily activities, albeit with reduced efficiency. At the end of the day, they may feel exhausted or fatigued, may suffer from backaches or headaches, and may be unable to do anything more than retire to the couch or bed. Even if patients possess sufficient physical energy to engage in activities, they may no longer have the interest or the desire to do so. In either case, the resulting decline in activity and accomplishment stimulates guilt, anxiety, or sadness. This process only serves to worsen depressive symptoms. The resulting exacerbations of problems with energy, motivation, and interest causes the lethargy cycle to repeat itself (see Figure 8.1).

INTERVENTIONS TO END THE LETHARGY CYCLE

There are three points of entry in breaking the lethargy cycle: the activity level, the mood symptoms, or the energy and motivation level (Figure 8.2). Medications can help to improve sleep and increase energy and motivation. Changing patients' activity levels is another way to intervene in the lethargy cycle. This might include helping patients to attend to important tasks that have been neglected, for example, paying bills, cleaning the house, or making important phone calls. Even small accomplishments can improve mood and leave depressed individuals feeling better about themselves and their abilities. Improvements in mood can increase motivation, interest, and energy, thus reversing the lethargy cycle.

The first step in interrupting the lethargy cycle is to provide patients with a rationale for the intervention. As patients come to understand how

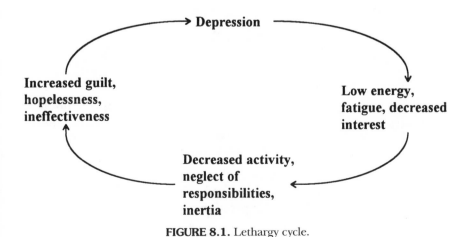

FIGURE 8.1. Lethargy cycle.

the cycle of lethargy influences their life, they can collaborate with the therapist to develop a plan for breaking the cycle. To begin, the therapist can ask patients to explain their inactivity.

THERAPIST: One of the things that is bothering you is that you believe you have neglected your household duties. Can you help me understand what happens?

MRS. NELSON: I just can't get going. My house is a mess. My husband and kids have had to cook for themselves, do their own laundry. I know they are embarrassed to bring friends home. I want to have a clean house. I am just so tired all the time. I just can't bring myself to do it.

THERAPIST: What kinds of housekeeping tasks need to be done?

MRS. NELSON: (*wringing her hands and staring at the floor*) Every room needs to be straightened up, vacuumed, dusted. Floors need to be swept and mopped. The laundry is piling up on the washroom floor. I need to iron my clothes. My garden is overgrown. The refrigerator needs cleaning, the bathrooms need to be scrubbed down. Then there are a thousand other small jobs, errands, and church activities. (*Begins to shake anxiously.*)

THERAPIST: It all sounds so overwhelming for you.

MRS. NELSON: It is.

THERAPIST: What goes through your mind when you walk into the house and see the work that needs to be done?

MRS. NELSON: First, I say to myself, "I have to get this work done. I'll do it

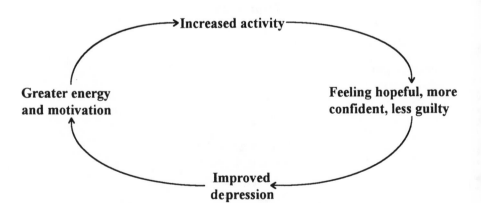

FIGURE 8.2. Reversal of lethargy cycle with increased activity.

today. I'll start with the kitchen." So I put my purse down, change my shoes and walk into the kitchen and that's when it hits me.

THERAPIST: Tell me what happens.

MRS. NELSON: It's like a wave comes over me. I can feel it from my stomach to my head. My chest gets tight and I have trouble catching my breath. I can see all the things that need to be done. It's like they fly toward my face. I have to leave the room.

THERAPIST: Does this happen in every room of the house?

MRS. NELSON: No. Not this bad. It's all so depressing. I hate looking at it, but I just can't seem to get started.

In this example, it appears that the volume of work to be accomplished is greater than the patient is capable of accomplishing. She sees housework as one large task that would mean days of work for her. She does not have the energy, motivation, or ability to mentally organize her work. For Mrs. Nelson it is an all-or-nothing venture, she either takes on all the housework or leaves it alone.

Graded Task Assignment

Graded task assignment (GTA) can be helpful in increasing a patient's activity. The goal of GTA is to take large, overwhelming tasks (like writing this book) and break them down into smaller, more manageable pieces (like writing chapters or paragraphs). The first step is to determine whether GTA is an appropriate intervention. Is the patient's inertia related to feeling overwhelmed? Is the patient unable to take the initial steps toward completing a backlog of tasks? Does the patient report being behind at work? Is there a big project that the patient has been avoiding? If so, GTA may be helpful in increasing activity.

To get started, patients list all the tasks that require their attention. Their level of inertia partly determines the level of detail in which tasks must be defined, because tasks will be assigned to the patient as listed on the sheet. The greater the inertia and the lower the energy, interest, and motivation, the greater the amount of detail needed in defining the tasks. For example, listing "clean the kitchen" may be sufficient for those patients who have enough energy to complete all the steps involved in this chore. For others, however, it will be necessary to divide this chore into each of the subtasks required, such as (1) wash the dishes, (2) put the dishes away, (3) sweep the floor, (4) empty the garbage, and (5) clean off the countertops. This approach allows the therapist to assign one or more subtasks at a time.

After a patient has made a project list, it is necessary to divide the tasks into smaller, more easily accomplished steps and devise a plan to guide the patient from one task to the next, avoiding the pitfalls that have contributed to inertia in the past. The first step is to prioritize the tasks on the project list by importance or urgency.

The items listed are assigned as homework at each therapy session. A few small tasks are assigned at first so that the likelihood of success is high. Ask patients to predict their likelihood of attempting this homework assignment. If they believe they are very likely to attempt the task, ask why they believe this is so. Remember that in the past it has been extremely difficult to initiate activities. What is different now? This may be an opportunity to illustrate how positive expectations can increase motivation. If the prediction of success is low, this gives the therapist an opportunity to explore the logic of this prediction. Ideas such as "I'm too lazy," "I can't handle stress anymore," and "If I try anything today, I'll just feel worse," can be evaluated with cognitive restructuring techniques (see Chapter 6). If GTA is successful, it will only be necessary for therapists to "assign" tasks at a few weekly sessions. When the inertia begins to lessen and motivation improves, patients can organize and execute tasks on their own. When this happens, therapists should follow up on the progress of the GTA tasks. This will provide an opportunity to positively reinforce their efforts with praise and to inquire about the effect of the activity on their self-evaluation, mood, and motivation. This reinforces the CBT model with a practical hands-on example.

Another variation on GTA is to divide tasks into two lists, those that are "high priority" (i.e., need to be done soon) and those that are "lower priority" (i.e., would be nice to get to, but can wait). The high priority items can be grouped together into the A list; the remaining tasks become the B list (Table 8.1). Because patients often state at first that all the tasks are equally urgent, it may be useful to focus their attention on the consequences of not completing each task. Those with the greatest or most immediate consequences if undone, such as paying bills, are A list

TABLE 8.1. Project Priority List

Project list	A list	B list
Wash dishes	Dishes	Closets
Do laundry	Laundry (2 loads)	Laundry (5 loads)
Buy groceries	Groceries (2-day supply)	Walls
Pay bills	Bills (those due now)	Garage
Clean closets		Groceries
Wash walls		Bills (those due later)
Clean garage		

tasks. Those with less severe or less immediate consequences if undone, such as washing the car, are B list tasks.

The items on each list should be further prioritized by importance or urgency. For example, they can be numerically ranked according to priority. A given chore, such as doing the laundry, can be reduced to smaller steps (e.g., seven individual loads of laundry) with some having higher priority than others (e.g., children's socks vs. linens); in this case, the chore may appear on both the A (socks) and B (linen) lists, as appropriate.

After the items on the project list have been prioritized, therapists can help patients select a few tasks to attempt before the next session. Patients may choose one or two high-priority items and one or two items that they believe to be less urgent. As with the master project list, the higher-priority items for the week become the A list, while the lower-priority items become the B list. Patients are instructed to attempt the A list items first. If time and energy are available, patients may then address one or two of the B list tasks (starting with those with the highest priority). As the inertia decreases, patients can begin to use this strategy on a daily basis to plan the next day's A list and B list activities.

Both GTA and the A list/B list interventions require considerable time in the first few weeks to plan for the execution of each activity. Ask patients to specify what materials are needed for each task (e.g., laundry soap); find out how to acquire additional supplies, if needed; and schedule each activity (i.e., day and time) when patients are most likely to have energy or when their motivation may be at its peak. It is best to have a backup plan in case an unexpected event should interfere with the original schedule (e.g., if a task cannot be done on Monday morning, the backup plan is Tuesday morning). In addition, therapists should try to anticipate and remove any obstacles that could interfere with the execution of the activity plans (see Chapter 5).

Mrs. Briggs, a working mother with severe depression, complained that she was overwhelmed with household, child care, and work-related tasks. When asked to provide an example of the types of tasks that she needed to accomplish, she retrieved from her purse a two-page list of things "to do." She said that whenever she made an effort to work on these tasks, she would first review the long list. Instantly, she would feel overwhelmed with the volume of chores and immobilized by the hopelessness of her situation. She had procrastinated for such a long time that tremendous guilt was now associated with her failure to accomplish her chores. As each day passed, her list grew longer, and her guilt and self-criticism grew stronger. The guilt and self-depreciation seemed to feed the depression.

"Catching up with life" was important to this patient, so completion of her "to do" list became an initial goal of therapy. The first step was to arrange her list of chores into a high-priority (A) list and a lower-priority (B) list. Each day the patient chose a limited number of tasks to put on her A list for that day. On one day, for example, she had to pick up her children from school, deposit her paycheck, and cook dinner; that became her A list. The B list consisted of tasks that she would like to accomplish or at least begin to work on that day (e.g., organize her office, vacuum her bedroom). It was important to match the number of items on the A and B lists to her level of energy and interest. Her task for each day was to accomplish the A list activities and to begin the B list activities only if time permitted.

When the patient returned for her next therapy appointment, she reported that this intervention had been very successful. She had accomplished the tasks on her A list and some items on her B list each day. As the weeks progressed, she was able to add to her lists and slowly reduce the backlog of chores that had overwhelmed her. Her ability to accomplish tasks decreased her feelings of guilt and anger with herself for her inertia. Her sense of accomplishment grew, as did her self-confidence. Although listed as chores, several of the tasks were enjoyable (e.g., taking the kids to the movies), which added some pleasure to her week. The long and overwhelming list of activities was slowly accomplished, and the accompanying guilt and anxiety were reduced. Once the patient had learned the principle of assigning a minimal amount of work to herself each day or each week, she was able to continue on her own without the therapist's coaching.

Overloaded and Overwhelmed

As the number of their uncompleted tasks increases, depressed patients often lose confidence altogether in their ability to handle work. They believe they are helpless in overcoming their inertia and have a sense of hopelessness about their ability to change. They blame themselves for their "failure" to keep up with life. Their sense of responsibility conflicts with their inertia and feeling of helplessness. They feel trapped, guilty, unable to function, and fearful of the consequences of their procrastination. Negative comments from others, such as bosses or spouses who are also disappointed, reinforce this self-depreciation.

When asked what happens when they think about approaching neglected work or daily tasks, these patients report being flooded by negative thoughts and feelings. Some become anxious or agitated; others ruminate about the consequences that they may have to face for their neglect. They say to themselves, "I just can't handle this today" or "I should be able to keep up, so there's no excuse." These dysfunctional cognitions may seem to exacerbate the inertia as well as the associated guilt. Identification of these negative thoughts allows the therapist and patient to examine each, test their validity, and correct any distortions. This process may help to lessen the inertia by giving patients more positive expectations for success.

There are several ways to identify the negative thoughts associated with inertia. Patients can monitor their automatic thoughts the next time they are faced with a task that has been neglected. Automatic Thought Records as described in Chapter 6 are used in this exercise. Another method is to ask patients to recall the thoughts that accompanied their last experience of this nature.

For example, they can imagine themselves confronted with a mountain of unfinished work. Ask them to describe the scenario in detail and to verbalize their feelings and thoughts. Have patients write down the feelings and thoughts evoked, and rate the intensity of each emotion and belief in each thought as described in Chapter 6.

This helps therapists and patients to select the specific feelings and thoughts most likely to interfere with the initiation of activity. These are usually thoughts accompanied by the most intense emotion and associated with the strongest beliefs. The interventions for modifying negative automatic thoughts that are described in Chapter 6 can be applied to the cognitions that accompany inertia.

The negative automatic thoughts associated with feeling overloaded or overwhelmed often lead patients to make negative predictions about their abilities to overcome their problems. Identifying these negative predictions serves three purposes:

1. It uncovers any basic assumptions (schemas) that may influence patients' self-perceptions and, thus, their confidence in their abilities.
2. It facilitates troubleshooting for factors that may interfere with patients' efforts to become more active, as it allows therapists and patients to develop a behavior change plan that maximizes the odds for success and minimizes the obstacles.
3. It permits therapists, after working with patients to increase their activity, to refer back to the negative automatic thoughts, predictions, and emotions to determine whether the behavioral intervention has had any influence on the patients' views of themselves, their ability, and the associated negative emotions.

Mr. Hawk, a 47-year-old accountant, is under pressure at the office and at home. He is behind in his work as he has been for months. He manages to get by at work but by the time he gets home he can only sit in front of the television until he falls asleep. He went to see the company psychiatrist after he saw a commercial on television about treatment for depression.

THERAPIST: Sounds like it has been a rough week. How have you been feeling?

MR. HAWK: Bad.

THERAPIST: What has been troubling you most?

MR. HAWK: My taxes. I haven't been able to finish them and the extension I filed ends next week. There is no way I can finish by then. I'm having to take work home from the office because I can't finish it by 5:00 P.M. My evaluation is coming up in a month so I have to put that first. There is no way to get everything done.

THERAPIST: How does that make you feel, Mr. Hawk?

MR. HAWK: Like it's futile. I'll never catch up. I'll always be behind.

THERAPIST: That's what runs through your mind. Can you tell me what the feeling or emotion is inside when you think about your prospects for finishing all this work?

MR. HAWK: Hopeless probably describes it best.

THERAPIST: Do you remember how we used that 0--100% scale to describe how intense the hopelessness feels right now?

MR. HAWK: Yes.

THERAPIST: How would you rate how hopeless you feel?

MR. HAWK: About 85%.

THERAPIST: What keeps it from being 100%?

MR. HAWK: I have managed to get enough done to keep my supervisors off my heels for now, but evaluations come up soon.

THERAPIST: What do you think will happen then?

MR. HAWK: I think it will all catch up with me.

THERAPIST: What do you mean?

MR. HAWK: When they look at all the late projects, requests for extensions, and piles on my desk, I'm going to be in a lot of trouble for not getting the job done on time or with the level of care they expect.

THERAPIST: What do you think will be the consequence?

MR. HAWK: I'm afraid that I'll be fired.

THERAPIST: How fearful are you, again on that 0--100% scale.

MR. HAWK: More than half, about 60%.

THERAPIST: Why only 60%?

MR. HAWK: I guess it's because I've been with the company a long time and have done good work for them in the past. I think there is a chance they will just give me a warning and put me on probation. Times are tough and there have been layoffs in several departments. They will no doubt have to trim the fat in my department and I can't perform like these kids right out of college.

THERAPIST: Let's use that 0--100% scale again but this time we're going to rate how strongly you believe that you'll get in trouble for not getting the job done.

MR. HAWK: About 80%.

THERAPIST: And how strongly do you believe that you'll be fired?

MR. HAWK: About 40%.

THERAPIST: It's not 100% because you think there is a chance that you'll only get a warning.

MR. HAWK: That's right.

THERAPIST: Going back to what you said earlier, how strongly do you believe that there is no way to get everything done and that you will always be behind?

MR. HAWK: Oh, I am 100% certain that I cannot get everything done. I'm only 90% certain that I'll always be behind.

THERAPIST: Do you get that hopeless feeling at work?

MR. HAWK: All the time.

THERAPIST: When do you notice it?

MR. HAWK: As soon as I sit at my desk. You should see it. It seems like the files are piled to the ceiling. I have so much to do, I have no space left to write.

THERAPIST: It sounds overwhelming. How do you think this affects your ability to focus on the work?

MR. HAWK: What do you mean?

THERAPIST: You are sitting there looking at piles of work and you are feeling hopeless. It all seems futile to you. How does this state of mind help or hinder your ability to focus or concentrate on each task? Is it motivating to you?

MR. HAWK: Are you joking?! I get in at 8:00 and I don't really get started until 9:30. I can hardly stand to sit there. I get up for coffee several times, check for messages, go to the mailroom, photocopy a few things, move files around my desk. I kill time until my anxiety quiets down enough to work.

THERAPIST: When you are feeling anxious, what is usually going through your mind?

MR. HAWK: There's too much to handle. I just can't do it. One hundred percent for each of those.

THERAPIST: Before this depression started, did you have this same reaction to piles of work on your desk?

MR. HAWK: No, but I was never this behind.

The therapist in this example has several choices of intervention. GTA is one option where the patient organizes and prioritizes tasks and develops a plan for completion including the possibility of deferring some projects to other staff members.

A second option is to change the physical cues that seem to precipitate the string of negative automatic thoughts that end with "I just can't do it." For example, he can remove the piles of paper from his desk that are constant reminders of how behind he is in his work. The visual cues alone seem to create a level of anxiety that interferes with his ability to get started. The paperwork not pertinent to the task of the day can be stored out of sight (e.g., in filing cabinets, on shelves, or on another work surface).

A third point of intervention is to evaluate the negative automatic thoughts that seem to accompany the patient's anxiety or hopelessness. Listening closely, it appears that Mr. Hawk is resigned to the permanence of his predicament. His resignation may likely keep him from developing or trying out new strategies for addressing his backlog of work. To examine the validity of these negative automatic thoughts, the therapist can help Mr. Hawk generate evidence for and against any of the statements generated. Three of the automatic thoughts (see Table 8.2) use words that imply absolutistic thinking—"always," "no way," "can't." This pattern can be pointed out and discussed.

Another method for examining the negative automatic thoughts is to have the patient imagine how he would feel about the backlog of work when he was not depressed. To begin this process, ask the patient to rate the intensity of belief in each automatic thought according to how he would feel when not depressed. Ask him to verbalize his alternative view. For example, if he were not depressed, the patient might believe "There is no way to get everything done" only 20%. The nondepressed view might be, "There is no way to get everything done at my current pace. I'm going to have to either put in more hours or get some help from others in the office." The next step would be to get the patient to think of methods for getting the work completed that he would have used if he were not so depressed. The advantages and disadvantages of each method can be

TABLE 8.2. Mr. Hawk's Automatic Thoughts about Work

Feeling (% intensity)	Thought (% belief)	Prediction
Anxiety (50%)	There's too much to handle. (100%)	I can't do it. (100%)
Fear (60%)	I'm going to be in so much trouble for not getting the job done. (80%)	I'll be fired. (40%)
Guilt (100%)	I'm lazy and worthless. (75%)	I'll never change. (80%)
Hopelessness (85%)	There is no way to get everything done. (100%)	I'll always be behind. (90%)

evaluated and methods that have the highest probability of success can be assigned as homework. Be sure to get the patient to rate his or her prediction at successfully completing the homework assignment and identify any potential obstacles to compliance with this task.

GUILT ASSOCIATED WITH INERTIA

As mentioned earlier, it is common for patients to feel considerable guilt for their decreased interest, motivation, and activity. Their personal explanations for their inertia may include character flaws, such as laziness, incompetence, or weakness. These self-denigrating thoughts worsen mood, which can, in turn, maintain the inertia. Using the cognitive intervention for generating alternative explanations for events (see Chapter 6), therapists can help patients generate alternative explanations for their inertia. If the patient is unaware that low energy and motivation are symptoms of depression, an explanation like the following can be provided:

"Each person has a certain number of energy units available each day. Generally, people have a sufficient amount of energy to accomplish the tasks required for a given day. There are times, however, when the amount of energy needed to complete activities exceeds the amount of energy that the person possesses that day. For example, a person who has 10 units of energy, but has 15 units of work to do, runs out of energy before the tasks are completed.

There are ways to acquire more energy, such as by refueling the energy system (e.g., by sleeping or eating) or by obtaining units of energy from someone else (e.g., by getting assistance from a family member). It is also possible to reduce the number of activities to match the level of energy available. When people are depressed, they have fewer units of energy available to them than they would normally possess. If they attempt to accomplish the same number of tasks that they did when they were well, they will run out of energy before they run out of work. The trick is to attempt the number of tasks equivalent to the amount of energy available."

Providing an explanation of this nature can help patients to understand inertia as a symptom of depression rather than as a sign of procrastination or laziness. This reframing of the problem often reduces guilt and anxiety associated with feeling overwhelmed by tasks.

Some patients intellectually understand that they are not capable of the same level of activity when depressed as when well (asymptomatic), yet they feel pressured to perform at the same level. For these patients, depression is an explanation, but not an excuse. If they misattribute the problem to a character flaw in themselves or to the behavior of others, it may be helpful to examine the evidence for and against their assumptions before generating alternative explanations. Helping patients to evaluate the validity of their own assumptions or explanations can be a more powerful intervention than attempting to convince them that the illness explanation is more valid. If patients do not themselves suggest that their inertia is a result of their depression, the clinician may find it useful to educate them about the symptoms of depression. For patients who readily accept or endorse this explanation, but discount it as an excuse for their own inertia, it is important to discuss and evaluate this line of reasoning objectively.

> Mrs. Freeman was usually very conscientious and responsible on the job, in school, and at home. When she sought treatment for depression, she was working part-time, taking three classes, doing volunteer work, and tending to her two children and husband. Her house was usually neat and clean; meals were ready when her husband arrived home from work. She still found time to take in stray animals, help her neighbors, and read for personal enjoyment. Although Mrs. Freeman may sound hypomanic, this pace was quite normal for her when she was not depressed.
>
> Once each year, Mrs. Freeman had an episode of depression; it began in the late winter and ended in the early summer. During that time, she suffered from insomnia, low energy, and decreased interest in most activities. Although she recognized her symptoms, she did not reduce her activities to accommodate her decreased drive. She was exhausted much of the time and felt very guilty for her reduced productivity. In the past, she had dropped one or more of her college courses because she was unable to maintain an A in the course. While she hated "giving up," she could not tolerate the thought of receiving a lower grade.
>
> At the time that she first sought treatment for depression, Mrs. Freeman was feeling very guilty for her poor performance at school and for not caring about her usual responsibilities at home. Although she had been through depression several times before and she actually understood how her symptoms interfered with her life, she could not excuse her underproductivity. When asked if she would expect herself to function normally if she were physically ill, for example, with the flu, she indicated that it would not be reasonable to expect as much if she were physically ill, but that depression was different. This led to a discussion of Mrs. Freeman's view of bipolar disorder, which included the unrealistic assumption that it should not interfere with her work.

THERAPIST: Help me to understand how it is possible to do the same amount of activity with only half as much of your usual energy?

After a lengthy discussion, Mrs. Freeman eventually accepted the notion that, when depressed, she was not physically capable of maintaining her normal level of activity and quality of performance. She was certain that her family members, especially her mother and husband, would not accept this as an excuse for her doing less, however.

In meeting with the family, it was clear that they did not understand her illness and its effect on her performance at home and at school. Although Mrs. Freeman herself had accepted the fact that she had this recurrent condition, her family did not understand the severity and chronicity of bipolar disorder. Knowing how capable and energetic Mrs. Freeman had always been, they believed that she could shake the depression if she truly wanted to and get on with her life as usual.

SO MUCH TO DO, SO LITTLE TIME

It is common for people to underestimate the amount of time needed to finish a job. Similarly, people often overestimate the amount of work that they can accomplish in a given day. When the day ends and there is still more to do, these people sometimes blame themselves for their "failure" to meet their productivity goals. The problem for these people may not be so much inefficiency, as it is their inability to set realistic goals. Not only must people take into account their available energy levels, but also their activity plan should allow a reasonable amount of time for each task.

Ms. Townsend sought treatment because she had many things to do and never seemed to have enough time to accomplish them. She viewed her failure to accomplish her work by the end of the day as inefficiency. When discussing the details of her daily activities, however, it became clear that she regularly scheduled 10 hours of work for a 7-hour workday. When it became apparent to her that she would be unable to accomplish her tasks in the 7 hours available, she would increase her pace. To "catch up," she missed lunch and worked late many days. Furthermore, she completed some tasks with less care than she liked. When queried about this situation, she replied, "I should be able to get these things done with time to spare." She added that she had no formal method for estimating the time required, but merely had a subjective sense of what she was capable of handling. Unfortunately, this sense may be particularly misguided in bipolar disorder patients, who may use the times of extraordinary productivity during hypomanic episodes as a reference. Although she faced some real external deadlines for her work, this patient often set personal deadlines far ahead of the real deadlines. She was able to meet her self-imposed goals on many days, but it was necessary for her to use all of her units of energy, including the several units of reserve energy that she saved for her personal interests. At the end of her workday, she had no mental or physical energy for non-work-related interests.

People with this working style are a dream come true for employers. Therefore, the workplace can reinforce or even foster the pattern of setting unrealistic personal goals and developing guilt associated with "decreased efficiency." These people are compulsive, driven, responsible, and self-motivated. They go the extra mile, care about the quality of their work, and are eager to please others. Often patients with bipolar disorder have jobs that capitalize on their high energy levels and drive (when not depressed), and they may accomplish a great deal in a short time period.

In the case of Ms. Townsend, a subjective standard of performance arbitrarily determined the number of goals set for each day. When she was consistently unable to perform at that level or could meet her goals only at great cost, she questioned her competency, not her standards. For this patient, GTA is the wrong intervention. Instead, the focus should be on an evaluation of her personal standards and goals, as well as a realistic assessment of the time that it takes to accomplish tasks at a level of quality acceptable to her. Once this evaluation is complete, daily activities can be more realistically planned.

As therapy progresses, it may be discovered that an underlying schema, or system of working assumptions, about needing to be perfect or being incompetent may be driving the patient's standards and/or behavior.

ALL WORK AND NO PLAY

Mr. Ricketts dreaded having to start the day. All the tasks that he did not finish yesterday, the day before, or the week before lay ahead. It seemed that he was living his whole life for work—work at home and work on the job. When he was not working, he worried about his personal and family problems. He found himself awake at night, thinking about all the bad things in his life and the ways that he had let his family down. Day after day, the pattern repeated itself. Month after month, negative events consumed his life. He could recall times when he used to smile and laugh with his wife and children. He could remember long walks through the woods, Sunday dinners, and ice cream cones with the kids. He believed that those days were gone, never to return.

Mr. Ricketts's story is not an unusual one. Many patients suffering from depression complain of a life consumed with work and problems. They see no way out of the daily grind. When they are not depressed, they still have problems, but they balance these problems with positive events. When they are depressed, they no longer engage in pleasurable activities because they lack the energy to plan and initiate them, as well as the ability to enjoy them.

When problems and demands dominate patients' lives, it can be helpful to restore balance by "prescribing" fun. The goal of the intervention is to improve dysphoria by prescribing tasks that are pleasurable to the patients, may lift their spirits, or change their view of life as all work and no fun. If successful, the patients may experience some relief from the depression and feel more competent to cope with existing stressors.

It is best to start this intervention with pleasurable activities that take little effort to arrange and execute. Patients can begin by making a list of things that they would enjoy doing. If they are unable to generate a list, the clinician can ask them what activities they enjoyed before the depression began. A pleasurable activities list (PAL) may include such activities as the following:

- Going to a movie
- Reading the comics on Sunday morning
- Watching a television show
- Reading a good book
- Taking the kids out for ice cream

Patients can choose one or two activities from the list to try before the next session. The activities chosen should have a high probability of success; that is, they should be activities for which patients are likely to have sufficient time, energy, and resources.

Initiating pleasurable activities may be stressful for some patients. If they are uncomfortable in social situations, for example, they may associate "fun" with potential scrutiny by others. If they suffer from panic attacks and/or agoraphobia, leaving the house to have fun can place them in anxiety-arousing situations. If they are critical of themselves for their shortcomings or their inability to cope when depressed, any failure of their plans for fun may give them further confirmation of their ineptitude or worthlessness. For these reasons, caution is necessary in assigning fun activities. Patients should not attempt pleasurable activities that place them at risk for experiencing rejection, anxiety, or a sense of failure.

There are two common problems with prescribing fun activities for depressed individuals. One is that they may not be able to derive pleasure from the experience. The second problem is that even if they can derive pleasure, their negative thinking may cause them to overlook any positive aspects and focus instead on the negative (e.g., my hair looked bad, the sound in the theatre was poor, we sat next to a loud party in the restaurant).

In the first scenario, patients sometimes say that they knew intellectually that they were engaging in a positive activity, but they did not feel a sense of pleasure. The therapist should be patient, but persistent, in the assignment of fun while they work on other aspects of the depression. Use the compliance model discussed in Chapter 5 to identify the obstacles to enjoyment of positive activities.

In the second scenario where the positive experience is viewed through a mental filter that only allows the negative aspects into awareness, it is essential that efforts be made to reduce the filter and evaluate events more objectively. Once an activity has been selected, ask patients to predict how they believe the event will go; this provides an opportunity to discuss ahead of time any concerns and to alter the plan accordingly. Some patients will find it difficult to imagine themselves having fun. They may be skeptical that small pleasures can have any effect on their depression. The homework can be conceptualized as an experiment that tests patients' predictions about pleasurable events and more objectively tests the effect of fun on mood, energy level, and overall view of life. If effective, improvements in at least one of these three areas should be noticeable. If no changes are noted, an exploration of the aspects of the experience that seemed to sustain, or possibly worsen, the person's mood and outlook on life may help to better understand his or her depression, can reveal underlying schemas that mediate responses to positive events, and can help in future activity planning. For example, a depressed patient who is attempting to repay debt accrued during a manic episode spending spree was assigned pleasurable tasks. He did not receive enjoyment from these activities. Exploration of the circumstances revealed tremendous guilt and a belief that he did not deserve to experience pleasure until his debt was paid. Taking time to play meant time away from work that could help pay his debt.

The Activity Rating Scale shown in Table 8.3 aids the evaluation of pleasurable activities. Just before attempting an activity, ratings are made for mood, energy level, and view of life on a 1–7 scale. A score of 1 means extremely low or negative and 7 means extremely high or positive. After completing the activity these are rerated using the same scale. At the next therapy session this information can be used to evaluate the accuracy of patients' predictions about their ability to experience pleasure. If ratings are made immediately preceding and following the event, it increases the chance that the event will be viewed without the interference of a negative filter. This will help patients to better evaluate their experiences between sessions and their mood without having to rely on the distortions of memory. If negative predictions were correct, the clinician and the patient can carefully review the event to determine what interfered with the plan's success, develop a new plan that takes into account the experiences on the first attempt, and discuss new predictions for the upcoming events, as well as any fears or concerns that the patient may have. If the prediction for the new assignment is a negative one, it is helpful to use the evidence for/evidence against procedure to help patients examine their prediction (see Chapter 6). If there is convincing evidence that the event will turn out badly, the plan should be altered. If

TABLE 8.3. Activity Rating Scale

Rate *mood, energy,* and *view of life* on a 1 to 7 scale with 1 being extremely low or negative and 7 being extremely high or positive.

		Mood	Energy	View
Activity _____				
Date: _____				
	Before	_____	_____	_____
	After	_____	_____	_____
Activity _____				
Date: _____				
	Before	_____	_____	_____
	After	_____	_____	_____
Activity _____				
Date: _____				
	Before	_____	_____	_____
	After	_____	_____	_____
Activity _____				
Date: _____				
	Before	_____	_____	_____
	After	_____	_____	_____

the prediction is based on emotional reasoning and has little or no objective basis, the event can be reframed as an experiment to test the prediction.

INDECISIVENESS

It took a while for me to write this section because I could not decide how to approach the topic. There are different kinds of indecisiveness. One type is when an individual is overwhelmed with too many choices. It is difficult to mentally organize all the stimuli, identify a desire or preference, and search through the choices until a match is found. A second type of indecisiveness is an inability to generate ideas altogether, a mental block of sorts (that's the type I had). A third type of indecisiveness is rumination over the advantages and consequences of each choice in a nonproductive way, that is, that the exercise does not lead to a conclusion. A fourth type is indecisiveness that stems from fear of making the wrong choice.

Too Many Choices

Mrs. Blumenthal stands in front of her closet staring at the clothes. She cannot decide what to wear. Mr. Pacheco opens the refrigerator, looks at its full contents, but does not know what to eat. This type of indecisiveness is quite common among depressed individuals. There are several different approaches to this problem. One easy, but often unacceptable, solution is to ask someone else to make the choice. Another solution that helps people mentally organize the options is to use a decision tree. The decision tree can be developed in session or can be given as homework. Figure 8.3 shows an example of a food decision tree. The goal is to eliminate some of the many food options by identifying general classes of preferences. "What should I wear today? Is the weather warm or cold? Do I want to wear work clothes, casual/play clothes, or dress more formally? What are my choices within each category?" It is best to walk away from the choices (the overstimulation), think about general preference, and then return to the task.

Another solution to this type of indecisiveness is to have a prearranged choice that is set aside for times of indecision. "When I don't know what to wear, I always wear the blue outfit." The time to make these kinds of plans is when the individual is not under pressure (e.g., not in a hurry). A menu for the week can be planned on Sunday afternoons. Wardrobe choices can also be made in advance to avoid last minute decisions.

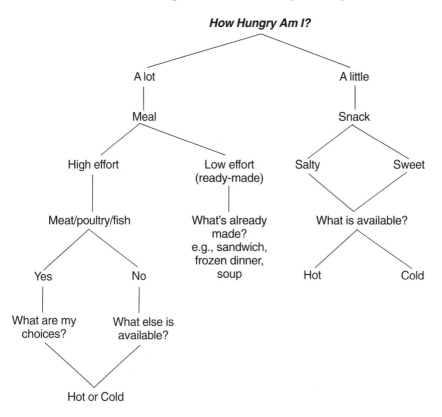

FIGURE 8.3. Decision tree.

Mental Block

"I don't know where to start." "My mind is blank." These are common complaints about work or other activities. The anxiety aroused by this type of indecisiveness further stymies creativity. The generation of new ideas requires a relaxed mind and freedom from distractions. The first two steps are, therefore, to relax and reduce distractions in the environment. It can also help to ask questions that organize one's thinking. For example, "What is the purpose of this task, letter, report, homework assignment, project, etc.?" "What do I hope to accomplish?" Depending on the task, it is sometimes possible to skip the beginning and jump into the middle. After being able to make some progress, it can be easier to return to the beginning of the task. For example, if the task is to write a letter, and the individual does not know where to start, they can begin with a conclusion or a piece that goes somewhere in the body, but is not part of the introductory paragraph. The rest of the letter can be built around this section.

Nonproductive Rumination

Mr. Castillo has had bipolar disorder for 15 years. He has had increasing difficulty in sustaining employment. He lives alone, is twice divorced, and is receiving some financial support from the county welfare program. He wants to work, but the rapid cycling nature of his illness makes it almost impossible. He can apply for benefits from Social Security for disability due to a psychiatric condition or he can persist in trying to obtain and then maintain full-time employment. "It would be nice to know a check is coming every month whether I'm feeling OK or not. But I can work, especially in the summer and sometimes in the spring. I don't want people to think I'm a freeloader. I hate these guys that use the system. A lot of them in my neighborhood get food stamps and then just sit around all day. I'm not like that. I'm a working man. Have been since I was 15. I'm so tired of being broke. I have to borrow from my mother. She's old and what little money she still gets from my father's retirement, she needs. I hate asking for money. I could fill out the forms for Social Security and look for a job and see which one comes first. But what if I get both? If I can get a job, I don't need social security. If I get a job, I may not be able to keep it."

Mr. Castillo has been repeating this conversation with himself for more than a month. He cannot reach a decision, so he makes no decision and continues to ruminate. He has many thoughts swimming through his head, but he gets nowhere in his analysis of the problem. With some help from his therapist, he examines the advantages and disadvantages of seeking employment as well as the advantages and disadvantages of applying for Social Security benefits (see Table 8.4). In this scenario, there are advantages and disadvantages of each choice. The advantages are equally compelling. The disadvantages of each choice are difficult to compare because they are qualitatively different for each choice. The disadvantages for work are the financial consequences of predictable times of unemployment. The disadvantages of Social Security surround the effect on self-esteem and the perceptions of others as well as a concern about being able to work periodically. Comparing money and self-esteem is a bit like comparing apples and oranges. This is what has made it difficult for Mr. Castillo to make a decision. Is there a way to maximize the advantages and minimize the disadvantages of either option?

TABLE 8.4. Evaluation of Job Choices

	Advantages	Disadvantages
Work	Feels good to work. Income is higher than Social Security benefits.	Have trouble keeping jobs when sick. Always "broke." I have to borrow from my mother. I hate to ask for money.
Social Security	Stable income.	Do not need it in the spring and summer. People will think I'm a freeloader. Makes me look bad. I will lose it if I work too much.

What If I'm Wrong?

Fear of the consequences of making a poor choice can keep patients from making decisions. These fears can be addressed with the logical analysis techniques covered in Chapter 6. For example, what is the evidence that a given consequence will occur if a given choice is made, what is the evidence against it? What are the consequences of making no choice?

The advantages/disadvantages technique can be used to evaluate the options available. This takes the focus off the consequences of making a bad choice and on selection of the option that is most likely to be useful and/or successful.

HOMEWORK NONCOMPLIANCE

The behavioral interventions described in this chapter require initiative by the patient between sessions. No matter how well the homework assignment is designed, and how supportive the therapist, execution of the assignment ultimately depends on the patient's willingness to give it a try. Patients can be ambivalent about reinitiating activities they have avoided for some time. Therefore, it may be necessary to reassign the same homework more than once.

If a patient returns to the next session to report that he or she did not complete the homework assignment, take time to determine what factors interfered. This information can be used to modify the assignment in a way that avoids these pitfalls. Caution should be taken, however, in how the therapist approaches the discussion of homework compliance.

Specifically, some patients will feel guilty for not completing an assigned task. They may be concerned about disappointing the therapist with their noncompliance. If the therapist communicates criticism or disappointment either verbally or nonverbally, patients may feel worse and the therapeutic relationship may suffer. Patients must feel like they are doing homework to help themselves, rather than to please the therapist. A therapist can do several things to reinforce this notion. First, when homework is assigned early in therapy, emphasize that therapy sessions only last 1 hour each week. To be helpful, the majority of the work of therapy has to be done between sessions. The pace of therapy is, to a great degree, dependent upon the amount of work patients do between sessions. Second, although guided by the therapist, homework tasks should be designed by the patient. This collaboration helps patients to "own" the homework task. Third, the therapist can ask patients to predict how they would feel talking to the therapist about being unable to complete the homework. Explore the patient's reasoning and provide corrective feedback about your own reaction.

Fourth, in designing a homework assignment, consider whether the patient has the resources to carry out the task. For example, before giving a lengthy reading assignment consider not only whether the patient has money to purchase a book, or has transportation to the library, but also whether he or she can concentrate well enough to read. Do not set a patient up for failure by not taking time to consider the feasibility of homework tasks.

Fifth, always take time to review homework at each session, preferably at the beginning of each session. This communicates that the assignment was important and worth discussion. Sixth, if the homework assignment was not completed, reevaluate its importance, usefulness, and feasibility before it is reassigned. Maybe after more thought the patient decided it was a bad idea or maybe he or she thought of another way to approach the task. If the therapist believes that it is better not to reassign the homework, cancel the task rather than leave it uncompleted. If not withdrawn from the patient's list of things "to do," homework can become as burdensome as other uncompleted chores.

CHAPTER SUMMARY

Lethargy, decreased interest in life, low motivation, fatigue, and indecisiveness are symptoms of depression that alter usual behavior patterns and activity levels of depressed patients. These changes can and often do include social withdrawal, impaired work performance, and neglect of household or family responsibilities. These changes can have both emotional and practical consequences. The guilt, hopelessness, and frustration associated with these declines in performance can exacerbate the depression and thus reinforce this cycle.

The lethargy cycle can be addressed through behavioral interventions that increase goal-oriented and pleasurable activities. GTA reduces overwhelming tasks to smaller and more easily managed subtasks that can be assigned as homework a few at a time. The A list/B list technique helps patients prioritize daily tasks. The affect of increased activity on self-esteem, motivation, and view of the future are monitored to determine its influence on reversing the lethargy cycle.

The inactivity associated with depression may be improved by addressing its cognitive aspects, for example, guilt, indecisiveness, unrealistic standards of performance, and self-depreciation. The lethargy and disinterest of depression often keep people from pleasurable activities. An imbalance of multiple problems and little joy validates the view of life as unpleasant, burdensome, and never changing. Systematic introduction of pleasurable activities can help restore balance through improved mood, increased motivation, and improved outlook on life.

The behavioral interventions for increasing activity require effort by patients between therapy sessions. This means initiation of activity that has been previously avoided. It is likely that most patients will have trouble with these exercises the first time they are assigned. This may be discouraging for both patients and therapists. Take care when discussing failed homework assignments so as not to communicate criticism or disapproval of the patient. If homework becomes yet another burdensome task to add to a long list of chores, it will be of little benefit to the patient and can weaken the therapeutic alliance.

NINE

Behavioral Changes and Problems in Mania

SESSION 13. BEHAVIORAL CHANGES IN MANIA

Purpose of the Session

The purpose of this session on behavioral changes in mania is to train patients to use fluctuations in their activity level as cues of the onset of hypomania or mania and to teach a method for limiting or containing the increased, but disorganized, activity.

Goals of the Session

1. Train patients to monitor their activity level.
2. Teach patients to set goals as a technique for setting limits on their activity before reaching problematic levels.
3. Discuss how to make use of feedback from others.

Procedure

1. Assess treatment compliance.
2. Review the homework from last session.
3. Provide a rationale for monitoring variations in activity level as a cue to the onset of mania or hypomania. Using patients' mood graphing homework from the last session, have them graph their activity level for the past week using the same scaling as specified for mood.
4. Provide a rationale for using goal setting as a means of setting limits on activity level when it begins to increase outside normal limits. Complete the Goal Setting Worksheet.
5. Discuss past experiences where others may have provided feedback to patients on their behavior changes. Was the information welcomed or rejected? Discuss how patients might be able to benefit from the feedback of others.

(cont.)

(continued from page 184)

6. Compare and contrast the patient's experiences of mastery and pleasure in normal, depressed, and manic states. Use the two cognitive restructuring exercises introduced in Chapter 6 if positive biased thoughts are present.
7. Assign homework.

Homework
Have patients monitor their activity level and mood over the next week using a Mood Graph.

The hallmark of mania is the striking behavioral change that takes place during a manic episode.

Mrs. Harper was a soft-spoken, somewhat shy woman of 50. She had been a housewife all her adult life. She had raised three children, attended church on Sundays, kept to herself in the neighborhood, and watched television for recreation. Her husband described the transformation that occurred when Mrs. Harper was in a manic episode: "I found her up in the kids' tree house, half-naked and yelling at the top of her lungs. I coaxed her down, but it took some time and the neighbors watched the whole thing." He also told of another episode: "One day I saw our car parked out in front of a local bar. I went in half expecting to see her hanging from the ceiling. There she was—drinking beer, hanging on to this drunk, and singing to the jukebox. The neighbors don't understand. I guess they think she's a lush. I hate talking badly about her, but I just don't know what to do with her when she's like that."

Many patients and their families tell similar stories. The changes in mood, speech, energy, actions, judgment, confidence, and activity are both fascinating and frightening. As one patient put it:

"I feel like a Cadillac, man. I'm smooth and fast and classy. I can do anything. I can run through this wall, man, and never feel a thing. I'm moving so fast right now that I can think a thousand thoughts at once. I can be a thousand places if I want to. I mean it, man. I'm like a Cadillac. Zoom!"

The fact that the behavioral changes of mania are often dramatic and easy to identify makes them excellent signals of the onset of mania.

Early recognition of a manic episode is essential because CBT is of little use once a patient is in a full-blown episode.

INCREASED INTERESTS, IDEAS, AND ACTIVITY

Perhaps one of the most enjoyable aspects of mania is the grandiosity. When manic, some patients with bipolar disorder believe that they can do anything:

> "I don't mean to sound conceited, but I am the smartest person in the world. I didn't get past the tenth grade, but I have had training on the job in science and engineering. I know enough to get a PhD right now. Honest, I have so many ideas that I can hardly tell you about them."

The proliferation of new ideas and projects, coupled with the overconfidence inspired by mania, creates a cycle of activity that can itself perpetuate and escalate the mania. Not all patients with bipolar disorder experience this symptom of mania. It is necessary to review each patient's history to determine if past episodes of mania included increased ideas or activity.

Because it usually begins slowly and builds over the course of the episode, the increased activity associated with mania can serve as a marker of the onset of mania. The patient's Mood Graph can be used to track the progression of increased ideas into increased activity and overstimulation. The first step is to help the patient draw a connection between changes in interest or activity level and changes in mood. As an example, the clinician may ask the patient to note on the previous week's Mood Graph his or her activity level for the past few days, using the same scale (e.g., −1 to +1 for the normal range). The clinician and the patient can then review the graph together to determine if there is an association between mood and interest or activity changes.

Figure 9.1 shows an example of such a Mood Graph.

> This patient began the week with more activity than usual and an elevation in mood. She had begun an exciting new project early in the week and she felt somewhat elated. She had been relatively inactive for several weeks and welcomed the opportunity to do something new. After a few days of feeling "a little too good," she began to watch herself more carefully. By 10/9 she had made the decision to decrease her activity. She had found herself taking control of the new project, assuming more responsibility than necessary. This was a familiar pattern for her and one that often left her feeling out of control.

Name of patient: _____   For week of: ___*10/6–10/12*_____

Completed by: ___*Patient*_____   Relationship to patient: _____

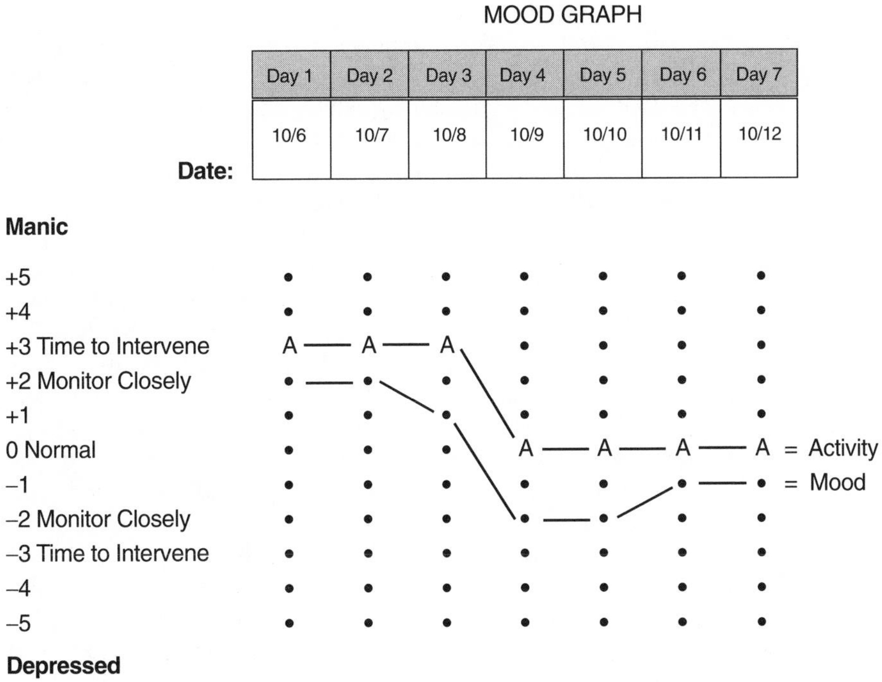

MOOD GRAPH

	Day 1	Day 2	Day 3	Day 4	Day 5	Day 6	Day 7
Date:	10/6	10/7	10/8	10/9	10/10	10/11	10/12

Manic

```
+5                    •     •     •     •     •     •     •
+4                    •     •     •     •     •     •     •
+3 Time to Intervene  A —— A —— A     •     •     •     •
+2 Monitor Closely    • ——— • ╲   •     •     •     •     •
+1                    •     •   ╲ •     •     •     •     •
0 Normal              •     •     ╲  A —— A —— A —— A  = Activity
−1                    •     •     • ╲   •     • —— •   = Mood
−2 Monitor Closely    •     •     •  ╲• —— • ╱ •     •
−3 Time to Intervene  •     •     •     •     •     •     •
−4                    •     •     •     •     •     •     •
−5                    •     •     •     •     •     •     •
```

Depressed

FIGURE 9.1. Completed Mood Graph.

For a few days after pulling back from the project, her mood dropped into mild dysphoria. She hated the fact that she could not handle the work without "getting sick"and she missed her friends on the job. After a few days of what she called "feeling sorry for herself," her mood began to improve.

The time to begin tracking interest and activity levels on the Mood Graph is when hypomania is suspected. Patients who know the time of year that they are most likely to experience mania can begin mood and activity graphing at least a month before this vulnerable time. This approach makes it possible to identify the changes in mood (affect), activity level (behavior), and interest (cognition) that are the precursors to mania. If these changes can be identified before they reach manic proportions, the increased stimulation can be contained to some degree and pharmacological interventions can be strengthened.

The objective of the intervention at this point is to help patients who are becoming manic choose a limited number of activities from their plethora of ideas and pursue those that have the highest probability of success and the lowest probability of negative consequences. The process is similar to that used to break the lethargy cycle (see Chapter 8). The difference is that, while the goal during a depressive episode is to increase activity, the goal during a manic episode is to limit activity.

To teach patients how to organize and set limits on their interests and activities, the clinician begins with an examination of their current activities. Using the first column of the Goal Setting Worksheet shown in Figure 9.2, the patient lists current activities, responsibilities, and interests, as well as future plans, in any order. The list should include daily home and work responsibilities, school requirements, regularly scheduled activities outside the home (e.g., church activities, bowling club), obligations to extended family members or friends, social activities, personal interests that are currently being pursued or planned (e.g., diets, reading), and new interests or ideas. In the second column, the patient lists the anticipated date of the activity or deadline, as applicable. If an activity is ongoing, the patient should note this fact in the date column also.

The next step is to organize the activities so that the patient focuses his or her efforts on the tasks with the highest priority. To accomplish this, the patient must attach a priority ranking to each of the activities. Therefore, in the third column of the Goal Setting Worksheet, the patient rates each activity as a high priority (H), moderate priority (M), or low priority (L). The therapist can ask questions or make observations that may facilitate this process, but the priority ratings must come from the patient. Once this task is complete, the patient assigns numerical rankings to assign priorities within each group of activities.

Finally, the patient selects a reasonable number of tasks to attempt in the following week. The grandiosity that accompanies hypomania may leave patients feeling that they can accomplish all the tasks on their list and, in fact, their extra energy and their decreased need for sleep may make it possible for them to do so. To make activity scheduling more effective, it is essential to include sleep on the plan for the week. With the help of the therapist, the patient sketches a rough outline of the time that activities will occur and the time that they will stop so that the patient can prepare for sleep. The clinician must make it clear, however, that the overstimulation caused by the increased activity can actually worsen symptoms. Patients may lose their concentration, become more and more disorganized, and be unable to complete tasks successfully. Setting limits on activity can help to contain the progression of mania.

Patients with bipolar disorder commonly report that, when manic,

Current activities, responsibilities, and interests	Date of deadline	Priority			Rank order
		High	*Medium*	*Low*	
_____	_____	H	M	L	_____
_____	_____	H	M	L	_____
_____	_____	H	M	L	_____
_____	_____	H	M	L	_____
_____	_____	H	M	L	_____
_____	_____	H	M	L	_____
_____	_____	H	M	L	_____
_____	_____	H	M	L	_____
_____	_____	H	M	L	_____
_____	_____	H	M	L	_____
_____	_____	H	M	L	_____
_____	_____	H	M	L	_____
_____	_____	H	M	L	_____
_____	_____	H	M	L	_____
_____	_____	H	M	L	_____
_____	_____	H	M	L	_____
_____	_____	H	M	L	_____
_____	_____	H	M	L	_____
_____	_____	H	M	L	_____
_____	_____	H	M	L	_____
_____	_____	H	M	L	_____
_____	_____	H	M	L	_____
_____	_____	H	M	L	_____
_____	_____	H	M	L	_____
_____	_____	H	M	L	_____
_____	_____	H	M	L	_____

FIGURE 9.2. Goal Setting Worksheet.

they start several projects, but rarely complete them. They become increasingly excited with each new idea and are anxious to begin the next project right away. With activity planning and prioritizing, the patient must agree to complete each given task before attempting the next.

As new ideas are formulated, they can be added to the Goal Setting Worksheet and prioritized accordingly. The purpose of this process is to create a cushion of time that allows patients to think through their new ideas and plans before they act. If the process does not slow activity, more aggressive pharmacological interventions are probably necessary.

SLEEP DISRUPTION

Clinical data have shown that sleep deprivation can induce mania or depression in people with bipolar disorder. Wehr and his colleagues (1987) proposed a model of the induction of mania caused by sleep deprivation or insomnia. They suggest that loss of sleep caused by external stimuli, such as noise or sick children, or internal stimuli, such as worry, racing thoughts, or physical illness, can cause shifts from depression or euthymia to mania. Their model is based on both clinical observations and empirical studies (Wehr & Wirz-Justice, 1982) of the effects of total sleep deprivation on patients with rapid cycling bipolar disorder in depressive episodes. They found that after one night of sleep deprivation most switched to mania or hypomania. When sleep was normalized, some patients experienced a return of depressive symptoms, for others the manic symptoms persisted.

Some patients with bipolar disorder find sleep disruption to be very distressing. They feel exhausted, but cannot slow down their thoughts or physical energy and drive enough to fall asleep; they may go days with little or no sleep. Their symptoms evolve into mania, often accompanied by psychosis. In contrast, other patients enjoy the unending flow of energy. Needing less sleep, they have more time for fun, adventure, and creative projects. Unfortunately, this euphoria soon turns sour. Irritability and paranoia can replace euphoria. Behavior becomes increasingly disorganized and thinking can be confused. No matter how a particular patient reacts, normalizing sleep as soon as possible after a disruption can help to reduce the risk of mania.

Nonpharmacological Methods
to Cope with Sleep Disruption

The best strategy for coping with sleep disruption is prevention. The key is to predict when normal sleep patterns are likely to be interrupted and to prepare an intervention to counter the change in the length of time that the patient is sleeping or at least to limit the number of nights that disruption occurs. Sometimes sleep disruption can be anticipated. People intentionally stay up later or wake up earlier than usual when they need more time to attend to important tasks.

> For example, Mrs. Costanza was up late several nights in a row to finish cleaning the house and preparing special foods for holiday guests. Ms. Dubois had a big report due in her history class and crammed over the weekend until she finished it. When Mr. Evans was writing the annual report for the next stockholders' meeting, he burned the midnight oil to double-check his figures. Getting less sleep than usual was risky for each of them, because all had bipolar disorder and knew that sleep loss could induce mania.

Some changes in sleep patterns are predictable, but outside the control of the individual. For example, travel across time zones may occur during normal sleep hours, thereby disrupting sleep, or it may reset the traveler's sleep–wake cycle. This is especially problematic when the traveler "loses" hours through time zone changes, but can also be troublesome when the traveler "gains" hours. Some people complain that they are unable to sleep well away from their own beds, which is a particular problem for bipolar disorder patients who work, vacation, or otherwise travel away from home. Other predictable, but uncontrollable, circumstances that may disrupt sleep include new babies that wake and need tending during the night; less predictable, but equally uncontrollable and disruptive, are noisy thunderstorms, physical illness, or bad dreams.

Good Sleep Habits Facilitate Normal Sleep and Reduce Disruptions

Sleep researchers recommend going to bed and waking up at the same times each day (Kryger, Roth, & Dement, 1989). Changes in schedule, such as late nights out or napping during the day, interrupt the sleep–wake cycle. Sleep electrophysiology can be disrupted without the patient's being aware of insomnia or restlessness. People without bipolar disorder can feel sluggish, easily fatigued, and mentally dull when their sleep routine is altered. In people with bipolar disorder, more dramatic symptoms can emerge. If not contained, sleep abnormalities can persist and worsen until they induce mania or depression.

To Nap or Not to Nap, That Is the Question

When tired, is it best to "make up" the lost sleep with an afternoon nap? This is not an unreasonable strategy as long as the nap does not perpetuate the nighttime insomnia. People respond differently to adding naps or sleeping late to compensate for sleep interruptions. Patients know their own bodies and usually know when it is best to compensate for or "tough out" sleep loss.

> Mr. Gilbert took a little nap to make up for the previous night when he could not sleep. He felt better, but then had difficulty falling asleep the next night because his nap had been too long. Finally, he fell asleep 2 hours after his usual bedtime. He slept late the next morning to make up for the loss of sleep, since it was a weekend and he did not have to go to work. Again, he found himself full of energy at the end of the day and stayed up late. The cycle persisted; as a result, he began to feel irritable and tired, and his thoughts began to race.

Minimizing Sleep Disruptions

Prevention or minimization of sleep disruption is important and advance planning can be useful in achieving this goal. Travel schedules can be arranged, for example, so that the person reaches his or her destination in time to get a full night of sleep. If he or she must change time zones so that bedtime is earlier than usual, a sleeping medication may be prescribed. If bedtime is later than usual, the individual should try to avoid overstimulation in the interim.

It may be more difficult to address sleep disruption caused by environmental changes, such as sleeping in a different bed or room, noises, or light. Keeping the environment as constant and comfortable as possible can facilitate sleep. Using a favorite pillow and linens, as well as wearing comfortable and familiar bedclothes, can be helpful. Ear plugs, eye shields, or white noise machines can reduce external distractions.

If possible, patients with bipolar disorder should share nighttime responsibilities, such as caring for newborn babies, ill family members, or animals, with other members of the household. Some sleep disruption may be inevitable, but it is important to reduce the number of sequential nights in which sleep is disrupted. Patients can negotiate an exchange in services for the period during which they are most vulnerable to the symptom-inducing effects of sleep disruption. For example, one family member may take care of a new puppy at night so that a patient can sleep without interruptions, while the patient takes over some of the family member's yard work in exchange.

Illness or injury can also disrupt sleep. Physical discomfort or breathing difficulties, for example, can keep a person awake. Medications for symptom relief may be necessary, but a physician or pharmacist should carefully consider the interaction between cold, flu, or pain medications and psychotropic medications.

Avoiding Overstimulation

Exercise is a healthy activity that has both physical and emotional benefits. However, some people find it difficult to fall asleep after exercise in the evening. They become physiologically overstimulated and cannot slow down sufficiently to sleep. For others, an evening walk after dinner is very relaxing and actually facilitates sleep. Each patient must experiment with the effects of exercise on his or her sleep habits and make adjustments to maximize the positive effects of exercise without the negative effect of sleep disruption. When patients find the exercise times that fit best with their daily routines, they should schedule these exercise periods regularly in order to normalize their physiological routine.

Caffeine is a common stimulant that can disrupt sleep, especially if consumed just prior to bedtime. Although usually associated with coffee, caffeine can be found in soft drinks, tea, and chocolate. For some, eating chocolate cake for dessert after dinner can disrupt sleep as much as drinking a cup of coffee. Some medications also contain caffeine. It is wise for patients to read labels and inquire about stimulants in both prescribed and over-the-counter medications. Limiting or avoiding caffeine altogether is recommended.

Drinking coffee is a socially sanctioned work and leisure activity. For those who are unemployed, as well as those who work throughout the day, coffee drinking can organize part of the daily routine (e.g., coffee first thing in the morning, coffee breaks, coffee after meals). It is not unusual for people with bipolar disorder to drink ten or more cups of coffee and/or caffeinated soft drinks each day. Eliminating caffeine can disrupt the usual social interactions or work routines. Rather than eliminating coffee breaks, for example, recommend that patients switch to decaffeinated products.

> Mr. and Mrs. Lum were busy with their careers, their family, and their home. They had two children in elementary school, and it seemed that the only time they could talk to each other without interruption was in bed. At this time, they ran through the activities of the day, planned for the weekend, talked about bills that needed to be paid, and even touched on current events in the news. Sometimes these discussions evolved into arguments. Many years ago, they had promised "never to go to bed

angry," so disagreements persisted until they were resolved or until one or both were too sleepy to continue.

These bedtime discussions occasionally left the couple with unresolved problems. Mrs. Lum could let go of issues, both intellectually and emotionally, and fall asleep. Mr. Lum could not. He thought about the problems, what had been said, what he "should have said," and continued to feel tense. He both admired and resented his wife's ability to sleep soundly after an emotional discussion. Although he tried to do the same, he often had to give up, go to another room, and watch television until he finally did fall asleep.

Mr. Lum had bipolar disorder that was fairly well controlled with medication. However, when he did not sleep well for a few days, especially during the spring, symptoms of mania would begin to emerge. The insomnia seemed to take on a life of its own. He began to feel "hyper," like everything inside him was moving faster. This was the beginning of hypomania.

Although it was convenient for Mr. and Mrs. Lum to use the quiet of bedtime for their discussions, it was also dangerous. Neither of them had drawn a connection between their talks/arguments and the exacerbations of Mr. Lum's symptoms. Once his therapist pointed out this pattern, Mr. and Mrs. Lum made appropriate changes. They set aside time before or after dinner to talk. If an issue was important, they made time to discuss it; if the issue was not urgent and time did not permit a full discussion, they tabled it until the next day or the weekend. The resulting disentanglement of bedtime and discussion made for fewer sleepless nights for Mr. Lum and, consequently, fewer symptom breakthroughs.

Relaxation Exercises

Relaxation exercises can be used by patients to decrease mental stimulation and muscle tension at bedtime. For some individuals these exercises reduce physiological and mental arousal and, in turn, facilitate sleep. There are many different relaxation techniques. No one method works for all people. To help patients identify the most helpful relaxation exercise, provide a sampling of inductions during therapy sessions and allow them to select one or more methods to learn. For patients who have difficulty in "turning off" stressful thoughts, relaxation techniques that help to focus attention on the relaxation task and away from distracting thoughts are often most beneficial. For those patients with muscle tension, especially tension that produces muscle aches (back, shoulders, neck) or headaches, inductions that focus directly on release of tensed muscles may be best. Imagery exercises are useful for people who have the ability to create and sustain mental images.

Relaxation inductions can be done during exercise, while driving a car, or while sitting at a desk. To induce sleep, relaxation exercises can begin long before bedtime as the individual slows his or her mental and physical activity at the end of the day. In fact, the best relaxation inductions are those used throughout the day to reduce tension or overstimulation as it begins to build.

The health club where Ms. Beach worked was noisy and full of activity. She taught aerobics there from 6:00 to 7:00 in the evening three times a week. The exercise was fun and good for both her mental and physical health. She met new people, saw her friends, and usually had a great time. Most evenings, she left work by 8:00. When bedtime came at 11:00, however, there were times when she could not slow down and fall asleep. She felt that she could exercise for another hour or two, but she knew the consequences of overstimulation.

Relaxation techniques helped Ms. Beach slow down. She began the relaxation intervention at work by sitting in the whirlpool after her class. This was usually sufficient to relax her. If she continued to feel energized or agitated on the drive home, she listened to soft music on the car radio. At home, she avoided television and played her favorite music while she prepared for bed. When she was a child, warm milk had soothed her before bedtime, so she often had a cup when she monitored her level of excitability on her Mood Graph.

Despite using all these techniques, Ms. Beach still felt too keyed up to sleep on some evenings. For these occasions, she learned a few muscle relaxation exercises from a friend. She bought an audiotape that helped her relax each muscle in her body. Listening to the tape and following the directions not only focused her attention, but also limited her distracting and self-stimulating thoughts.

When prescribing a relaxation program, a clinician generally begins with those techniques that the patient has found helpful in the past such as an evening walk or a warm bath. Some people with bipolar disorder relax by praying, meditating, or doing crafts, such as knitting. Reading helps some people slow down and fall asleep, but action-packed novels that are difficult to put down may not be ideal at bedtime. When tense or upset, it can be difficult to generate ideas to induce relaxation. A preplanned list kept at home can be helpful. Table 9.1 shows an example of a list of relaxation activities developed by a patient with bipolar disorder.

If new relaxation exercises are introduced, keep them simple, for example, slow and controlled breathing. *Clinical Behavior Therapy* (Goldfried & Davison, 1994) includes several relaxation inductions that are easy for therapists to administer. The following is an example of a simple relaxation induction based on techniques presented in their book:

TABLE 9.1. Relaxation Activities

1. Take a walk.
2. Take a deep breath and slowly exhale. Repeat.
3. Go to my room and close the door.
4. Listen to music.
5. Lie down.
6. Take a warm bath.
7. Do an outside task (e.g., take out garbage,
   take time to notice the stars).

"Find a place to relax that will have as few distractions as possible. Turn down the lights. Turn off the television. Ask others to avoid interruptions. You can lie down or sit comfortably. Before you begin to relax, think of a number between 0 and 100 that describes how tense you feel. One hundred means the most tension you have ever felt and 0 means no tension at all. Write the number down somewhere so that when you have finished this exercise you can rate your tension level again to see if it has improved. Now take a deep breath in through your nose and let it out through your mouth very slowly (*pause*). You can close your eyes if you would like (*pause*). Try to let go of the tension in your body by allowing yourself to sink heavily into the bed or chair (*pause*). Loosen your fingers (*pause*). If you teeth are clenched, loosen your jaw and allow your lips to part slightly (*pause*). Let your arms and legs move into a more comfortable position (*pause*). Imagine yourself to be a rag doll or puppet lying limply on the bed or chair (*pause*). Feel the tension leaving your body. Your body feels more relaxed than before (*pause*). Now take another slow, deep breath in through your nose and out through your mouth (*pause*). You can let your eyes close if they are still open (*pause*)."

Some patients can relax when they close their eyes and imagine a relaxing scene. Others are more comfortable with their eyes open, as they find it harder to control rapidly moving thoughts with their eyes closed. In this instance, it may be more effective to use a technique in which the patient concentrates on a small object in the room while breathing slowly and deeply.

Turning Off Thoughts and Worries at Night

Rumination differs from racing thoughts, but is equally disruptive to sleep. Worry seems to beget worry, especially at bedtime. Patients may complain that they cope well during the day, but that the worries, ideas, thoughts, and questions encountered during the day stream into their awareness just when their conscious mind has decided that it is time for sleep. Typically, thoughts or pictures stream by effortlessly. Some people lie in bed and make mental lists of things to do, questions to ask, and problems to solve. They add items and review the list repeatedly to be certain that they do not forget anything. At that time of day, everything seems urgent and sleeplessness continues.

Some people can tell themselves to stop thinking, turn off the mental lights, and go to sleep. Stopping disruptive thoughts is most effective if the individual replaces the rumination with thoughts that facilitate sleep. For example, organization of the disturbing thoughts can replace repetition. For some patients, actually getting out of bed and making a list of concerns on paper allows them to put aside worry about these tasks.

To take this technique a step further, a patient can organize the list of items in order of priority so that he or she has the beginnings of a plan to address them. The next day, the patient should allocate time to begin working on the listed items in the prioritized order. The patient can then add new issues to the list as necessary and cross off old issues that have been resolved or determined to be unimportant. This exercise is most effective when time is scheduled each day to think about problems before bedtime. If bedtime is the only feasible time for this exercise, the patient should make the list before going into the bedroom.

Distraction sometimes reduces ruminative thoughts that interfere with sleep. Any mental activity that interferes with rumination, such as prayer, meditation, or mental organization, can serve as a distraction. Imagery is effective for some patients. The image should be sufficiently detailed to require concentration. A relaxing scene is best, especially if it is a place that the patient has visited in the past. The image progresses through an exploration of the scene, including the colors, sensations, sounds, and feelings, and ends with a picture of the individual falling asleep in a comfortable place within the scene (e.g., on a hammock, on the beach, under a tree on a spring day, in a sleeping bag under the stars). Exploring the details and working through the image gives the individual time to relax and fall asleep as he or she reaches this final scene in the image.

Pharmacological Methods to Cope with Sleep Disruption

Insomnia, which can be a symptom heralding the onset of either a major depressive, manic, hypomanic, or mixed manic episode, should be a sign or symptom that is carefully followed in the management of patients with bipolar disorder. Sleep onset insomnia is more common with the onset of manic or mixed manic episodes, while middle insomnia or terminal insomnia (waking up during the middle of the night or waking early in the morning and staying awake an hour or more prior to usual time to wake) are often heralds of the onset of a major depressive episode. In addition, hypersomnia may herald the onset of a major depressive episode. The usual treatment for sleep complaints (insomnia or hypersomnia) when associated with the onset of a major mood episode should be adjusting the medications aimed at the bipolar disorder itself (e.g., lithium, anticonvulsants, antidepressants). Occasionally, it is appropriate to add, for a brief period of time, hypnotic agents in the case of insomnia. It is not appropriate to treat hypersomnia with medications. Useful medications for insomnia include virtually all of the hypnotic drugs (e.g., chloralhydrate, flurazepam, temazepam, triazolam). These medications should be in the usual doses prescribed for transient insomnia but should not be continued for a prolonged period of time because their efficacy may wane, and sometimes the patient may become habituated to the drug and require ever increasing doses to attain the same therapeutic benefit. The onset of insomnia or hypersomnia should cue the clinician to more frequently see the patient, assess for other symptoms of the potential and pending episode, and caution the patient against treating the insomnia on his or her own with either the excessive use of alcohol or other substances of abuse. Substance abuse behavior is more likely to lead to the full expression of the episode and subsequent complications. There is no evidence that hypnotic drugs have a negative interaction with any of the other medications used in the management of bipolar disorder.

BEHAVIOR PROBLEMS IN MANIA

Irritability and Aggressiveness

On occasion, Mr. Jones had ferocious arguments with his mother. Sometimes an argument was resolved by his acquiescence to her stubbornness; other times, by her acquiescence to his stubbornness. On occasion, the arguments escalated until Mr. Jones lost his temper. The holes in his bedroom wall and door were evidence of his angry, aggressive, and sometimes violent outbursts. He had never hit his mother, but they were both fearful that the time would come when he would lose control and hit her.

These arguments seemed to come in cycles. There might be several months with minimal conflict, aside from the usual playful bantering of sarcasms that they both seemed to enjoy. There were times, however, when an irritable edge replaced the playful tone in Mr. Jones's voice.

When his mother heard this, she asserted her authority in an attempt to control his inappropriate behavior. Instead, she added fuel to the fire, and an argument ensued.

Neither Mr. Jones nor his family members recognized that his anger and irritability were the early symptoms of mania. The family's response to his irritability further escalated the symptom until Mr. Jones was out of control. The anger and hurt that Mr. Jones felt after a fight with his mother made it difficult for him to sleep at night. He lay in bed with his mind moving at an accelerated speed. He felt edgy and could not get comfortable. He paced in his room. Nothing seemed to help with the agitation.

To help patients such as Mr. Jones, their families must come to recognize the increased irritability as a symptom of mania. Then they must learn an alternative response that addresses the symptom rather than merely reacts to it. Once aware of the symptom, the patients themselves can intervene in various ways. For example, they can review their Symptom Summary worksheet to determine if they have any other manic symptoms. The presence of any additional symptoms suggests that a patient is in the early stages of mania. In some cases, the patient and the therapist work out a treatment plan for such events, and the patient can initiate treatment by calling for help. If irritability is the only manic symptom, mood graphing may be helpful to monitor the course of the irritability.

It may be prudent to discuss with the therapist this differential assessment of the symptom. The clinician will want first to determine if the patient has been taking the prescribed medications regularly. If not, they can work together to resume the appropriate regimen and monitor its effect on the irritability. It may be necessary to modify the medication regimen if the symptoms continue or worsen.

Another way to address irritability is to try to improve sleep, often through the strategies outlined earlier in this chapter. If stress at home is exacerbating a patient's sleeplessness, it will be necessary to address family problems. The intervention can be as simple as drawing the family's attention to the cycle of conflict that is feeding the patient's irritability. When the patient's symptoms remit, family therapy may be appropriate to help the family learn new ways to cope with problems at home.

As any of these interventions are introduced, the patient's level of irritability should be closely monitored. The sequence of interventions used depends on the special needs of the patient and the preferences of the clinician. Although pharmacological management may be the best frontline strategy for some patients, the cognitive-behavioral approach provides an alternative or complementary response.

Extravagance

"Is it hypomanic spending or just a good bargain?" Mrs. Neale voiced her confusion. "My husband says I'm getting manic again. I say I went on a little shopping spree. I put off buying things I needed because I wasn't in the mood to shop. Now I'm feeling better, and I needed a few things that were on sale." Mrs. Neale also spent money when she was becoming manic. It usually started with small amounts and increased. She and her husband had limited resources, and spending sprees were definitely not in the budget. During manic episodes in the past, her shopping had been out of control. For example, she bought several suits in the same style, but in different colors. She did the same with blouses and shoes.

Mrs. Neale was not selfish. She bought things for others as well: a new jacket for her husband, earrings for her mother, and a birthday present for a friend at work. The amount that she and her husband owed on their credit card accounts climbed as Mrs. Neale ordered repeatedly from spring catalogues. The end result was a $5,000 debt and insufficient funds to meet this obligation. "But this time it's different," Mrs. Neale said. "I only spent $100."

For patients who spend extravagantly during manic episodes, it is sometimes difficult to determine when the spending is normal and when it is symptomatic. There are two ways to approach this question. The first is to examine the nature of the spending itself. Were unusual or unnecessary things purchased? Can the patient inhibit any additional spending? Poor judgment about expenditures or an inability to control them is likely to be a symptom of mania. The second approach is to determine if the individual is experiencing any other symptoms of mania. If so, the spending may be one of a cluster of symptoms. Whether symptomatic or not, the patient can monitor shopping urges, mood, and other symptoms on the Mood Graph until certain that mania is not returning.

Mrs. Neale resented her husband's accusations. She thought that he was "cheap" and always used her illness as an excuse to restrict her spending. The Mood Graph settled their arguments. The therapist had shown both spouses how to monitor the symptoms of depression and mania (see Chapter 4), and the Symptom Summary helped guide their observations when necessary. They resolved any differences in view with a call to the therapist. It had been agreed that, until any difference was resolved, Mrs. Neale would stop spending money. If she were unable or unwilling, it was understood that her husband's suspicions about mania might be correct.

When Mr. Dansen went on a buying spree, he headed to the hardware store to purchase supplies for a new home improvement project. His garage was full of "great ideas" that never quite got off the ground. He had learned from these experiences, however. When the hardware urge came upon him now, he stayed away from tempting "bargain day" sales and "two-for-one" offers. He talked about his new ideas with members of his family before he went to the store. Although they sometimes overreacted when he said he was going to buy light bulbs, he generally respected their views and heeded their warnings.

When spending money excessively is a symptom of mania, it can be used as a cue that action must be taken to control symptoms. This means contacting therapists and/or psychiatrists, limiting stimulation, and putting some restrictions on spending money. Some patients use the 24-hour rule whereby they delay purchases for 24 hours. If it still seems like a good idea a day later, the purchase is made. Others talk to family members or friends before spending, or put themselves on a budget.

Some people report that shopping makes them feel better when they are depressed. Unfortunately, the relief is usually very temporary and leaves them with unwanted debt. When hypomanic, spending money can be as compelling as an addiction and just as difficult to control. People who find shopping addictive make it a practice to not carry credit cards, a checkbook, or cash that is needed to pay bills or cover daily expenses. In designing an intervention for excessive spending, encourage patients to set their own limits. Therapists should never be the ones who hold patients' purse strings.

ALCOHOL AND SUBSTANCE ABUSE

Mrs. Goldberg thought that she had control of her drinking. She drank two to three glasses of wine each night. Sometimes, she finished a whole bottle on her own with a good meal. However, her attitude was, "A problem? No, I don't have a drinking problem."

Alcohol affected Mrs. Goldberg in different ways. When she was depressed, alcohol disrupted her sleep, and she felt tired and nauseated in the morning. When she was lonely, alcohol alleviated her sadness temporarily, but left her feeling more depressed after weeks of continued use; she vowed to stop drinking each time. When she was hypomanic and wanted to party, alcohol made it easier for her to make friends and fit in with a group that otherwise made her uncomfortable.

Hypomania impaired Mrs. Goldberg's judgment. When she was drinking, she was more likely to act on her impulses. If she was lucky, she was able to avoid trouble. In the past, however, she had given in to her impulse to drive too fast, act impulsively, and made poor decisions. Furthermore, the alcohol had potentiated her hypersexuality and grandiosity. The results of her behavior have not yet been life threatening, but she may not always be so lucky.

Alcohol use in mania is very tempting. It extends the high for some, calms agitation or anxiety, and sometimes helps people to fall asleep. Unfortunately, a significant proportion of people with bipolar disorder suffer from alcohol abuse or dependence. This requires specific treatment that is not within the scope of this treatment manual. Alcohol/medication interactions are dangerous. Work with the treating psychiatrist to develop a plan with the patient on how and when alcohol can be taken or how treatment of an alcohol or a substance abuse problem should proceed.

CHAPTER SUMMARY

The behavioral changes that accompany mania and hypomania can be very engaging, seductive, humorous, and sometimes entertaining for the patient and for others. This is particularly the case when patients have spent a great deal of time depressed. The rush of hypomania is a pleasant change for patients and for their loved ones. The positive aspects of hypomania are not usually long-standing and are not without consequences. Many people with bipolar disorder have tried to walk the tightrope of hypomania, pushing the limits while believing that they can keep themselves from the fall into mania.

The CBT approach to the management of the behavioral symptoms of hypomania advocates control of the behavioral changes as a means of forestalling a full episode of mania. As with the other CBT interventions, this chapter emphasizes methods for sensitizing patients to the early behavioral changes that cue the onset of mania. Early interventions discussed in this chapter include pharmacological and nonpharmacological strategies for normalizing sleep. Goal setting is introduced as a method for organizing and containing activity. Some common behavioral problems associated with mania such as spending money excessively and irritability and aggressiveness are addressed.

TEN

Psychosocial Problems and Bipolar Disorder

SESSION 14. PSYCHOSOCIAL PROBLEMS

Purpose of the Session

This session changes the focus of the therapy from symptoms of bipolar illness to discussion of their psychosocial consequences. It sets the stage for the next training segment that includes the assessment of, interventions for, and resolution of psychosocial difficulties, including interpersonal problems.

The plan for this session is to begin to examine some of the psychosocial difficulties the patient may be experiencing as a direct or indirect result of bipolar illness.

Goals of the Session

1. Open discussion of psychosocial problems faced by people with bipolar disorder, by providing examples of common psychosocial problems associated with bipolar disorder.
2. Facilitate discussion of problems that patients may have experienced in the past or are currently facing that may be directly or indirectly related to their mental illness.

Procedure

1. Assess treatment compliance.
2. Review patients' mood and activity graphs. Discuss the association between feelings and behavior.
3. Provide an explanation of how psychosocial or interpersonal problems can exacerbate or be exacerbated by symptoms of depression or mania.

(cont.)

(continued from page 203)

4. Ask patients to describe any psychosocial difficulties that they have experienced that were related to the illness. Inform patients that in the next session you will be discussing these difficulties in more detail.
5. Assignment homework.

Homework
Mood and/or activity graph is assigned.

SESSION 15. ASSESSMENT OF PSYCHOSOCIAL FUNCTIONING

Purpose of the Session
In this session, we take the first step toward addressing psychosocial problems by conducting a thorough evaluation of patients' psychosocial and interpersonal functioning, both strengths and weaknesses. If patients identify acute problems/crises in their current interpersonal relationships, you may wish to encourage them to bring their significant others to therapy sessions to attempt to work out these difficulties.

Goals of the Session
1. Assess for psychosocial problems that may be troubling patients.
2. Assess patients' interpersonal strengths (e.g., resources, skills) and weaknesses.
3. Establish treatment goals to address psychosocial problems.

Procedure
1. Assess treatment compliance.
2. Review mood and activity graphs.
3. Assess the quality of patients' current interpersonal relationships including social network, amount of contact with others, quality of these interactions, degree of perceived support from others, and any current difficulties in primary relationships.
4. Assess for any current psychosocial stressors.
5. Help patients identify their strengths that facilitate psychosocial adjustment and weaknesses that may interfere with everyday functioning.
6. Assess any sources of support available to patients.

(cont.)

(continued from page 204)

7. Utilizing the above information, assist patients in setting treatment goals to be addressed in the remaining sessions.
8. Assign homework.

Homework
Ask patients to continue working on the problems list and goals sheet.

SESSION 16. PROBLEM-SOLVING
SKILLS DEVELOPMENT

Purpose of the Session
Patients and their significant others may have difficulty organizing their discussion of troublesome issues in a way that leads to effective problem resolution. It is often useful to follow a structured stepwise approach to addressing problems. The purpose of this session is to teach a structured procedure for resolving psychosocial problems. The procedure can be used with individual patients or in conjoint therapy sessions with family members or significant others.

This basic problem-solving procedure should be modeled by the therapist in resolving problems in session as they arise, including problems with compliance, scheduling, or crisis resolution.

Goals of the Session
1. Teach a structured procedure for identifying and defining problems.
2. Teach a structured procedure for resolving problems.
3. Practice the procedure in session.

Procedure
1. Assess treatment compliance.
2. Select a psychosocial problem identified in the last session and apply the problem-solving procedure.
3. Assign homework.

Homework
Apply the problem resolution procedure with a moderately troublesome issue. Implement the solution and evaluate the outcome.

Although the specific neurobiological mechanisms are not well under-stood, it is well accepted that bipolar disorder is a biologically based illness. However, looking retrospectively at the course of bipolar disorder, research suggests that the expression of the illness may be stress related. Specifically, a very high percentage of individuals with this illness experience significant psychosocial stressors just prior to their first episodes as well as later episodes of mania and depression. Such stressors include bereavement, divorce, and job loss (Aronson & Shukla, 1987; Clancy et al., 1973; Hall, Dunner, Zeller, & Fieve, 1977; Krishnan, Swartz, Larson, & Santoliquido, 1984; Perris, 1984). For example, in a 1979 study, Ambelas interviewed 67 patients admitted to the psychiatric unit of a general hospital over the course of 2 years, as well as a matched group of patients admitted to the same hospital for surgery. Ambelas (1979) found that 28% of the manic patients had experienced a significant life event prior to admission, compared to only 6.6% of the surgical patients, suggesting a stronger association between stress and illness in manic patients than in surgical controls. Kennedy et al. (1983) compared a group of 20 manic inpatients to a control group of orthopedic inpatients matched for age, sex, marital status, and social class. Patients were interviewed to determine the occurrence of undesirable life events in the 4 months preceding hospitalization. Negative life events were found to be significantly more common among the bipolar patients than among control patients.

Evidence from studies of patients with unipolar depression offers further support for the importance of considering life events, particularly interpersonal stress or conflict, in the course of bipolar disorder. In their research with depressed women, Brown and Harris (1978) found that interpersonal "separations" were the most commonly reported stressful events that precipitated depression. Similarly, Paykel et al. (1969) and Billings, Cronkite, and Moos (1983) report that interpersonal "exit events" were more likely than other types of events to precede episodes of depression.

HOW DO BIOLOGICAL
AND PSYCHOSOCIAL FACTORS INTERACT?

Studies of the course of affective disorders (e.g., Leverich, Post, & Rosoff, 1990; Post, Roy-Byrne, & Uhde, 1988; Roy-Byrne et al., 1985) have consistently shown that episodes of mania and/or depression become increasingly frequent over the course of illness. Episodes occurring earlier in the course of the illness are more likely to be associated with the occurrence of stressful life events than later episodes.

Post (1992) suggests limbic kindling and behavioral sensitization as models to help understand the interaction of psychosocial and biological factors in the course of bipolar disorder. The notion of kindling (Goddard, McIntyre, & Leech, 1969) comes from observations that rats who received repeated electrical stimulations to the brain, each of which was not strong enough to cause seizures, eventually began causing seizures. These seizures continued long after the electrical stimulation was stopped. Post proposes that these electrical stimulations may be analogous to life events or other psychosocial stressors; that is, an accumulation of stress eventually leads to depression or mania in a biologically vulnerable individual. Episodes of depression and/or mania may be like kindled seizures in that episodes which initially had an identifiable "trigger" (stressful life event) eventually occur spontaneously, when there is no longer a stimulus present.

Another possible explanation for the association between life events and episodes of depression or mania, particularly earlier in the course of the illness, is behavioral sensitization (Post, Rubinow, & Ballenger, 1986). This is based on the observation that individuals who repeatedly take psychomotor stimulants (e.g., cocaine) seem to, over time, need smaller doses of stimulants to produce the same response as the person becomes sensitized to the drug. In bipolar patients, life events can be thought of as analogous to stimulants, with progressively fewer or less severe stressors needed to precipitate an episode of depression or mania as the illness progresses.

Because evidence from research with patients with affective disorders suggests that stressful life events can play a significant role in the course of illness, prevention of relapses and recurrences of depression and mania may, in part, be achieved by controlling stress. Therefore, this chapter focuses on evaluating and addressing psychosocial problems experienced by people with bipolar disorder.

Unfortunately with individuals who have suffered from bipolar disorder for some time, stress and illness do not have a simple cause and effect relationship. While distress, like that caused by loss of a loved one, can lead to depression, the depression itself can create other psychosocial problems for the individual as described in the example below.

Mr. Phillips lost his mother to cancer and he became seriously depressed for the first time in his life. During the first few months of the depression, the symptoms had little effect on Mr. Phillips's psychosocial functioning. His energy had been a little low, but with some extra effort, he could keep up with his work. His job started to seem boring, however. He became less concerned about the quality of the work; he just wanted to get it done and get out of there. At home, the children got on his nerves;

he found them too loud or too demanding. All his wife seemed to do was complain about money. It seemed to him that they argued often. He was doing the best he could. His family just did not appreciate his efforts. Mr. Phillips began to have trouble sleeping at night. In the morning, he would sleep through the alarm. His boss accepted the excuses at first, but later began to see Mr. Phillips's tardiness as another example of his careless attitude toward work. Layoffs were coming, and Mr. Phillips inched his way to the top of the list until he was finally let go.

After several months, Mr. Phillips's depression began to dominate his life and the lives of his wife and children. He no longer worked. He stayed locked in his room, refusing even to answer the phone. When his wife and children were home, he was irritable and argumentative. He refused to get help. His wife watched the children develop problems at school and with their peers. They competed for her attention, fought with each other, and cried when their father rejected them. Mrs. Phillips wanted to leave, but felt trapped by her own sense of obligation and commitment. Furthermore, she felt guilty when she thought of leaving her sick husband when he needed her the most. Her income as a secretary was not enough, and their debts were accumulating. The creditors were demanding payment. The stress of it all worsened his depression until he began to think of suicide as the only alternative.

Episodes of mania can occur without a particular precipitant, but the behavioral sequelae of mania can produce psychosocial stressors—for example, accrued debt due to financial extravagance and poor judgment, marital conflict due to hypersexuality and promiscuity, or legal problems resulting from illegal actions. When the mania clears, the individual sometimes finds that his or her life is in ruins. As the realization of the damage occurs, it is not unusual for the person to become increasingly distressed, frustrated, and hopeless. In this case, the residual psychosocial stressors produced during an episode of mania could help to instigate an episode of major depression. The distress or dysphoria can come from the self-deprecation and guilt for "creating" problems, the natural consequences of the events (e.g., losing one's home), and the inability to solve the problems effectively. The feelings of frustration, hopelessness, and being overwhelmed can block creative and effective problem resolution. When the problems remain unresolved, they sometimes worsen, growing in intensity (e.g., like interest on overcharged credit cards) or complexity (e.g., marital conflict developing over financial problems) until it seems impossible to identify any clear way to address the difficulties.

MARITAL THERAPIST: Well, Mr. and Mrs. Dimelo, how can I help you?

MRS. DIMELO: (*turning to her husband*) You tell him. This was your idea.

MR. DIMELO: I don't know where to start. I have bipolar disorder. It's pretty well controlled for now, but it's been hard. (*Pauses and looks down on the floor.*)

MARITAL THERAPIST: Tell me more about it.

MR. DIMELO: I got a little carried away during my last round of mania.

MRS. DIMELO: A little?

MR. DIMELO: I ruined our credit and nearly caused us to lose our house. You know how it is. The idea seemed foolproof at the time. I put up a lot of our money, even the kids' college fund.

MRS. DIMELO: I tried to tell him. But would he listen? Oh no. Him and his great ideas.

MR. DIMELO: I was sick!! The doctor explained that to you.

MRS. DIMELO: You weren't too sick to go to the bank and clean out our life savings. The girl at the bank said you were fine, happy, sure you had found a way to get rich quick. My father warned you. He said the only safe way to the top is hard work. He worked in a factory all his life, took care of his family, and put all his kids through college.

MARITAL THERAPIST: Mrs. Dimelo, it sounds like you are very proud of your father's accomplishments and rightly so. But it also sounds like you are very angry with your husband for what has happened. I really want to hear your side of the story. It would help me keep things straight in my mind if we could let your husband finish his part and then turn the floor over to you. Would that be all right with you?

MRS. DIMELO: That's fine.

MARITAL THERAPIST: Mr. Dimelo, please go on.

MR. DIMELO: Anyway, I got us into this stupid land deal and it fell through, leaving us with nothing. Thank God I was able to keep my job or we'd be on the streets by now.

MRS. DIMELO: *You'd* be on the streets by now.

MARITAL THERAPIST: Mrs. Dimelo.

MRS. DIMELO: Sorry. I'll be quiet.

MR. DIMELO: When I told my wife what happened, she exploded. She had every right to be mad. I'd fix it if I could (*starting to cry*). It just seems to get worse each day. I try, but she gets madder, the kids hate me, the neighbors won't talk to me. I'm on probation at work and the cops want to talk to me about the deal. I didn't know it was crooked.

MARITAL THERAPIST: You sound pretty overwhelmed with it all. You say you want to make everything right, but you are stuck for right now. (*Mr. Dimelo nods.*) Mrs. Dimelo, tell me what I can do for you.

MRS. DIMELO: I don't know. My husband and I have been fighting like never before. I'm so angry with him, I can hardly stand looking at his face sometimes. The kids talk to him out of respect, but they would like to stay away or give him a piece of their minds, especially the oldest. He's in college right now.

MARITAL THERAPIST: You said in the beginning that it was your husband's idea to come here.

MRS. DIMELO: Yeah, that's right. You helped some friends of ours and so he thought you might be able to help us.

MARITAL THERAPIST: Mrs. Dimelo, do you want help?

MRS. DIMELO: Yeah. I hate fighting, but most of all I hate seeing my husband like this.

In this scenario, the problems are many and complex, as they are fueled by a great deal of emotion in all parties. The therapist must untangle the conflict, define each specific problem, including those that have to do with hurt feelings, and facilitate the couple's attempts toward resolution.

IDENTIFYING PSYCHOSOCIAL TARGETS FOR CHANGE

The most important step in addressing psychosocial difficulties is to clearly define the nature of the problem. What is it exactly that is bothering the patient? This sounds fairly straightforward, but it can actually be quite difficult. Usually, an individual can identify the person with whom he or she is having trouble (e.g., spouse, mother-in-law, boss, creditor) or the arena in which the problems are occurring (e.g., at home, at work), but it may be harder to describe the specific nature of the problem (e.g., the precise behavior or circumstance that are causing the stress).

Some problems are easy to identify: "My car broke down, and I don't have enough money for repairs." "My unemployment benefits are running out, but I don't feel well enough to go back to work." "My mother is sick, but she won't see the doctor." Interpersonal problems are more difficult to pinpoint. Patients often incorrectly assume that they have figured out the source of an interpersonal problem, when, in fact, they have usually erred by not including themselves in the equation.

Mr. Boyd complained that everyone took advantage of him at work. He was expected to help others with their projects, be efficient, and work hard, yet he never seemed to be rewarded. As a result, he resented his boss and coworkers. His sense of responsibility and his professionalism drove him to do his best when he really felt like telling them all to go away and leave him alone. He needed this job and probably could not find another that had all the conveniences of this one.

Mr. Boyd defined the problem as existing outside of himself. He felt helpless to make changes, victimized, unappreciated, and overwhelmed. In his definition of the problem, Mr. Boyd missed his own failure to communicate his feelings about the job to his boss and his coworkers. He never attempted to set limits, assert himself, ask for assistance, or look out for his own interests. Defining the problem accurately means looking at each party's contribution.

Mrs. Turnby's life was not going the way she thought it should. She was dissatisfied with her work, her home, and herself. She ruminated about problems on the job while she was there and even when she was not. She questioned her future. Her children were a constant source of irritation. She felt as if she were going nowhere. She hated the city that she lived in, the people, the traffic, the noise, and the crowds. She felt guilty for not taking good care of her health, not finishing school, ignoring her husband, gaining weight, and not being more accepting of others. On a particularly bad day, she blamed herself for her son's poor grade on a spelling test, and she saw only catastrophes in the future. She contemplated skipping work, but instead succumbed to the guilt of letting her coworkers down. She was irritated with this memo she got on the changes in the vacation policy at work. Her in-laws were due to visit and she knew how *that* would go. Mrs. Turnby has so many troubles, she does not know where to begin in addressing them. She is exhausted from worry and stress. She thinks that more troubles are just around the corner. She had put off seeing her therapist for a month. She wondered if her lithium level was low or if she had become immune to its effect. She finally took off a half day from work to see her doctor.

For this example, Mrs. Turnby is faced with a number of difficulties and it is not clear which needs the most immediate attention. In this scenario, it appears as if all the issues raised were deemed to be of equal importance or at least worthy of equal amounts of energy. To begin the process of resolving problems, it is necessary to identify a few targets of change, those with greater urgency and importance.

To begin to delineate problems, the patient can list all the issues that have consumed his or her physical, emotional, and mental energy in the past week. Mrs. Turnby's list is presented in Table 10.1. The second step is for the patient to order the items on the list according to the amount of energy that they consumed, with the item that consumed the greatest amount of energy over the past week ranked 1, the item that consumed the second greatest amount of energy ranked 2, and so on. Items that seem to be part of the same problem can be ranked together. In Mrs. Turnby's example, her dissatisfaction with herself included her health, education, weight, and acceptance of others. This step tells the therapist which problem is most troublesome to the patient. From the rankings on Table 10.1, we can see that her job consumed the most energy this week, and her personal well-being ranked lowest.

The third step in this exercise is for the patient to prioritize the items in terms of their importance or urgency. This is indicated in the column labeled "Priority." Ideally, the greatest amount of energy should be given to problems that are highest in priority or importance and the smallest amount of energy should be given to problems that have the lowest priority. In devising a treatment plan for resolving psychosocial stressors, the highest rated priority items should be addressed first. This step in the exercise is important because a great deal of emotional energy can be spent on issues that may have little importance for the patient's overall quality of life.

In the above example, Mrs. Turnby's energy allocation did not match her priorities. Things that were less important to her (e.g., the vacation

TABLE 10.1. Mrs. Turnby's Problem List

Energy consumed	Problem area	Priority
1	Vacation memo	12
2	Dissatisfied with work	5
3	Job problems	
4	Prospects for the future on this job (going nowhere)	5
5	Upcoming in-laws' visit	8
6	Children irritating (dissatisfied with home)	1
7	Hated her city (people, traffic, noise, crowds)	11
8	Dissatisfied with self:	
	Poor health maintenance	7
	Did not finish school	6
	Gained weight	7
	Not accepting of others	9
9	Attention for husband	2
10	Son's grades on spelling test	10
11	Lithium level	3
12	Needs to see doctor	3
13	Exhaustion	4

memo) were receiving more of her energy than things that were of great importance to her (e.g., her children, husband, and herself). Such an imbalance suggests that the patient is wasting energy on things not worth her time and, in turn, neglecting things more critical to her overall life satisfaction. This contributes to her sense that her life is in disarray.

Clinicians should guide patients in reviewing their lists and comparing energy allocations to priority ratings. This process organizes patients' problems so that a systematic intervention can begin. The items rated highest in importance and/or urgency should be the first targets for change. The list can also be used to remind patients to set limits on the amount of energy expended on relatively unimportant issues when more pressing problems need attention. For example, if Mrs. Turnby finds that she is complaining about problems at work during her family time, she can remind herself that she is wasting her family time energy on her work when her work has a lower priority for her than her husband and kids. This refocuses attention on issues that are more important to patients, resolution of which has a greater chance of reducing distress.

COPING WITH STRESS

People with bipolar disorder may have psychosocial problems in a number of different areas: family, work, health, finances, and so on. Stress from psychosocial difficulties can exacerbate symptoms such as impaired concentration, fatigue, and distractibility which, in turn, can further interfere with effective coping. Therapists can help patients begin to cope with stressors by helping them to define and prioritize problems that need to be addressed in therapy. These become goals for therapy against which progress can be compared.

Patients have usually tried to resolve their problems on their own before presenting them to a therapist. Therefore, before developing a new treatment plan, it is helpful to determine what strategies patients have already used and how effective they have been in coping with stress. Therapists may ask questions such as:

- How have you coped with problems in the past?
- How have you dealt with similar problems?
- Have you tried to apply those strategies to current problems?
- What kept those strategies from working for these new problems?
- What do you believe is the next strategy to try?

Taking the time to inquire about past efforts to deal with stressors serves several purposes. First, it facilitates treatment planning; therapists can suggest interventions that patients have not yet tried or perhaps a modification of strategies that patients have attempted without success. Second, inquiring about patients' previous attempts at coping with problems makes it clear that the therapist respects the patient's intelligence and resourcefulness. Third, it establishes clinicians as consultants to patients in coping with stressors, providing expertise in areas in which patients need assistance. This emphasizes the view of the therapeutic relationship as a collaboration rather than a "fix-it shop" where patients passively bring in problems to be fixed and therapists do repairs and send bills.

Coping Resources

When developing a treatment plan to address patients' psychosocial stressors, the therapist generally thinks about ways to maximize patients' coping resources. The fact that patients are not coping well does not mean that they are devoid of internal and external resources. Internal resources include:

- Intelligence
- Practicality
- Analytical-mindedness
- Common sense
- Fortitude
- Assertiveness
- Sensitivity
- A sense of humor
- Time
- Personableness
- Organizational ability
- Resourcefulness
- Energy
- Stamina
- Creativity
- Self-esteem
- Money
- Confidence
- Self-perceived competency
- Ability to seek out and accept help from others
- Perseverance

External coping resources include assistance from others, such as family, friends, therapists, coworkers, support staff on the job, and housekeepers. External resources can also include services that are purchased, such as a maid service, income tax services, clerical support services, babysitters, banks and other financial institutions, or real estate agents.

Obstacles to Effective Coping

Although mobilizing patients' existing resources or acquiring new resources to cope with psychosocial stressors may sound simple, many factors can interfere. To understand fully the context in which problems have developed and persist, patients' weaknesses and the obstacles to effective coping must be identified. In patients with bipolar disorder, the symptoms of the illness can produce problems. For example, the impaired judgment associated with mania may lead to ill-conceived financial ventures that leave the family in financial ruin. Sexual promiscuity can stress existing relationships. Similarly, the emotional distress and fearfulness associated with depression can create obstacles to effective coping by overriding patients' logic and keeping them from actively attending to their problems. Neglected problems can compound over time. Perhaps emotion is the most common obstacle to effective coping.

> Ms. Allen often lost perspective when she was distressed. She let her emotions govern her decisions and actions because she believed that she had good instincts. However, her instincts regarding the appropriate way to handle problems differed depending on whether she was calm or upset. In the peak of emotion, her actions appeared impulsive to others and there were often repercussions, which seemed to worsen her problems overall.
>
> Ms. Allen recognized this pattern after the fact. "I get so upset that I can't think straight, I can't think of the right thing to say, and I often say things I later regret. Later on, I calm down and realize how I should have handled it, but it's usually too late by then." She worked with her therapist to adjust her coping strategies to compensate for her emotion, either by slowing down the problem-solving process or by delaying her decisions until she was less upset.

Several other internal and external factors can interfere with successful coping. Internal factors, such as fearfulness of the outcome, can keep patients from taking direct action to solve their problems. Not having sufficient information can impede problem solving, as can being unaware that there is a problem. External factors, such as other people over whom patients have little, if any, control, can produce, exacerbate, or maintain difficulties. When patients are faced with competing demands, impossible deadlines, and/or a mounting work load, they may not have time to resolve their problems. Instead, they struggle to keep their heads above water for another day. Some patients may have the time to work out their problems but may lack sufficient resources to do so. Money, for example, may be needed to solve financial problems and other problems of daily living. If patients are unemployed and have only limited sources of support, financial problems will linger.

The goal is for patients to recognize obstacles to effective coping, make use of existing coping resources, and attempt to reduce or eliminate the obstacles that preclude active coping.

PROBLEM SOLVING

Most people engage in problem solving every day. It occurs automatically for many of the small decisions needed to navigate through each day's activities. For example, "Should I get up now, or can I sleep 10 minutes longer?" Quickly, the possible choices and the relative risks and benefits of obeying the alarm clock or sleeping later come to mind. More sophisticated problems are as easily addressed. For example, "I have three tasks that need to be completed by the end of the week. How am I going to get them all accomplished?" After considering the possible strategies, one is chosen and implemented. If it proves ineffective, an alternative strategy is implemented. People who can define problems, consider options, make choices, and implement a plan have all the basic skills required for effective problem solving. Reminding patients that they can make decisions may increase their confidence in their ability to handle more complex difficulties.

Even when patients have the necessary skills, obstacles to effective coping can impede problem solving. In these cases, a more formal step-by-step procedure for defining problems and for generating and implementing solutions can be useful. The following are step-by-step procedures for helping patients and their family members to solve problems. They are fairly generic and can be applied to many different scenarios.

1. Problem identification and definition
   a. State the problem as clearly as possible. If there are multiple participants in the therapy session (e.g., family members), each individual should have a chance to state the problem from his or her perspective (e.g., "I don't have enough money to pay the bills").
   b. Be specific about the behavior, situation, timing, and/or circumstances that make it a problem (e.g., "I need to pay the phone and credit card bills, and I don't have enough money to cover both this month").
   c. If there is more than one participant, some discussion may be necesssary until there is an agreed upon statement of the problem.
   d. If the problem is a personal hurt, state the specific action that caused the hurt feeling (e.g., "You hurt my feelings when you said I couldn't handle the money").

2. Generation of potential solutions
   a. List all possible solutions without evaluating their quality or feasibility.
   b. Try to list at least 15 solutions; be creative and forget about the quality of the solution.

    c. Eliminate less desirable or unreasonable solutions.

    d. Order the remaining solutions in terms of preference.

    e. Evaluate the remaining solutions in terms of their pros and cons.

    f. Specify who will take action.

    g. Try to select a solution that will allow each person to take some action (e.g., "I'll go to the doctor if you will take me").

    h. Specify how the solution will be implemented.

    i. Specify when the solution will be implemented.

3. Implementation of the solution

    a. Implement the solution as planned.

    b. Evaluate the effectiveness of the solution.

    c. Decide whether a revision of the existing plan or a new plan is needed to address the problem better.

    d. If so, return to step 2 to select a new solution, and repeat remaining steps or return to step 2 to revise the existing solution, and repeat remaining steps.

Problem Definition

The most difficult step in resolving psychosocial problems is identifying and defining the problem in a way that facilitates its resolution. Because the definition must be as objective and specific as possible, the problem should be described in terms of observable phenomena rather than subjective feelings.

> Mr. Washaw's complaint that he "can't cope" is too general. To define the problem more precisely, it is necessary to specify the situations in which he has difficulty coping (e.g., disciplining the kids). Is it always a problem in this particular situation? (No.) If not, when is it more or less a problem? (It is more a problem with his son than with his daughter.) What has happened when he has tried to address the problem? (He gets very angry, says things that he does not mean, and later regrets what he said.) A more specific definition of Mr. Washaw's complaint, therefore, is that he gets too angry and overreacts when he disciplines his son. The situation is defined in observable, operational terms. That is, outsiders would understand "I have difficulty in disciplining my son" more easily than they would understand the meaning of "I can't cope."

To facilitate problem definition, therapists can ask the following questions:

- What is the problem?
- When is it most likely to occur?
- Are other people involved?

- How do they help or make the problem worse?
- How would the therapist know if the problem were occurring?
- Would anyone else notice?
- In what way does it cause a problem?
- What are the consequences?
- How often does the problem occur?
- Are there circumstances that make it better or worse?
- In general, what, when, where, how, and with whom is it a problem?

If the problems involve other people, it is very likely that each participant has a somewhat different view of the situation.

> Mr. Fujitsu complained that his wife could not be trusted to pay the bills properly, making it necessary for him to find time in his busy schedule to do so. The problem appeared to be the manner in which his wife paid the bills (i.e., paid only the minimum balance when it was possible to pay more). Mrs. Fujitsu saw things differently. According to her, the problem was that her husband procrastinated in paying the bills so long that she had to do it. She might pay only the minimum amount, but at least she paid them! So, it appeared that the problem was more compli-cated than Mr. Fujitsu had originally suggested. In this case, there were two problems: getting bills paid on time and paying an agreed upon amount.

Some practical problems (e.g., unemployment, financial problems, or schedule problems) are easily defined. More existential problems (e.g., dissatisfaction with life or low self-esteem) are more difficult. If patients make general complaints about themselves or their lives, therapists can help by inquiring about the situations in which their dissatisfaction is more apparent.

> "I hate my life," complained Ms. Louise. "Nothing is going right. Work, my social life, my body, my family—it all stinks." When asked to specify which element in each of these domains was troubling her, Ms. Louise replied, "All of it, the whole package." Her therapist was skeptical that there were problems in all aspects of the patient's life. A different tactic was necessary to hone in on Ms. Louise's problems. Taking one topic at a time (e.g., work, social life), the therapist inquired about what was going right for Ms. Louise in each domain. What parts of her job did she like or dislike? Was it the task, the environment, the people, or the pay? What was it about her body, her family, and her social life?

Defining complaints about other people requires a somewhat differ-ent strategy. The offenses that people commit against one another are generally defined by the meaning that each party attaches to the event rather than by what is observable.

> Mr. Magoo made an extra effort to get home early to prepare dinner for the family. He made his specialty, set the table, and called everyone to dinner. His wife was not hungry and declined to eat. Mr. Magoo was hurt and angry. There was no discussion about dinner, but a quiet coldness pervaded the household. To Mrs. Magoo, there was no reason for her husband's detached demeanor. She just was not hungry. She appreciated his effort, although she may not have mentioned it at the time. So why was he so angry and hurt? He knew that his wife did not eat when she was not hungry. The problem was in Mr. Magoo's interpretation of his wife's behavior. It conveyed to him that she did not care about the marriage, that she did not appreciate his efforts, and that she did not care about him or love him. When the therapist asked Mr. Magoo to explain this to his wife, she understood, clarified her feelings, and apologized for contributing to his hurt.

GENERATING SOLUTIONS

Once the difficult task of defining the problem has been accomplished, efforts can be initiated to resolve it. It is particularly useful to assess a patient's coping resources, previous coping strategies, and obstacles to effective coping (i.e., strengths and weaknesses) before attempting to generate new solutions. Brainstorming for potential new solutions should proceed without stopping to evaluate the merits of any one idea. In addition, because obstacles prevent the patient from making use of existing coping resources, the solutions generated to handle problems should include a plan for eliminating the patient's weaknesses while utilizing the patient's strengths. For example:

Mr. McNeeley's strengths included:
1. Creativity
2. Organizational skill
3. Assertiveness
4. Ability to get along with others
5. Knowledge about aspects of work

His weaknesses were:
1. Impatience
2. Irritability
3. Unwillingness to compromise
4. No time to deal with problems
5. Aggressiveness

Mr. McNeeley was angry about a new procedure implemented at his job site because it increased his work load and sacrificed quality for higher volume. He complained (weakness 5) to his superiors and demanded immediate action (weakness 1). He did not see any response to his complaints, so he returned to his boss's office, demanded to be seen (weakness 1), angrily (weaknesses 2 and 5) criticized management for their lack of foresight, and told them how to rectify their errors. Mr. McNeeley made little progress, but began to have stomach problems and tension headaches. He told his therapist that he thought he should quit his job (weakness 3).

The solutions that Mr. McNeeley attempted seemed to have no effect. His weaknesses appeared to have impeded his progress. Once he recognized this, he was able to use his creativity (strength 1) and organizational skill (strength 2) to generate a new plan that incorporated his strengths. He solicited the assistance of his colleagues (strength 4) to monitor their productivity and track occasions when they were unable to complete their work or had to compromise quality for speed (strength 5).

After documenting these findings, he made an appointment to talk with the management (strength 3) about his data and their implications. He and his therapist worked out a strategy that kept him from appearing angry and uncompromising.

DECISIONS, DECISIONS

Life transitions, such as changing jobs, moving to a new neighborhood, and making new friends, can be very exciting. New opportunities often bring stress and uncertainty, however. Individuals may ask themselves, "Am I making the right decision? What if it doesn't work out? Am I just running away from my problems? What should I do?"

Patients with bipolar disorder often find themselves immobilized by indecisiveness. When poor concentration, low self-confidence, racing thoughts, and stimulus overload muddle their thinking, even the simplest decisions seem laborious. Fear of the consequences of each choice feeds rumination; in turn, past experiences, when change led to failure, feed this fear. Ideas, options, and fantasies flash through the mind of the manic or hypomanic patient. Disjointed details flood the patient's thoughts while the urge toward impulsive acts grows stronger. The depressed patient often makes decisions by default, when the failure to act becomes a decision or when others take over and make decisions. In either state, the outcome is not always in the best interest of the patient.

The clinician can facilitate decision making by teaching patients to slow down the process and organize their thoughts. Providing a structure for systematically evaluating choices can alleviate the mental wheel spinning and move patients toward active decision making. Committing these thoughts to paper allows the patient to make some constructive use of the mental energy spent ruminating about the options. It also buys the hypomanic patient some time to slow down and evaluate the choices objectively before impulsively acting.

The first step in this structured approach to decision making is to define each choice. For example, (1) I can change jobs, or (2) I can remain at the existing job. The second step is to list the advantages and disadvantages of each choice (see Figure 10.1). There will be some redundancy across lists, with the advantages of one choice paralleling the disadvantages of the other. The patient should explore all aspects of each choice, considering the pros and cons of each. When the four lists are complete, the patient can begin the third step, an evaluation of the choices.

As the third step in the decision-making process, the patient reads through the lists and places three stars (***) next to the items that he or she considers most important, two stars (**) next to items that are very important, and one star (*) next to those that are important. The patient can ignore the remaining items for the time being. Examining the starred items to ·determine the primary or strongest advantages and disadvantages of each choice (see Figure 10.1) simplifies the decision-making process by focusing the patient on the key issues. The patient can then compare the main advantages and disadvantages of the various choices relative to one another. When the evaluation is complete, the patient can proceed with the fourth step.

	Stay on This Job	Change Jobs
Advantages	It's close to home * Good secretary * I know everybody	*** Can make more money Larger office ** More independence in decision making Get away from boss
Disadvantages	Business has been poor *** Stuck with current boss *** No raise this year Bad neighborhood No room for creativity	The work schedule may require more weekend work *** May have to move the family The new boss could end up being a jerk

FIGURE 10.1. Advantages and disadvantages of job changes. *** most important item; ** very important items; * important items.

In this final step, the patient considers the possibility of maximizing the advantages of each choice (e.g., asking for a higher starting salary on the new job), while minimizing the disadvantages (e.g., negotiate for a limit on weekend work). This process often requires the patient to gather additional information on each option before making a decision.

TIMES FOR FORMAL PROBLEM SOLVING

Although people make decisions every day without going through each step in the problem-solving sequence, there are times when casual decision making does not adequately address the issues. The most common time to use formal problem solving is when there are obvious difficulties in everyday activities, for example, when there are unresolved problems at home, on the job, or in interpersonal relationships. Formal problem solving is most useful when (1) the problem persists despite the patient's efforts, or (2) the patient has been unable to identify a reasonable solution to the problem.

> Mrs. Romero's psychiatrist could see her only in the afternoon. This was not a good time for her, however, because she did not have a babysitter for her youngest child and she had to pick up her older kids from school by 3:00 P.M. Often, Mrs. Romero had to wait to see her doctor and, therefore, was late to pick up her children from school. She wanted to keep appointments, but often canceled them at the last minute because she became anxious and overwhelmed at the thought of her tight schedule.
>
> Trying to solve this problem on her own, Mrs. Romero worked within the constraints that she received. Her solutions had included (1) taking her youngest child to the appointment with her; (2) working out a fail-safe plan in which she left the doctor's office by a certain time, even if she had not yet been able to see the doctor; (3) finding the quickest route from the doctor's office to the school; and (4) picking up her children early from school and bringing them all to her appointment. These solutions had caused Mrs. Romero considerable stress. She understood how important it was for her to see the doctor regularly, however, so she did her best to comply.
>
> Mrs. Romero's solutions had been creative, but were based on three assumption that may not be valid. First, she assumed that the doctor's schedule was inflexible and that she must see him during a time that was inconvenient for her. This kept her from asking for a more convenient appointment time. Second, she assumed that she had to handle this scheduling problem on her own, which kept her from asking for assistance from others. For example, she did not like to impose on family

members to care for her youngest child and could not afford a babysitter. She did not want to inconvenience others, so she did not ask friends or neighbors to pick up her children from school and keep them until she returned. Third, the assumption that her psychiatrist was the only doctor who could help her kept her from requesting a referral to a doctor with a more flexible schedule. Mrs. Romero was feeling locked in to her current situation with no prospects for improvement. Using formal problem solving to define each component of the problem and to generate a list of potential solutions helped to free her from the constraints that she herself helped to maintain.

CUES TO ACTION

Identifying and defining problems requires an awareness that problems exist. There are various internal and external cues to the need for problem solving. As part of their training in problem solving, it is useful to explore with patients the various types of cues and the ways in which these cues bring problems to their attention.

Physical Cues

Sometimes, the cues that problems need attention are physical discomforts, such as headaches, indigestion, muscle tension, fatigue, hives, and tightness in the chest. Even when individuals are not consciously aware that there is a problem, their bodies can speak for them.

> Ms. Colon had suffered from headaches for the past 2 weeks. She believed that the headaches were caused by environmental allergies. She took decongestant medications and over-the-counter pain relievers, but they gave her little relief. When asked if she was having stress-related headaches, Ms. Colon quickly responded that she was under no more stress than usual. After inquiring further, it became apparent that she had many things on her mind. None of her concerns were overwhelming in and of themselves, but they had a cumulative effect on her that fueled her tension headaches.

> When Mr. Fabre was informed that his company would be laying off several employees over the next month, he took the news well. He did not know if he would be laid off, but decided to develop a plan for finding a new job just in case he needed it. He was skilled and would probably have little difficulty in finding another job. His wife worked, and they had saved some extra money for emergencies. If he were to be unemployed for a time, they would not suffer financially.

Mr. Fabre began to suffer from indigestion. He attributed it to spicy foods, lack of exercise, bad restaurants, and aging. He modified his diet to avoid those things that were most difficult for him to digest. His diet became more and more restricted; his consumption of antacids, more frequent. He saw his doctor at his wife's insistence. The doctor explained that the stomach problems were most likely caused by stress. Although Mr. Fabre could use his analytical thinking ability to deal with this problem, his logic could not completely eliminate his underlying anxiety about losing his job.

These examples of physical manifestations of stress are common, but are not always identified as stress related. Medications can provide symptomatic relief, but do not address the underlying problem. Patients can be taught to use physical discomforts as cues that psychosocial problems need immediate attention.

Emotional Shifts

For patients with bipolar disorder, emotional shifts can serve as cues to initiate problem solving. At first, the focus should be on determining how to cope with the emotional shift itself. Defining the problem, in this case, means analyzing the situation and deciding whether the mood shift is an independent event or has resulted from a stressor. As noted in earlier chapters, the events, cognitions, and actions associated with the mood shift can provide clues about its source. The solutions generated to cope with the mood shift will depend on the identified source of the problem. If the cause of the mood shift is a belief or negative cognition regarding an event, the solution may be to use cognitive restructuring strategies. The patient can then evaluate and modify the emotion-laden thoughts about the event that are fueling the mood shift.

If the source of the emotional shift is a stressful event or problem itself, formal problem solving may be required. It is best if, before they begin the problem-solving process, patients try to reduce the intensity of the emotional shift by gaining emotional distance from the problem or by using other mood-stabilizing methods. The solutions that patients generate while they are extremely upset are often colored by the intensity of the emotion. Gaining emotional distance reduces the likelihood of impulsive responding and gives patients more control over troublesome situations.

Input from Others

"My wife is always nagging me. She's never satisfied. I do the best I can, but it's never good enough. I think she's just going through one of those mid-life things and is taking her own problems out on me. I just ignore her and read the paper. She eventually shuts up until she gets the next bee in her bonnet."

Input from others can take the form of complaints and criticism. It is common for people to see complaints from others as unjustifiable and unworthy of concern. Although the complaints or criticisms from others may indeed be unsubstantiated, they are cues that something is wrong. Patients should be encouraged to hear criticism as a cue that a problem exists, whether it be in their own behavior, in the behavior of others, or in their relationships. Defining criticism as a cue may allow the patient to move beyond defensiveness to begin to evaluate the situation objectively. If the problem can be identified, it has a better chance to be solved.

Family members, friends, and significant others are often good observers. They may be able to identify problems before they become noticeable to the patient, particularly when the patient's judgment and insight are colored by mania or hypomania. Unfortunately, patients in this state do not always welcome the observations and comments of significant others. Many therapists discuss with their patients ways in which significant others may help patients identify areas where active problem solving can be useful. It can be very useful to include the family in such a discussion if the patient is comfortable with the plan. During a conjoint meeting, the therapist can address (1) when the family should talk with the patient about problems, (2) how to present problems in a way that the patient can hear them, and (3) what to do when the patient is unable or unwilling to respond to the family's concerns. The therapist may also:

- Explain how the symptoms of the disorder interfere with the process of information.
- Find out how the family has dealt with similar communication problems in the past and how successful their attempts have been.
- Use the problem-solving model to generate solutions to any difficulties that may arise in the family's communications with the patient about anticipated or observed problems.

SCHEDULED ASSESSMENT

Patients need not wait until problems emerge before using formal problem solving. While it is most often used for putting out fires in the patient's life, problem solving can be *pro*active rather than *re*active. Patients and their significant others can schedule time at regular intervals (e.g., every

3 to 6 months) to evaluate their progress and to address problems, either with the assistance of a therapist or on their own. At these scheduled progress checks, patients take stock in their lives, compare their goals with their progress, and identify any areas of dissatisfaction. Difficulties or impediments to progress can become targets for change.

After each self-evaluation or progress check, patients can decide when the next evaluation is to occur. It can be helpful to pair the exercise with a regularly occurring event, such as the next medication clinic visit. For example, Mr. Peters and his wife make time at the end of the month, when they are paying their bills, to check on their progress. Ms. Carlson schedules her progress check every 6 months and writes it in her professional and home calendars as reminders.

The scheduled progress check should include a review of goals and an assessment of functioning in the following areas.

- Symptom control: To what degree is the patient maintaining his or her treatment gains? Is he or she taking the medication as prescribed? Are the symptoms of depression and/or mania under control?
- Interpersonal sphere: Are relationships progressing as expected and/or as desired? Are there any sources of tension in ongoing relationships? If so, what attempts have been made to resolve problems? Is there any need for professional intervention?
- Occupational sphere: Are there any problems on the job? Is the patient able to function on the job as expected? How is job attendance? Are there any problems in getting along with others on the job?
- Social sphere: Are social relationships progressing as desired? Is the patient maintaining an active social life consistent with his or her goals, needs, and desires? Is there sufficient social support? If not, what is keeping the patient from gaining support from others?

PREDICTABLE TIMES OF CHANGE AND STRESS

Major life events are associated with increased stress and can precipitate an exacerbation of symptoms in the patient with bipolar disorder. Stressful events, especially catastrophic events such as the death of a friend or family member, severe financial crises, major accidents, or illnesses in patients or their significant others, can tax a patient's internal coping resources. Positive life events can also be stressful. They require alterations in routine, including eating and sleeping patterns, and may affect symptom control. During these times, the patient may need to rely on more formal problem-solving strategies to cope with the changes associated with the event.

> Mrs. Wilber's elderly mother had been hospitalized with a major illness. Although she was steadily improving and her doctors said that she would recover completely, Mrs. Wilber was worried. She stayed awake at night worrying about her mother and wondering what she would do if her mother died. When Mrs. Wilber was deprived of sleep, she usually began to experience symptoms of mania. Knowing her usual pattern, Mrs. Wilber took time to figure out a solution to her sleeplessness, which helped to prevent a return of her manic symptoms.

Life events can affect other spheres of a patient's life. For example, Mrs. Wilber's preoccupation with her mother might interfere with her work performance, reduce the time that she has available to be with her children, and cause some financial strain. She might not become aware of the effect that her mother's illness is having on her daily life until a problem emerges on the job or at home. Measures can be taken to prevent such problems, first, by formally surveying the areas in a person's life (e.g., work, relationships, finances) that the life event could potentially affect and, second, by taking appropriate action. Thus, Mrs. Wilber could talk with her children about her preoccupation and the effect that it is likely to have on their time together. She could make extra efforts to compensate for her time away and check with her kids to monitor any negative effects of the event. If difficulties emerge, problem solving can be used to address them before they become severe.

Life changes generally have an impact beyond the arena in which they are occurring. For example, job changes can affect life at home and vice versa. Periods of change, therefore, are also times in which more formal problem solving can be useful. Expected role transitions can be similarly stressful and place the patient at increased risk for an exacerbation of symptoms. Role transitions can affect the patient directly (e.g., getting married) or indirectly by means of changes in other family members (e.g., the youngest child moving away from home). Developmental role transitions, like any other change or event, can be disruptive to the patient's mental health.

CHAPTER SUMMARY

Psychosocial stressors, while common to all individuals, are particularly problematic for people with bipolar disorder. Research examining the relationship between stressful life events and the onset of depression and mania has found a convincing association. In particular, episodes of depression and mania occurring early in the course of the illness are likely to follow a significant and stressful life event.

Psychosocial problems also emerge as a result of the actions of an individual during the course of depression or mania. For example, financial problems can develop from loss of employment resulting from the inertia, fatigue, and low motivation of depression or as the result of financial extravagance and impaired judgment of mania.

Coping with both the illness and the psychosocial consequences can be overwhelming. Failure to resolve problems can exacerbate stress which places the individual at an increased risk of relapse. This chapter describes methods for the identification and resolution of psychosocial problems.

Problem solving includes the following steps: problem identification and definition, generation of potential solutions, selection and implementation of the solution, and evaluation of the outcome. Patients and their significant others can be taught to resolve problems using this stepwise method.

Before issues are presented for discussion in psychotherapy, patients have usually made attempts to resolve them on their own with varying degrees of success. Problem-solving training should build on the existing skills of the person, survey the coping resources of patients, acknowledge their competencies, facilitate collaboration, and expedite the therapy process. It communicates respect for the individual's capacity to cope and engages the person as an active participant in their care.

ELEVEN

Interpersonal Problems: Communication

SESSIONS 17–20. RESOLUTION OF PSYCHOSOCIAL PROBLEMS

Purpose of the Sessions

The purpose of the problem-solving sessions is to attempt to resolve the ongoing psychosocial difficulties identified in the assessment phase that continue to be a source of stress for the patient.

At least one session should be allocated for each of the treatment goals outlined in the assessment phase. Multiple sessions may be necessary to address a complicated problem. To facilitate the process, divide the main treatment goal into subgoals and address each individually using the problem-solving procedure.

Over the remaining sessions, discuss how and when the problem-solving procedures can be incorporated into everyday life. Although problem-solving procedures can be applied with the assistance of a therapist, patients must learn to apply these skills in the course of their everyday lives. Help patients to identify times when problem-solving should be initiated.

Goals of the Session

Address one problem area defined in the previous sessions using the problem-solving procedure.

(cont.)

(continued from page 229)

Procedure

1. Assess treatment compliance.
2. Follow the procedure outlined in the Problem-Solving Skills Development session. Take sufficient time to address one problem area. If time allows, move on to attempt resolution of a second problem area.
3. Discuss how problem identification and problem-solving methods can be used at times when increased stress is likely. This may include major life events or developmental role transitions. Other cues that problem evaluation and resolution may be needed are when symptoms worsen, stress increases, or others recognize problems that involve the patients. Regularly scheduled assessments of psychosocial functioning can help to head off problems before they occur.
4. Assign homework.

Homework

Attempt implementation of the solutions generated during the problem-solving discussion. Evaluate how well the solution addresses the problem and implement a new or revised plan if the proposed solution proved ineffective.

SPECIAL COMMUNICATION PROBLEMS OF PEOPLE WITH BIPOLAR DISORDER

Oversensitivity

For people with bipolar disorder, oversensitivity to rejection or criticism occurs more often during depressive or mixed episodes than during manic episodes. Patients often state that their feelings are hurt easily, that they anticipate rejection or criticism before it occurs, and that they overreact when these events do occur. It is difficult for these individuals to distinguish between real rejection or criticism and their own cognitive distortions. Sometimes, patients are able to recognize intellectually that others' behavior was not intended to be rejecting or critical, but they are unable to inhibit or reduce their strong emotional reaction (e.g., sadness, guilt, embarrassment, or anger) to that behavior.

Interpersonal conflict may ensue if the "offender" responds to the bipolar disorder patient's oversensitivity by becoming defensive or counterattacking in response to the "unjustified accusations" of the patient. For example, the offender may say defensively, "You always accuse me of criticizing you. I didn't say a damn thing." Even if an argument does not develop, the patient may withdraw, further exacerbating his or her depressive feelings.

Several interventions may be helpful for the overly sensitive individual and his or her partner. The first is to teach the patient to evaluate the validity of the assumption that he or she has been rejected or criticized. Appropriate action can then be taken, depending on the outcome of this assessment (see Chapter 6). The easiest way to determine if feelings of rejection are warranted is to discuss them with the offender. To introduce the topic, patients can use the following fill-in-the-blank statement: "When you said/did _____ on _____ [specify time] _____, it made me feel _____." Sometimes, it is best simply to ask: "When you said/did _____ on _____ [specify time] _____, did you mean _____ [assumption of rejection] _____?"

> Ms. Salinas and two coworkers had lunch together on Wednesday. Ms. Cain had not been asked to go with them; she had been invited on other occasions, though she rarely accepted these invitations. When she saw the three ladies laughing as they entered the office after lunch, Ms. Cain felt left out, rejected, and saddened. Her therapist had instructed her to discuss her feelings of rejection with the suspected "offender" as a first step in coping with the lingering hurt that often followed these events. Following this instruction, Ms. Cain said to Ms. Salinas, "When I saw you and the other two ladies return from lunch today, I really felt left out. Are you mad at me or something? Is that why you didn't invite me?" Ms. Salinas apologized for leaving Ms. Cain out and added that it was not the group's intention to exclude Ms. Cain, nor was she angry with her. The group had planned to eat at a restaurant that they knew Ms. Cain disliked, so she was not included. Ms. Cain reluctantly accepted the apology and explanation. After a period of mild sadness, she was able to put the event behind her.

In a second intervention for coping with interpersonal sensitivity, the therapist may teach the offender to recognize when the patient is feeling hurt and to respond by attempting to understand the situation from the patient's perspective. Rather than explaining or defending his or her position, the offender can express sympathy for the patient's hurt. For example, a partner may say, "I'm sorry that your feelings are hurt. That isn't what I intended." Another effective response is to focus on the patient's emotional state; for example, "I know that when you are having a bad day you get your feelings hurt easily. I'm sorry if I accidentally hurt your feelings." For offenders inclined to respond to the patient in anger or frustration, these responses take a considerable amount of coaching.

Pessimistic View of Self, Others, and the Future

When depressed and, perhaps to some extent, when euthymic, bipolar disorder patients see the world through blue, cloudy, and myopic lenses. They feel hopeless about their prospects for a happy life, disheartened by what they see as a slim chance for improvement in their relationships (and/or partner), and unhappy with their current status, yet too immobilized by pessimism to consider, let alone attempt, change. When a pessimist and an optimist meet to work out the problems of daily life, plan for the future, or attempt to have fun, their fundamentally different views of the world can create tension and conflict.

Research on the negative views of patients and their spouses suggests that the pessimism of the patient is not contagious (Prager & Basco, 1995). That is, the dysfunctional or negative attitudes, low self-esteem, and feelings of hopelessness reported by depressed patients are not reported by their spouses any more often than they are reported by individuals who have never suffered from depression. It is helpful for both the patient and his or her significant other to learn to recognize when their differences in perspective are influencing their interaction. The patient can then evaluate the validity of his or her pessimistic views by using cognitive restructuring interventions (see Chapter 6). The partner can alter his or her responses to the patient by discontinuing the discussion before it worsens or, with considerable guidance, by attempting very carefully to help the patient examine his or her thinking for potential distortions.

Brett and Patty Smythe had been married for 10 years. Despite treatment, Mrs. Smythe had been depressed for much of their married life. She was well educated, very attractive, creative, and talented. When her depression remitted, she had a lovely sense of humor. She viewed herself very differently from the way that others viewed her. She was exquisitely aware of her own imperfections, faults, and errors. She believed that the praise received from her husband was patronizing and insincere. She easily overlooked the positive features of her relationships, but had a highly sensitive radar that identified and recorded most negative events.

Mr. Smythe, a man who prided himself on his analytical thinking, attempted to explain to his wife how her pessimistic views of herself, of him, and of their future together had no logical basis. He pointed out her strengths, his love for her, and their potential for happiness. However, her pessimism was not only unresponsive to his attempts to reason with her, but also angered her because she thought that her husband lacked a true appreciation of her feelings. Despite his failure to convince her that she was a wonderful, intelligent, creative person, he continued to use analytical reasoning in his battle against her negativity. As the process continued, tension, frustration, and distance between them increased.

It can be very frustrating for the spouses of depressed patients to cope with their seemingly illogically negative outlook. Attempts at "talking them out of" their negativity generally fail and may even worsen the conflict. The pessimistic spouse accuses the optimistic spouse of overlooking problems, while the optimistic spouse accuses the pessimistic spouse of finding problems where none exist. It takes tolerance, commitment, and love to stay married in these situations.

Paranoia

One of the more severe symptoms of mania and, occasionally, of depression is paranoia. In the early stages of paranoia, the patient may appear overly sensitive or suspicious of others. Furthermore, the onset of paranoia feeds the process by which patients presume that others have malevolent intentions. Not all bipolar disorder patients experience paranoia as part of their symptom picture, however.

Mr. Patterson knew that one of the symptoms of his mania was paranoia. He often imagined people at work talking about him behind his back and even colluding against him. While he knew that he could be overly sensitive to things at times, several "real" things had happened at work that could be construed as attempts to exclude him. For example, he had not been invited to attend several important policy-forming meetings at his company, even though they directly affected his department. People often talked and laughed in groups that quickly quieted and dispersed when he approached them. Someone heard a rumor that several management positions were about to be eliminated, and Mr. Patterson had less seniority than did other managers in the plant. When his superiors approached him to discuss productivity problems in his department, he was openly defensive.

At home, Mr. Patterson was tense. He told his wife about the conspiracy to get rid of him at work. She was well acquainted with his paranoia and tried to help him reason through the events of the day. He sensed that she did not believe him and convinced himself that she was against him as well. An argument quickly ensued. His wife encouraged him to get a good night's sleep and agreed to talk more about the problem in the morning.

The paranoia subsided after Mr. Patterson had sufficient sleep, and he was able to talk with his employers to determine if his job was in jeopardy. Feedback that his position at work was secure allowed him to look at his reaction more objectively and recognize that his suspiciousness, coupled with real events, had contributed to his distress.

The paranoia affected his interaction with people at work. Perhaps others sensed his irritability and tension, and they may have avoided him to escape his sarcasm and short temper. Having experienced his paranoia several times before, his wife had lost her ability to be sympathetic, especially when there was reason to believe he was overreacting to coincidental circumstances. Mr. Patterson was correct in his assumption that his wife was unempathetic. Until he was able to gain some distance from the problem, however, he was unable to examine his contribution to the uncomfortable interpersonal events.

Irritability

Like paranoia, irritability can be a symptom of either depression or mania. It can accompany paranoia, oversensitivity, or a pessimistic view of the world, but it can also exist independently of other symptoms. Irritability affects the way messages are sent to others and colors the interpretation of messages received from others. It can make a person quick to anger, can precipitate arguments, and can lead to intense anxiety or agitation. No matter how "reasonable" or "careful" a spouse may believe that he or she is being, interacting with an irritable partner can be like walking through a mine field; even stepping lightly, the spouse never knows when the next explosion will occur. While irritability can affect many individuals, regardless of their psychiatric history, it is particularly troublesome for those experiencing depression or mania.

Mrs. Westin had a history of severe depression with bouts of irritability. During these episodes, she was edgy and quick to anger. In fact, she sometimes became so intensely angry that she said and did things that she later regretted, even physically assaulting her husband. Her husband, a generally nonaggressive individual, occasionally "restrained" her in self-defense to minimize injury to himself. On one of these occasions, his "restraint" broke her arm.

The extent to which Mrs. Westin could inhibit her irritability and aggressive behavior was not always clear. On occasion, her husband responded to her irritability with reason. The more he used reason, however, the more irritable she became. It was as if his insistence on reason fueled the fire of her irrationality. Mrs. Westin knew that her irritability was a symptom of her illness and that this emotional state distorted her perception of reality. He responded to each of her angry statements by attempting to change her view. He could not; instead, he became more angry and frustrated, which, in turn, contributed to the downward spiral of conflict.

In this situation, rather than engage an irritable person in a discussion or argument about the validity of their statements, it is preferable to not respond. One useful strategy is to refuse to fight and then leave the scene for some period of time. This gives the irritable person time alone to cool off and regain some control. Another strategy that may be used in conjunction with the first is to express empathy for the person's hurt or angry feelings and to apologize for contributing to the person's troubles. For example, "I'm sorry that your feelings were hurt by my statement earlier. I can understand how it would make you angry to be left out, but I did not intend to hurt you." Giving an apology after being unjustly criticized is very difficult, but it can prevent an altercation with the irritable person. A third strategy is to draw the patient's attention to the irritability before it reaches a high level and to talk about whether it is a warning signal of the onset of a depressive or manic episode. Suggesting to the patient that he or she call the doctor to discuss the irritability can do more to address the "real problem" than arguing.

Pressured Speech

Mr. Alegro talked his wife's ear off when he was hypomanic. When she came home after a long day at work, she was preoccupied with tending to the children, cooking dinner, or trying to unwind. Mr. Alegro wanted to tell her about all the things that happened during work that day. At times, he felt a strong "need" to talk that he just could not inhibit, no matter how hard he tried. "I just need to talk to someone or I'll burst." Mr. Alegro's wife needed quiet time, not an incessant monologue of stories, jokes, plans, or observations. This conflict of needs caused her to withdraw from him, diminished her tolerance, and increased her own irritability. She did not notice the pattern of symptoms that began with his pressured speech and developed into mania. Instead, she tried to ignore him.

Although generally a symptom of hypomania or mania, pressured speech or increased talkativeness can occur outside an episode of illness. This talkativeness can be socially adaptive in that it facilitates entry into new social groups, reduces social anxiety, and is often enjoyable to or even envied by others. At home, it may be less valued, burdening other family members.

Mr. and Mrs. Bronson made an agreement that he would listen to her talk for at least 30 minutes if she would give him time after work to unwind and relax so that he could be more receptive to her.

This type of quid pro quo agreement provides a way for couples to cope with their competing needs and can be applied to other types of relationship conflicts.

Cognitive Impairment

Changes in a patient's cognitive functioning can make it difficult for him or her to process information, formulate thoughts, or make decisions. Such a cognitive impairment may be evident in decreased concentration, mental confusion, indecisiveness, sensory overload, distractibility, and flight of ideas. These symptoms may accompany depression, mania, or hypomania and may interfere with the patient's ability to operate on the job, at home, or in social situations.

Mr. Macias found that, when his thoughts were "jumbled," he could not think clearly. He made poor decisions that he later regretted, interpreted the actions of others incorrectly, and forgot what he was doing or what he had to do. To others, he appeared to be a "scatterbrain." His wife and his boss became irritated with him on such occasions. Mr. Macias's attempts to cope with a variety of problems (e.g., marital problems, job problems, decisions about moving, preparation for vacation or holidays, plans to begin weight loss or exercise) seemed to exacerbate his mental confusion. He knew that cloudy thinking might indicate a symptom breakthrough and that he must carefully monitor his symptoms to avert an early relapse of depression or mania.

Patients can be taught to use the symptoms of cognitive impairment as cues that the onset of an episode of depression or mania may be imminent. They should watch for other symptoms and consult their clinician. In the meantime, it is best to encourage patients who are experiencing a cognitive impairment to avoid making any important life decisions and to reduce the number of problems that they are trying to cope with until their cognitive functioning improves.

It is difficult to know whether it is the mental confusion that interferes with normal coping abilities or if it is caused by trying to deal with too many issues simultaneously. In either case, reducing stimulation may help to prevent the psychosocial sequence from developing and may reduce the severity of the cognitive impairment.

DIMENSIONS OF COMMUNICATION

Even without the complexities of bipolar disorder, communication with others can be very complicated and often fails. One reason is that each message is actually made up of several different levels of messages that are communicated simultaneously. These levels can be thought of as dimensions of communication. The verbal dimension consists of the words that are said. For example, "Oh, I see you cleaned the kitchen." Communication can become problematic when the words imply more than the message sender is saying directly: "Oh, I see you *finally* cleaned the kitchen." The addition of one simple word can turn a neutral comment or an acknowledgment of a positive event into an implied criticism of the times that the individual had not cleaned the kitchen.

The nonverbal dimension of communication includes the tone of voice in which the message is conveyed (e.g., angry, pleasant, sarcastic), as well as the message sender's facial expression (e.g., smiling, frowning), body posture (e.g., arms crossed), volume of speech (e.g., loud, soft), rate of speech (e.g., fast, slow, frequent pauses), and the timing of the message (e.g., during an argument, as soon as the message sender walks into the house). A husband who comes home from work and, with a sarcastic tone, a smirk on his face, and his hands on his hips, says to his depressed wife, "Oh . . . (*with surprise in his voice and followed by a long pause*), I see you finally cleaned the kitchen," sends one message. A mother who comes home from work and, with a pleasant tone, a smile, and a pat on her child's shoulder, says, "Oh, I see you cleaned the kitchen," sends a very different message—even though she uses nearly the same words.

The third dimension of communication, content, involves not just the choice of words, but the general idea that is being conveyed in a message. The husband, for example, sends a message that says he cannot believe she has done something good; that he perceives her generally as a failure; and that he is, therefore, surprised that she cleaned the kitchen. In her message to her child, however, the mother is acknowledging that her child has done something to be appreciated and that the mother is very pleased.

The relationship value of the message, the fourth dimension of communication, is generally conveyed through the message sender's choice of words and nonverbal behaviors. This dimension of the message indicates the way in which the sender views his or her relationship to the receiver. For example, when teachers give information to a class of students, they are communicating that they are in charge, know more than the students, and expect the students to behave with respect. Messages sent from employer to employee, physician to patient, and parent to child may have a similar relationship value. Although the relationship message communicates something about the status of the sender and receiver(s) as perceived by the sender, this perception may not reflect the true status differences. For example, the sarcastic husband's message suggests that he sees himself as superior to her, when they may actually be more equal than his tone suggests.

The fifth dimension of communication is the consistency between the intended message and the received message. The intended message is what the sender wants to communicate to another person. Although the verbal message that is sent may be accurate, the nonverbal information sent along with the words may alter the meaning in a way that makes the received message different from the intended message. The husband's intended message, for example, may have been to acknowledge his wife's accomplishments, perhaps because her psychiatrist said that it is important for him to notice and acknowledge her positive activities and to give her credit for taking small steps toward recovery. The message that she received, however, was that her husband is disgusted with her. In addition, she received the nonverbal message that he thinks she is merely doing what she should have done long ago. Therefore, the message did not make her feel that she is taking positive steps toward recovery, but that she is merely digging herself out of the deep hole of previous failures.

Not only can a sender convey much more than just words, but also the receiver can alter messages by "reading in" more than the sender is conveying. Sometimes a listener hears a different nonverbal tone or relationship message in a speaker's voice than actually occurred or hears the negative part of a message while "not hearing" the positive part. For example, a wife may kiss her husband and ask to hold hands while they watch television together. In these nonverbal and verbal messages, the husband hears, "She wants to have sex. She doesn't care that I've had a bad day, I'm tired, and I need to sleep. She's going to get her feelings hurt or be mad if I say no. This is so unfair."

Communication problems can result from the absence of information from any of these dimensions. For example, when one spouse says "I love you" and the other says nothing, the first may perceive the absence of a response as rejection. Failing to reciprocate nonverbal messages (e.g., not returning a smile or not responding to another person's attempt to make eye contact) can also cause tension between people.

When the various dimensions of a message are inconsistent with one another, the receiver may become confused. He or she usually "believes" the component of the message that is the most powerful or that resonates best with his or her internal mood state. A parent who is upset with a teenager for staying out too late may yell angrily (nonverbal message), "Can't you see that we love you and don't want you to get hurt?" (verbal message). The teenager is likely to hear the nonverbal message of anger, rather than the verbal message of love and concern. If a physician says to a patient in a compassionate tone, "Just call me if you have any problems" (verbal message), but delays returning the patient's call (nonverbal messages), the patient is likely to hear insincerity, lack of concern, or rejection.

DIAGNOSIS OF COMMUNICATION DIFFICULTIES

Context

The first step in evaluating a patient's communication difficulties is to identify the context in which communication problems occur. With whom does the patient have difficulties communicating, under what circumstances, how often, how predictably, and to what degree does it upset the patient? Some individuals find it difficult to communicate effectively at home, at work, and on social occasions. It is not unusual, however, for a patient to be an eloquent or effective communicator with friends, coworkers, and strangers, but to have considerable difficulty in talking to his or her spouse.

It is also common for people to be able to communicate well about some topics, but not others. For example, a couple may have no difficulty in discussing the children, work, finances, or current events, but may see their communication deteriorate or explode into an argument when the topic of love, affection, or sex is raised.

Skill Deficit versus Performance Deficit

In diagnosing the communication difficulty of an individual or couple, it is important to determine whether the difficulty arises from a skill deficit or a performance deficit. A skill deficit implies a lack of the basic speaking, listening, and/or problem-solving skills necessary to communicate effectively. A person who has a skill deficit is likely to have trouble communicating with several individuals, especially in stressful situations, such as those involving problems in a relationship or at work. In this case, the intervention should include teaching the individual some basic communication skills.

Individuals who communicate effectively, at least under some circumstances and/or with some individuals, already possess basic communication skills. Environmental contingencies or stimuli prevent these individuals from making use of their existing communication skills. The most commonly observed example of such a performance deficit is an argument between two verbally skilled individuals, often a husband and wife, whose emotional state (often frustration or anger) causes them to "forget" to use their skill and leads them to resort to more primitive attack and defend behaviors, such as blaming, name-calling, or sarcasm. It is not necessary to teach these individuals basic communication skills, but rather to help them identify the factors that interfere with their ability to communicate effectively. In identifying these factors, it is helpful to ask the following questions:

- Are there predictable situations in which their communication is less effective?
- Is there something that one person says that predictably elicits a strong emotional reaction in the other?
- Are there certain topics of discussion that regress into arguments?

The goal is to develop new coping strategies for the situations identified as problematic in order to diminish or eliminate the obstacles to good communication.

Manifestations of Communication Problems

The most common manifestation of communication difficulties is conflict. It can range in intensity from disagreement, petty sarcasm, or "dirty looks" to serious verbal aggression. Occasionally, conflict escalates into character assassinations, humiliation of others, and threats of rejection or physical harm. At its extreme, conflict can include physical violence. The less severe forms of physical violence, such as throwing objects, breaking things, and pushing or shoving others, are common in family arguments. A less frequent, but more serious, problem is physical assault, such as slapping, hitting, biting, kicking, or using a weapon. The intervention for the management of verbally or physically aggressive conflict involves the diffusion of anger and training in problem-solving skills.

Conflict avoidance is also a manifestation of communication difficulty. In this case, individuals fail to communicate with each other about important and often problematic issues. These individuals are generally uncomfortable with confrontation and/or fearful of conflict. Teaching communication skills to conflict-avoidant individuals can be more difficult than working with those who have a more verbally aggressive style. The conflict-avoidant person must first be willing to initiate discussion and, therefore, risk conflict. The interventions for conflict avoidance are (1) to deal with the concerns that maintain the avoidance; (2) to teach assertiveness and communication skills so that patients know how to discuss problems and to cope with anger, both their own and that of others; and (3) to provide opportunities for repeated practice with these skills. Practice in discussing difficult topics can be framed as an experiment to test the patient's hypothesis that discussing problems can be hurtful.

ASSESSMENT OF COMMUNICATION SKILL

A structured evaluation of the individual's or couples' communication problems before any attempt is made to address those problems serves two functions. First, it guides the therapist in the decision to include communication training in the treatment plan. Second, a baseline communication assessment provides an objective standard against which to compare posttreatment change. Such a standard is useful for the clinician and the patient to monitor the progress of therapy and to determine if changes in the treatment plan are needed, as subtle changes in communication behavior over a long period of time may be difficult to detect.

The two most commonly used methods for evaluating communication problems are self-report measures and direct observation. The Marital Satisfaction Inventory (MSI; Snyder, 1979) is a 10-subscale self-report measure of satisfaction in various areas of marriage, for example, recreation or sexual relations. Husbands and wives independently rate each of 280 statements as true or false for their relationship at present; then their scores are compared. Higher scores indicate greater dissatisfaction in this area of the marriage.

The MSI contains two communication satisfaction subscales. The Problem-Solving Communication (PSC) subscale measures the degree to which the respondents are satisfied with the way in which they solve problems through discussion. It includes statements such as "Minor disagreements with my spouse often end up in big arguments" and "My spouse seems committed to settling our differences." The Affective Communication (AFC) subscale measures the degree to which each individual is satisfied with his or her partner's expression of feelings, affection, and caring; empathy and understanding from the partner; and self-disclosure in the relationship. Some examples of items on this subscale are "There is a great deal of love and affection expressed in our marriage" and "Sometimes my spouse just can't understand the way I feel."

Evaluating communication problems from direct observation can be as simple as casually watching the way in which the parties interact in the therapist's office or as sophisticated as the microanalysis of verbal and nonverbal behaviors.

Many different observations can be made about the interactional style of patients, couples, or the clinician–patient dyad. The dimensions of communication discussed earlier in this chapter can be assessed by looking at the individual statements made by each person or by the overall flow of the discussion. Specifically, the nonverbal messages can provide a wealth of information about the speakers. For example, it is possible to make some judgment about the status of each person with respect to the other(s). To make this assessment the questions to consider include the following: Does one person appear to have more control over the interaction, are the participants of equal status, and does one defer to the other?

The speakers' choices of words and nonverbal messages can also provide information about the emotional tone of the interaction. Simply, emotional tone can be categorized as positive, negative, or neutral, or it can be more qualitatively defined as angry, loving, collegial, tense, productive, conflictual, etc. Verbal messages can provide some clues about the communication skill of the speakers. Do they express themselves well? Can they make themselves understood? Are their thoughts organized?

It is also possible to make observations about the degree to which there is consistency between the messages that the speaker intended to send and the information that the listener received. Inconsistencies would be evidenced in an escalation of anger, misinterpretations of messages, defensiveness by the sender, and confusion by either party.

These casual observations about the communication process can be made by observing others interacting, observing oneself in relation to others, listening to reports from the patient about interactional events, or assessing the participants' responses to a structured communication task. A variety of communication games or tasks can be assigned. The interaction can be observed by the clinician in the office, from another room through a two-way mirror or video monitor, or at a later date from a videotape of the interaction. If the clinician is observing the interaction of others, it is best that he or she be minimally involved in the interaction. The best method, which is impractical for most clinicians, is to leave the room and observe the participants through a monitor or two-way mirror.

In research on interpersonal communication, semistructured games or tasks are occasionally used to acquire a sample of the interactional behavior of couples or families. These tasks provide enough structure for the interaction to make the situation comparable across many subjects. For individual patients, however, their responses to these standardized tasks may not provide an accurate representation of their day-to-day behavior.

A stimulus task for assessing everyday communication problems should approximate typical real-life scenarios. An interaction that takes place in the clinician's office is not likely to be as natural as those that take place at home. However, this assessment can provide some clues about what the patient is capable of under relatively neutral conditions (i.e., without interruptions, with constraints on use of inappropriate language or actions, and with focus on a specific topic). This type of assessment will help the clinician to determine if the patient or the couple has a communication skill deficit or a performance deficit. If the patient or couple does well at this task, but has difficulty at home, it is likely that they have a performance deficit. In this case, the clinician's job is to determine what factors interfere with their ability to communicate effectively.

If the patient or couple have difficulty with the communication task, appear disorganized, fail to state the problem clearly, or are unable to make progress toward resolution, it is likely that they have a skill deficit. In this case, the intervention required is training in basic communication and problem-solving skills.

While much can be learned from observing people interact, it is helpful to formalize or structure the evaluation of communication behavior. Many researchers have tried to quantify good and poor communication behaviors. The pioneers in this area (e.g., Gottman, 1979; Hops, Wills, Patterson, & Weiss, 1972) developed elaborate coding systems for categorizing each verbal statement and significant nonverbal behaviors made by couples, family members, or strangers participating in standardized communication tasks. Gottman's (1979) Couple Interaction Scoring System and Hops et al.'s (1972) Marital Interaction Coding System, two of the earliest coding schemes, continue to be used in interactional research today. The categories of behavior in these coding systems include positive statements such as praise or agreements, neutral statements such as definitions of the problems, and negative statements such as blame or insults. A tally of the total number of statements falling into each category and summed across groups of happy couples (presumably good communicators) and unhappy couples (presumably ineffective communicators) allows for the investigation of systematic differences between these groups. From this early research much has been learned about the behaviors that constitute effective communication skill. Communication training, a hallmark of the behavioral approach to marital and family therapy, stems in part from this early research.

Microanalytic coding schemes, while important in research, are not practical for the individual clinician, nor are the summary of individual behaviors easily interpretable for each patient or couple. Several more portable assessment measures have been developed that can be used with individual couples. These include the Communication Skills Test (Floyd & Markman, 1984) and the Communication Rapid Assessment Scale (Joanning, Brewster, & Koval, 1984). These measures, while easier to use, also require special training in communication assessment. The Communication Style Q-set (Stephen & Harrison, 1986) is a card sorting task which assesses interactional "style."

The Clinician Rating of Adult Communication Scale (CRAC; Basco, Birchler, Kalal, Talbott, & Slater, 1991) is a "user-friendly" clinician rating scale developed by clinicians for clinicians. This 20-item scale helps clinicians to structure their assessment of couples' interaction by focusing their attention on verbal and nonverbal behaviors important to good communication and problem solving. The original CRAC (Basco et al., 1991) includes six background information items for clinicians to document their clinical impressions of the couple. The abbreviated version of the CRAC presented in Figure 11.1 consists of only the 14 behavioral items that include involvement in the discussion, clarity of communication, listening skill, verbal aggression, problem solving, and attribution of blame. After watching a 10-minute sample of communication, clinicians rate couples' levels of skill in each of the 14 behaviors and sum the scores for each spouse (both spouses summed provide a total couple score). Each skill is rated as being better (1 point), similar to (2 points), or worse (3 points) than typical couples who present for treatment. The therapist can use this information to determine if communication training is necessary, and, if so, what behaviors should be the focus of training. This structured assessment provides a standard against which posttreatment progress can be compared.

ERRORS IN COMMUNICATION

Communication Filters

Thoughts and feelings filter messages, influencing each of the five dimensions of communication and accounting for discrepancies between the message that the sender intends and the message that the listener actually receives. A communication filter can be a mood, a belief, an attitude, a physical state, or any other thing that influences the way that a person speaks to others and interprets messages from others. When a person is angry, for example, the messages sent can sound harsh, sharp, negative, or sarcastic; anger becomes the filter through which that person sends messages. Similarly, oversensitivity to criticism or rejection can be a filter that distorts messages as the listener receives them; in this case, the sensitive person's filter can magnify a minor negative comment.

Communication filters can be transient, such as a "bad" mood or fatigue, and only temporarily alter communication. They can also be more permanent, such as a belief or an attitude (e.g., "People will take advantage of you if they can" or "Men are superior to women"). Filters

Couple _____ Rater _____ Date _____

From a standardized sample of marital communication (with therapist absent), rate husband and wife separately on each of the following dimensions. In rating these items, consider the average couple presenting for treatment. Rate the present couple as they might compare to that population.

For the purpose of this communication sample the topic of discussion is _____

---

1. Degree of Participation in the Discussion

   Husband   Wife
   ( )   ( )   contributed/participated more in the discussion than the average distressed spouse
   ( )   ( )   contributed/participated as much in the discussion as the average distressed spouse
   ( )   ( )   contributed/participated less in the discussion than the average distressed spouse

2. Communication Defensiveness: overtly defending self against real or imagined attack as in making excuses, denying wrongdoing, or rationalizing

   Husband   Wife
   ( )   ( )   less defensive than the average distressed spouse
   ( )   ( )   as defensive as the average distressed spouse
   ( )   ( )   more defensive than the average distressed spouse

3. Communication Clarity: rater is able to clearly comprehend content level of spouses' messages

   Husband   Wife
   ( )   ( )   conveyed message more directly and clearly than the average distressed spouse
   ( )   ( )   conveyed message as directly and clearly as the average distressed spouse
   ( )   ( )   conveyed message less directly and clearly than the average distressed spouse

4. Listening/Attending Skills: maintained eye contact, acknowledged messages, demonstrated interest

   Husband   Wife
   ( )   ( )   listened/attended better than average distressed spouse
   ( )   ( )   listened/attended as well as the average distressed spouse
   ( )   ( )   listened/attended less than the average distressed spouse

FIGURE 11.1. Clinician Rating of Adult Communication (CRAC).

[*]Top item = 1 point, middle item = 2 points, bottom item = 3 points. [**]Agreement on who is responsible = 1 point (each says that responsibility is shared or both agree that one spouse is to blame), total disagreement = 3 points (e.g., each blames the other), partial agreement = 2 points (e.g., husband says responsibility is shared, wife says it is her fault).

(continued)

5. Communicated Understanding: demonstrated appreciation of and/or empathy for spouse's thoughts/feelings

   Husband   Wife
   ( )   ( )   communicated understanding better than the average distressed couple
   ( )   ( )   communicated understanding as well as the average distressed couple
   ( )   ( )   communicated understanding less than the average distressed couple

6. Quality of Nonverbal Behaviors[*]
   Husband   Wife
   ( )   ( )   generally positive (e.g., eye contact, smile, touch, positive voice)
   ( )   ( )   generally neutral (e.g., neither overtly positive nor negative)
   ( )   ( )   generally negative (e.g., harsh voice tone, arms crossed, little eye contact)

7. Display of Verbal Aggression: blaming, sarcasm, name-calling, criticism, shouting

   Husband   Wife
   ( )   ( )   less verbal aggression than the average distressed spouse
   ( )   ( )   as much verbal aggression as the average distressed spouse
   ( )   ( )   more verbal aggression than the average distressed spouse

Does the couple report history of physical violence when arguing?
   Yes ( )   No ( )

8. Overall Emotional Tone of Discussion[*]
   ( ) generally positive
   ( ) generally neutral
   ( ) generally negative

9. Amount of Agreement between Spouses
   Husband   Wife
   ( )   ( )   agreed with partner more than the average distressed spouse
   ( )   ( )   levels of agreement and disagreement similar to the average distressed spouse
   ( )   ( )   disagreed with partner more than the average distressed spouse
   ( )   ( )   lack of data

10. Effectiveness of Observed Level of Participation in Facilitating Problem Solving
    Husband   Wife
    ( )   ( )   more effective than most distressed spouses in facilitating problem solving

FIGURE 11.1. *cont.*

()   ()   as effective as most distressed spouses in facilitating problem solving

()   ()   less effective than the average distressed spouse in facilitating problem solving

11. Ability to Stay on Original Topic as Specified by the Task[*]

( ) generally stayed with topic throughout the discussion
( ) significant digression by one or both spouses, but eventual return to original topic
( ) failed to focus on original topic or multiple topic changes

12. Closure[*]

( ) reasonable solution(s) verbalized and agreed upon
( ) solution(s) verbalized with no specific agreement or plan of action
( ) no solutions verbalized

13. If Solutions Generated, Should Husband or Wife Change?[**]

Husband Wife

( )   ()   self
( )   ()   both spouses are responsible for change
( )   ()   spouse
( )   ()   no data

14. Attribution of Blame[**]

Husband Wife

( )   ()   this spouse accepted primary responsibility for the problem
( )   ()   responsibility was shared
( )   ()   blame attributed primarily to spouse
( )   ()   blame attributed to outside circumstances or individuals outside of the dyad

can also be specific to communication with particular individuals. For example, a husband and wife who often argue may be on the defensive when speaking to one another. As a result, they can become hypersensitive to perceived attacks, fail to listen to one another, and initiate counterattacks. No one else may feel that these two individuals are defensive or argumentative, because the filters that are influencing their interaction with each other are not present with others outside the home. The intervention for reducing communication filters is to identify their existence and then to factor them in when communicating with others. Practically, this means that when people are "feeling bad" they compensate for this by monitoring their words and nonverbal behaviors when speaking to others. This can mean controlling an angry tone of voice or sarcasm. When listening to others, the "feeling bad" filter can affect how messages are interpreted or received. The listener has to tell himself or herself, "When I'm feeling bad, I'm a lot more sensitive. I get my feelings hurt more easily. Maybe I am reading more into what others are saying because I'm feeling bad."

This process takes time, effort, and the coaching of a therapist. Usually, people are unaware of their communication filters and need others to help them identify and label them correctly.

Incorrect Assumptions

Mrs. Clark complained that her husband was angry with her because she had worked late two nights ago. "It's just not fair. He expects me to work hard all day and still be there to cater to his every need. He has no right to be angry. After all, my earnings helped to buy his new golf clubs. Oh, he claims he's not angry, but I know that look. He's just saving it up to let me have it later. We argued about it all night." The therapist, being uncertain about the reason that Mr. Clark would be so angry, inquired about the interaction. "What did your husband say to you that indicated he was angry at you for working late?" "He didn't have to say a word," she replied. "I could just tell. And besides, he didn't even bother to kiss me when I came in from work." In fact, Mr. Clark had been talking on the telephone with a coworker about a problem on the job just before Mrs. Clark came home. Because he was upset about work, he was frowning and was not very interested in talking when Mrs. Clark came home. Mrs. Clark personalized his nonverbal behavior and assumed that he was angry with her.

Mind reading, a common communication error, stems from the incorrect assumption that, after knowing another person for some time, it is possible to know how that person thinks and feels—sometimes even before that person knows. If another person responds to situations in a consistent fashion, it may be possible to make good guesses about that person's thoughts and feelings, but there is always room for error in guessing. It is true, for example, that Mr. Clark has been angry with his wife in the past when she had worked late, but he was not angry with her at all this time. Her anticipation of his anger prepared her to behave defensively when she returned home. This set the stage for the argument that followed. Clearly, mind reading or making assumptions can produce conflict.

Teaching people to ask questions instead of making assumptions is the key to reducing mind reading. In this example, Mrs. Clark needed to ask her husband, "Are you angry at me?" It is difficult to get people to ask questions. Their assumptions will be correct some of the time. This reinforces the notion that they know others well enough to not have to ask questions. Patients must be convinced that mind reading can create trouble. Practice in asking questions to evaluate the validity of their assumptions can begin the therapy.

Misattributions

Attributions are guesses or explanations about people and situations that help an individual to understand the cause of a given event. Misattributions are erroneous or inaccurate attributions (e.g., "You slammed the door just to irritate me"). A misattribution may not be verbalized, however, so there is no means of evaluating its validity. It feels right to the person holding the attribution and, therefore, in the mind of that person, it is right. As with mind reading, reacting as if the misattribution is correct can lead to misunderstandings, tension, and even arguments.

Some common types of misattributions are certain to cause bad feelings or conflict with others. Most commonly, misattribution of the negative or malicious intentions of others may occur when a person feels that others caused a troublesome situation. Some examples of misattributing intentions are "she wanted to make me late for my appointment" or "he did that just to be spiteful." The person who makes this type of assumption often does not discuss it openly with the source, but instead may share these thoughts with others, keep them to himself or herself while silently fuming, or act them out in an angry countermove.

The source of the problem can also be misattributed. Blaming others for things that they may not have done generally precipitates an attack-and-defend interaction that resembles a tennis match, where each person sends blame across the net and the receiver defends against it. The defense can take the form of a rational explanation or justification of a particular position, or it can take the form of a counterattack. For example, "You made me late for my appointment, and I looked like an idiot walking in after the meeting started" (blame). "I did not make you late; you were the one who couldn't find your keys" (explanation). "That's because you moved them" (blame). "I had to move them; they were in the middle of the dinner table" (justification). "Well, if you were a better housekeeper, there would be a clear space on the counter near the door where I could put my keys" (counterattack). "Well, if you weren't so cheap, we could hire a housekeeper . . . , etc." (counterattack).

The presumption of the deliberateness or purposefulness of the actions of others is another misattribution that can lead to conflict. An extreme example is paranoia. Patients with paranoia assume that others have malicious intentions to be hurtful. In everyday interaction, it is not unusual for these patients to assume that others purposefully acted to produce a negative outcome, when, in fact, there may be no evidence to support this assumption. "You did that on purpose." "No, I didn't. It was an accident." "I don't believe you."

The intervention for correcting misattributions is the same as that for correcting negative automatic thoughts (see Chapter 6). First, misattributions are identified. Second, their validity is evaluated by gathering evidence for and against the attribution. An alternative approach is to generate other explanations for the event for which there may be some evidence. If the therapist is working with a couple for whom misattribution is a common communication problem, the misattribution can be discussed in a way that allows the accused person to explain his or her position without counterattacking the partner.

Failure to See the Reciprocity of Behavior

When examining how a problem has evolved, how an argument started, or why a problem continues despite attempts at discussion and resolution, it is easy to see how *others* are responsible. Most interpersonal problems, however, result from the actions of two or more individuals. This is especially true for communication problems. Each statement made by an individual is both a response and a stimulus for the next response, which, in turn, is a stimulus for the next response, and so on. This is called reciprocity.

Although most people would agree with the basic concept of reciprocity if it were brought to their attention, few people, even very skilled people, are aware of it when they are in the middle of an interaction that is going badly. If individuals could recognize their own contribution to poor communication, they could alter their responses so as to change the course of the interaction. For example, if the husband and wife described earlier knew that each defensive counterattack was escalating their anger and frustration, one or both could take another direction that might lead to a resolution of the conflict.

HELPING PATIENTS TO IMPROVE
THEIR COMMUNICATION

Communication problems generally occur between at least two individuals, and it is easier for a therapist to help resolve such problems if both parties are present. This is not always possible or appropriate, however. In some cases, the second party is a boss, someone who lives a great distance away, or someone the patient is not likely to see again.

When it is possible and appropriate for a therapist to work with both parties in helping to resolve communication problems, the role of the therapist is similar to that of a referee. (It may be useful to come to the session equipped with a whistle and a striped shirt.) The therapist's job is to help the two participants follow the rules of the communication game and play fairly. If things get out of hand, the therapist blows the whistle, calls a time-out, and redirects the interaction by informing each player of the type of foul that he or she committed and the way to proceed differently.

Playing the Communication Game

Before the communication game starts, the therapist may find it helpful to assume the role of coach. The therapist teaches the players the basic rules, demonstrates each behavior, has them practice in and between sessions, watches them play, and provides feedback on ways that they can improve their skills.

Rules of the Communication Game

In normal daily interaction, it is not usually necessary to impose any structure on communication. Structure is useful when communication is ineffective or exacerbates relationship difficulties, however. When a discussion of potentially conflictual issues approaches, it is useful to review the basic rules of the communication game as listed in the following:

- *Be calm.* It is counterproductive to attempt to discuss difficult issues when angry or stressed in any way. An angry person may let emotions dictate the choice of words and the solutions offered. Solutions that seem reasonable in the heat of anger may prove inappropriate when examined later. It is better to wait until the emotion subsides than to risk making bad decisions.
- *Be organized.* It is best to approach the discussion of troublesome issues after having taken the time to think through what the problem is and what must happen in order to resolve it. Furthermore, it is useful to have a plan for discussing the issue.
- *Be specific.* Global complaints (e.g., "I'm not happy," "You're irresponsible," "I just can't take this anymore") cannot be easily resolved. It is necessary to specify the action, event, or process that is problematic: What does it look like? How would I know it was happening if I were watching you? What causes the discomfort?
- *Be clear.* Beating around the bush or speaking in vague terms leaves much room for misinterpretation of the message. It may appear that the intended message was received, but the message may not have been received accurately.
- *Be a good listener.* The best way to be heard is to be a respectful listener. Attentive listening without interrupting is important. The

listener should not merely use the other person's talking time as an opportunity to prepare a response (or defense).

- *Be flexible.* The resolution of problems between individuals requires give and take. Although a plan to resolve the problems may have been developed before the actual discussion began, it is important to consider others' ideas before selecting a solution. Moreover, others are likely to have a different view of the problem, and all participants should approach the discussion as if the others' perspective is as valid as their own.

- *Be creative.* In generating a solution to a specific problem, it is useful to look beyond strategies used in the past, to be imaginative, and to try out new plans. If they do not work, another method can be used.

- *Keep it simple.* Those with communication difficulties should solve one problem at a time. When discussing a problem, they should describe it as simply as possible. If the conversation begins to digress into other areas, stop and redirect the conversation back to the original topic.

Communication Game Strategy

The first step in the communication game is to prepare for the discussion. Each person should prepare a clear definition of the problem and a list of who is affected by it and in what way each person is affected. Statements of the problem that do not criticize or blame others are most constructive. For example, an objective statement such as, "The problem is that our bills aren't getting paid on time, and I'm worried that our utilities may be turned off" is more effective than a blaming statement such as, "You are being totally irresponsible. Don't you care about anything but yourself? You said you'd pay the bills, and you haven't even bothered to touch them. You won't be happy until the electric company turns off our electricity."

As part of the preparation for discussion, it is also useful for each party to consider what actions may be necessary to solve the problem and to generate a list of potential solutions. Timing is important in successful communication, and the discussion should be scheduled at a time that is convenient for all parties. As a final preparatory step, each party should take time to be in a calm emotional state before beginning the discussion of troublesome issues.

The first goal in the problem-solving discussion is to define the problem. Each party may have a different definition of the problem and should have an opportunity to give his or her perspective. The clinician can help the participants to generate a mutually agreeable definition of the nature of the problem. It is essential that there be agreement on the definition of the problem before resolution is attempted.

The second goal of the discussion is to select a solution to the problem. The participants may begin this process by simply listing all possible solutions to the problem without stopping to evaluate the feasibility of each. After eliminating from the list those solutions that are unlikely to resolve the problem, the parties should evaluate the probability of success, the practicality, and the acceptability of the remaining suggestions. The best solutions are those that require action from all parties involved. For example, "I'll pay the bills on time, if you will remind me when it is time to pay them." The solution chosen must specify (1) who will take action, (2) what that action will be, and (3) when the action is to be accomplished.

It is helpful to specify a means for evaluating the success of the intervention. That is, how will the parties know if the solution was effective? It is also helpful to set a time to evaluate the success of the intervention. For example, "Let's try this out for the next 2 months to see if it works."

Overcoming Communication Failure

The most common source of disruption in communication is emotion. As discussed earlier, intense emotion such as sadness, frustration, or anger can influence the way in which information is conveyed and received. If any person's emotional level becomes uncomfortable or appears to interfere with the interaction, the discussion should stop until the intensity of the emotion has substantially decreased. It is essential that a plan be made to resume the discussion at a specified time. To stop the interaction, the individual can say, "I'm getting too upset to talk about this. Let's stop and talk about it again after dinner." Another way to stop the interaction is to talk about the communication process itself. "This isn't going the way I hoped it would. We're getting angrier instead of working out the problem. Let's stop for now and try it again later."

It may be possible to save the discussion by following the communication rules in a structured way. A "cheat sheet" or list of problem-solving steps can provide this kind of structure. If the discussion continues to flounder, it may be helpful for the parties to write down the information that they want to communicate to each other. For example, it may be helpful for each to write down a definition of the problem, as well as a list of potential solutions.

If it becomes clear that the parties cannot resolve an issue through discussion, it may be necessary to bring in a third party, such as the therapist. The mediator should not be someone who is deeply involved in the problem, a family member who is likely to "take sides" (e.g., the mother-in-law), or someone who may be negatively affected by the process of discussion (e.g., a child). It may be helpful if each party talked individually with the therapist to gain assistance in defining the problem or in generating solutions.

OTHER COMMON RELATIONSHIP PROBLEMS OF BIPOLAR PATIENTS

Selective Monitoring of Negative Events

It is not unusual for people in unhappy relationships to be acutely aware of every error committed by their partner. Similarly, depressed persons seem to attend to negative events selectively, "missing" more positive events. Depressed individuals in troubled relationships may report with absolute certainty that "nothing good" has happened in their relationships lately. To determine if this is true, the clinician may instruct the couple to keep a log of every positive thing each partner does. This exercise broadens the negative focus of both partners to include the tracking of positive interactions. A more balanced report on events allows the clinician to determine whether there is a perceptual inaccuracy or an actual imbalance in the number of positive and negative events in the marriage that needs attention.

Decreased or Increased Sex Drive

Depending on the intensity of the change in the sexual interest of the patient and the interest and drive of the partner, fluctuations in libido can place stress on relationships. The stress caused by decreased interest, which is more common in depression, differs from that caused by increased interest, which is more common in mania. Decreased sexual interest is generally accompanied by a reduced energy level, a lack of motivation, and a blunted ability to enjoy activities in general. For the partner, the patient's decreased libido can take on other meanings about the relationship, for example, that the patient no longer finds the partner attractive, is no longer in love with the partner, or must be having an affair with someone else.

In counseling couples where sexual drive has diminished, it is useful to ask each partner what he or she believes this shift in interest means. Often, the intervention most helpful to the couple is to provide them with an alternative and less damning reason for the diminished sexual interest. This can be accomplished by educating both partners about the common symptoms of depression and the way in which these symptoms interfere with sexual intimacy.

Increased sexual drive is particularly problematic if the patient is in a monogamous relationship, but impulsively becomes sexually involved with others. The patient may never disclose his or her sexual promiscuity to the partner. If the partner finds out, however, it is often very difficult for him or her to accept and forgive such behavior as merely a symptom of the illness. In these cases, the couple may require counseling to resolve this issue and develop a plan for preventing its future occurrence.

Unrealistic Expectations for the Relationship

When two people enter a relationship, they generally have specific expectations for each other and for the relationship. Most expectations are unspoken and may even be outside the individuals' conscious awareness. They originate in what the individuals observed, learned, and imagined as they became adults. Some people expect to duplicate what they observed at home; others expect to do just the opposite in an attempt to have a lifestyle different from the one that they experienced as children.

If two people marry before the onset of the first episode of depression or mania, they have no way of knowing how the disorder will affect their lives. Old expectations may no longer be achievable. The spouses of patients describe feeling compassionate and concerned for their partner, while simultaneously feeling angry and "tricked" because the marriage they now have is not the one that they anticipated in the beginning. Spouses of bipolar disorder patients understand that their mates are ill and feel obligated to stand by them despite the hardships. Some never know that their spouses have an illness, however, because the problems were so great that the marriage ended before a diagnosis was made.

Denial of the severity or recurrent nature of the illness by the patient and the spouse may prevent them from adjusting their expectations for the behavior of the spouse and for the stability of the marriage.

Mrs. Okuma thought that she could manage the children, her job, and her many other civic and family responsibilities despite recurrent depressions. She assumed responsibilities with the same vigor that she had shown before the onset of the disorder. She took on more than she could handle, felt guilty and angry with herself for not being able to complete all tasks to perfection, and became immobilized.

In contrast, Mrs. Iinuma set limits on the amount of work that she accepted, making adjustments to fit her energy, interest, and concentration levels. Her husband, however, had not adjusted his expectations of her and communicated with negative nonverbal behavior that he was disappointed when she failed to complete household tasks, prepare meals, or put in a sufficient number of hours on the job. She felt torn between trying to please him and trying to take care of herself.

In either scenario, it may be useful for the clinician to meet with both partners to renegotiate a relationship contract in which each person spells out what he or she expects from the other and is willing to do to make the marriage work. As with any contract, it is important to define the terms clearly so that both partners know what is expected of them and what they can expect of their partner.

CHAPTER SUMMARY

Some of the more common psychosocial problems experienced by people with bipolar disorder are interpersonal in nature. Getting along with others can be difficult, particularly when depression and mania interfere.

Negative thinking or dysfunctional attitudes or beliefs can greatly affect both mood and actions. When interacting with others, the problem is compounded as each person may make negative assumptions or have unrealistic expectations of the other. Usually, these negative beliefs are not discussed but are acted upon, thereby leading to impaired communication and open conflict.

This chapter reviews communication difficulties and other relationship problems that may be encountered by patients. Guidelines for the evaluation of communication weakness and for improving communication skill are provided.

TWELVE

Putting It All Together

SEQUENCE OF SESSIONS

In this final chapter we discuss how to put the intervention together. In most cases, depending on the symptom status of the patient, you will be able to proceed through sessions 1–20 in the sequence we prescribe. In some cases, the presentation of the patient will force the therapist to alter the sequence of the intervention, for example, when emergencies occur or when the patient presents with a particular issue or symptom that would best be addressed by an intervention covered in a later chapter or session. In this case, it makes more sense clinically to jump ahead a bit to take advantage of a good learning opportunity and then return to the original sequence.

If it is necessary to deviate from the designated sequence to address a crisis, the problem should be addressed from a cognitive-behavioral perspective, for example, explaining the problem in terms of the model when it applies. There are times when it will obviously not apply directly, for example, when the patient experiences a severe medication side effect. In this case, it is not appropriate to try to talk the patient out of his or her side effect, nor to suggest that it is the result of dysfunctional cognitions. However, the CBT model can explain the fear or frustration resulting from the side effect, desires to discontinue the medications, and other cognitive, affective, or behavioral outcomes precipitated by the event of having a side effect.

It is likely that for some sessions or interventions, it will take longer than the number of sessions recommended to adequately teach the intervention. Use more sessions if needed. It is time well spent if it helps the patient to better understand the purpose of the intervention, the proper way to execute the intervention, or how and when to apply the intervention in their attempt to control or prevent symptoms. If after two or three additional sessions the patient still does not understand or cannot apply the CBT strategy, it may be better to skip it and go on to the next intervention. Return to the topic when possible or substitute another CBT intervention with the same purpose.

Only a selected subset of cognitive-behavioral techniques are presented in this treatment manual. Experienced cognitive therapists will know other techniques that may be as helpful or more helpful to a given patient. The therapist drives this intervention and therefore should always use his or her best clinical judgment in introducing additional CBT techniques or personally preferred variations on those techniques covered in this manual. We believe that is good to be creative clinically, but best for the patient (i.e., least confusing) if the therapist sticks with one explanatory model that underlies all the interventions introduced in this treatment program. This is why we emphasize selection of techniques which fall within the rubric of CBT.

Another stimulus for deviating from the session sequence is the belief that the patient already knows and understands the material to be covered. This is particularly tempting when the patient is well read on the subject of bipolar disorder, attends lectures or support groups, or has had a great deal of experience with the illness personally or in family members. Our experience has been that even the most knowledgeable individuals benefit from a review of basic information about the illness or its treatment. People forget facts, misinterpret information, or may have been educated on the topic at a time when less was known about the illness or its treatment. Some people will feel insulted by the elementary nature of the initial education sessions. The educational sessions are intended for patients and their family members. In most cases, the information covered will be new to at least some of the participants. To avoid insulting well-read patients, we suggest a disclaimer similar to the following:

> "I know that you are very well read on the topic of bipolar disorder. You will very likely teach me a few things as we go along. I am going to review several facts about the illness and its treatment that you may already know. I apologize if this seems a little boring to you, but I have found that it can be helpful to go over basic information. It will help to make sure that you and I start off on the same foot, that is, that we both have the same understanding about the illness. If there is something I cover that you disagree with or have not heard before, please let me know so we can clear up any confusions."

It is critical that therapists listen attentively to what their patients have learned from their experiences with the illness. They know about bipolar disorder from an intimate perspective that can greatly enhance therapists' appreciation for and understanding of the illness. Taking time to learn from the patient will also facilitate the establishment of rapport. Some patients will question your ability to treat an illness that you have not had yourself. This is a problem common to many types of psychotherapy. Rather than attempting to convince the patient that you know a great deal about bipolar disorder, acknowledge that you do not have the same personal knowledge about the illness and let them tell you what it is like for them to live with bipolar disorder. You will no doubt learn a great deal about the infinite variations in the presentation of the illness and how the symptoms interact with various treatments and with the individual strengths and weaknesses of each patient.

PATIENT AND THERAPIST CREATIVITY

It is our intention that the session-by-session instructions presented at the beginning of each chapter be followed as closely as possible. It is also our intention to provide a treatment manual that is practical and flexible enough to allow the therapist to work with a variety of patients with bipolar disorder, not just "perfect research patients" with no comorbid medical or psychiatric problems. The overriding clinical goal is to serve the patient well. The therapist must use "common sense" in applying the manual to individual patients' needs. When the therapist must deal with a particular problem or patient need for which there is no instruction in the manual, the therapist should follow the CBT model as best as possible and handle the problem in a way that makes sense for the patient. In this way, proper execution of the manual rests on the good sense and clinical skill of experienced therapists.

The CBT interventions covered in this manual are fairly simple and easily modified. The usefulness of the interventions is greatly enhanced if they are personalized for each patient. The best example is with the Mood Graph. In our practice, each patient is asked to design their own Mood Graph that best captures their personal experiences with the fluctuating nature of the illness. If you have the luxury of a word processor in your office (or better yet, a secretary), you can design homework forms during the session. We begin with a skeleton of a Mood Graph like the one presented in Chapter 4. We change the anchor words, add columns for multiple daily ratings, change the scale, and print out the graph for the patient to take home. Encourage patients to play with the homework forms at home and make a version that best suits their needs. Take time to type it up for them so that it can be used for future sessions and for use with other patients.

When possible, make photocopies of patients' completed homework sheets for future reference. Have patients keep the originals in a folder or binder so that they can review their work at a later date when the same intervention is needed. The Symptom Summary Worksheet described in Chapter 4 will be used repeatedly in therapy as well as the Goal Setting Worksheet. These should be kept handy.

RECORDING THERAPY SESSIONS

Audiotaping or videotaping the therapy sessions can be very useful for the therapist and the patient. In a research study, these tapes are used to judge the competency of the therapist and his or her compliance with the protocol. In this case, a random sample of tapes can be rated by an "expert" using a structured scale to periodically assess the therapist's behaviors. Audiotapes or videotapes can be helpful to the therapist who is learning this intervention so that he or she might review the session alone or with a supervisor to evaluate progress. Some patients like to audiotape therapy sessions so that they can listen to them again. This can help them to review instructions for a complicated or confusing intervention and is particularly helpful with the multistep cognitive restructuring interventions. As with any form of psychotherapy, the sessions can arouse considerable emotion. Emotional arousal can interfere with learning. A review via the audiotapes is particularly helpful and can save time in therapy.

Some patients have found the audiotapes of sessions useful in examining their behavior during therapy. After listening to an audiotape of a therapy session, one patient returned the following week with some important observations. She heard herself interrupting the therapist repeatedly and occasionally changing the subject at inappropriate times. This self-observation validated the criticisms of her family members and gave her a new target for change. She made efforts to hold her comments or questions until the therapist was finished. She also asked herself if she had finished a topic before she introduced a new one. This patient listened to another tape some weeks later and was able to hear her progress.

STRUCTURED VERSUS PATIENT-DRIVEN
SESSION AGENDAS

In traditional cognitive therapy, the session for each agenda is defined at the beginning of each session. The therapist may have an idea ahead of time of the type of intervention to be introduced at a given session to address problems presented at previous sessions. The patient helps to set the agenda by selecting topics for discussion, generally surrounding psychosocial problems or significant shifts in mood that occurred since the last session. This CBT manual for bipolar disorder differs in that the agenda is preselected for the first 20 sessions. The remaining sessions follow a more traditional cognitive therapy format in that the agenda is not preselected but is driven by the patient. In the first 20 sessions, however, it is important that the therapist find ways to address the presenting concerns of the patient at each session. This can be done by taking time before beginning the session procedure to listen to the patient's concerns. Sometimes the problem raised by the patient can be addressed within the session's agenda. In this case, let the patient know you will be covering a new CBT technique that session which may address the presenting problem.

At other times, it will be necessary to forego the planned agenda to deal with a more pressing problem presented by the patient. Some examples might include suicidal ideation or family crises. In these cases, the therapist should use a CBT model to define and address the problem, but will be less likely to emphasize teaching the patient a new technique. For most psychosocial crises, the problem-solving model presented in Chapter 10 can be applied. When the crisis has passed, the therapist can review the problem-solving process used to resolve the crisis. There may also be an opportunity to use the crisis as an example of how stimulus events elicit strong emotions that influence and are influenced by one's view of the event. These feelings and thoughts, in turn, influence the course of action taken by the patient. We believe it is critical that patients understand the cognitive model. We use every available opportunity to illustrate and reinforce the model with the patient.

THERAPEUTIC CHALLENGES

We provide a few examples of how we have coped with some common therapeutic obstacles or complexities within the constraints of this manual. We cannot hope to provide answers to all therapists' questions. We can, however, provide a model for overcoming problems and staying within the framework of the manual. We close this section with a number of false assumptions or beliefs that therapists may have about using this manual, followed by our rational responses to each of these dysfunctional beliefs.

Crisis Intervention

In the course of therapy, it is not unusual to be sidetracked by a major crisis such as an unwanted pregnancy, a lawsuit, a threatened divorce, a car accident, or child or adolescent behavior problems. The therapist has to decide when and how to deviate from the treatment package and how to return to the planned agenda. Some patients always seem to be experiencing crises, both minor and major. Can the protocol be followed in these cases?

Crises cannot be ignored or disregarded. They must be discussed to some extent during the session. To not acknowledge their importance is to risk damaging the therapeutic alliance with the patient. Sometimes the patient will need assistance in resolving the crisis. Sometimes he or she will have already developed a plan or will have taken action toward resolving the crisis and merely wishes to report to the therapist what has transpired. Telling the story, however, can fill an entire session. The therapist should quickly assess whether or not the crisis has been resolved and how much time will be needed for further discussion. This can be accomplished at the beginning of the session when the agenda is being set. Sometimes patients will begin telling their story as soon as the door closes and the session begins.

Ms. SPENCE: You will not believe what has happened this week. I am disgusted beyond belief. You remember that guy I told you about? He showed up at my job and started yelling at me and threatening me. He said he was going to kick my "you know what" if I ever stood him up again. I didn't stand him up, I told him I didn't want to go to the party. He just assumed I was going to go because he insisted.

THERAPIST: I can see that you are really upset about this. Should we put this on our agenda to discuss today? I had planned for us to talk about combating negative thinking. Do you need some help in dealing with this guy?

Ms. SPENCE: I took care of it. I called store security and had him kicked out. They called the city police, made a big fuss. The jerk was humiliated. He knows not to mess with me.

THERAPIST: Maybe we should spend some time talking about what happened, but maybe only 15 minutes or so. Would that be enough?

Ms. SPENCE: That's probably more than we need.

Sometimes the crisis can be the content around which a CBT intervention is taught. For example, a patient might present with a problem about getting their income tax forms completed on time. The goal setting, GTA, or problem-solving interventions can be taught using taxes as the example. If the therapist is lucky, a problem will be brought in by the patient that matches the planned agenda for the session.

Patients as Passive Recipients of Care

Unfortunately, many institutional settings inadvertently socialize people with bipolar disorder to be passive recipients of care rather than to be active consumers of or participants in their care. When severely ill, people with bipolar disorder are sometimes unable to care for themselves. These are times when hospitalization is often needed. While many institutional settings are working toward changing these environments that foster passivity to advocate active patient participation in care, those adults currently in treatment for bipolar disorder may have already "learned" to behave passively in their treatment.

A passive view of the patient's role in treatment is in opposition to the collaborative view espoused by this treatment manual. Therefore, in many cases, the therapist will have to take time to socialize patients to this new collaborative role early in the course of treatment. Countering the institutional belief of patients as passive recipients of care can be accomplished by eliciting active participation. This means encouraging them to ask questions, asking their opinion, and providing ample opportunities for them to tell their personal stories.

> Mrs. Niko was a once gregarious, 55-year-old artist. She began to suffer from severe depressions in her mid-20s, but did not have her first manic episode until her early 40s. She had been treated with tranquilizers and antidepressants for her depression, with some response. The depressions sometimes gave her a perspective on her art that she appreciated and even thought she needed to be successful. Unfortunately, over time, hospital stays were becoming more common, more dreaded. Then, she happened upon a psychiatrist who "put her on a medication" that seemed to prevent her depressions from recurring. While "curing" her depressions, the medicine also took away her joyful bouts of hypomania and with them her spirit and her creativity. She painted infrequently now and sold few pieces, but was able to support herself on a disability pension. From Mrs. Niko's perspective, the doctor had "cured her" and the "cure" had taken with it her artistic talent. "I just need to keep following the doctor's orders and I'll be fine."

Many would argue that there is nothing wrong with Mrs. Niko. She is psychiatrically and financially stable and is able to occasionally enjoy her hobby of painting. Her attitude toward treatment, while at face value seems appropriate and would be welcomed by many health care providers, is passive. She views forces outside of herself as being responsible for the quality of her life. Although not ideal, she accepts the life that she is given.

To cultivate a collaborative relationship with the patient, the therapist asked Mrs. Niko what she thought about her care, her diagnosis, her health care providers, her medication regimen, and her life. When she repeated what her doctor had told her to do, the therapist asked Mrs. Niko what she thought about the doctor's recommendations.

THERAPIST: What medications do you take?

MRS. NIKO: Lithium, bupropion, and Benadryl sometimes.

THERAPIST: How do the medications help you?

MRS. NIKO: I'm not sure. My doctor says the lithium and bupropion control my depression. I take the Benadryl at night if I have trouble sleeping.

THERAPIST: Does the medication work?

MRS. NIKO: Yes, I think so. I have not had to go to the hospital in 2 years. I still get a little depressed sometimes, especially when the weather is bad and the sky is gloomy.

THERAPIST: Do these medications seem right for you?

MRS. NIKO: Yes, I think so. I have tried others. They only seem to work for a while or they make me feel worse. These medicines seem to do better than other things I have tried.

THERAPIST: Do you plan to keep taking them?

MRS. NIKO: Yes, I do.

The therapist also asked her how she combated her depression, what methods worked the best, the least; and what had she discovered along the way about controlling her illness. This gave the patient a chance to share what she had learned and to educate her therapist about bipolar disorder. When Mrs. Niko offered a personal opinion, the therapist was particularly attentive and validated the patient's ideas.

THERAPIST: You mentioned that you still experience some depression when the weather is bad. How do you cope with these times?

MRS. NIKO: At first I keep to myself, sleep more, sip hot tea, and think about the past. Then I realize that I am on a path straight back to depression. I make myself do the opposite of what I really feel like doing.

THERAPIST: What do you mean?

MRS. NIKO: I make myself get up at my regular time even though I am tired; I get dressed and go out. I ask a friend to lunch or to visit an art gallery. I get us to talk about the good times we have had.

THERAPIST: So it sounds like the medications help you a lot, but when the depression sneaks in, you take control of the situation by making yourself do things you know will make you feel better.

MRS. NIKO: That's right.

THERAPIST: You really know how to take care of yourself.

Patients who are accustomed to a passive role will sometimes ask the therapist for advice or guidance. The helpful therapist will feel inclined to provide such guidance. A strategy that is helpful and that encourages patients to be active problem solvers is to ask them how they have coped with similar problems in the past. Here is an example of an evening telephone conversation from a distraught patient.

MR. ENRIQUEZ: Dr. B., I hope I'm not bothering you, but I'm feeling bad and I can't sleep. My mom is getting on my nerves. My sister is getting on my nerves. The other people at the clubhouse were bothering me and asking me for money. I got in an argument with one of them today. What should I do? I'm very upset.

THERAPIST: This has happened before, hasn't it?

MR. ENRIQUEZ: Yeah.

THERAPIST: What helped you to feel better the last time this happened?

MR. ENRIQUEZ: I just kept to myself. I stayed in my room and listened to music until I fell asleep or I called a friend. You told me to call you if I needed you.

THERAPIST: That's right. It sounds like the problem right now is that you are too upset to get to sleep. People are getting on your nerves. What do you think you need to do now?

MR. ENRIQUEZ: I just need to get some sleep. If I don't sleep, I'll be worse tomorrow.

THERAPIST: What usually helps you to fall asleep?

MR. ENRIQUEZ: I already took my medicine. I just need to relax, stay away from my mom and my sister.

THERAPIST: Anything else?

MR. ENRIQUEZ: I'll listen to the radio and just try to calm myself down.

THERAPIST: That sounds like a good plan. Call me tomorrow and let me know how you did. At your next visit maybe we can take some time to talk about your sister and your mom. I think you are right to put them out of your mind for now and just focus on relaxing and getting a good night's sleep.

Developmental Delays Due to the Illness and Their Impact on Therapy

For many people with bipolar disorder, symptoms of the illness began in young adulthood or adolescence. It is during these years that people learn to relate to others in an adult manner. It is also during this time that young people begin to develop their own ideas about who they are and what they believe. They begin to examine and challenge the beliefs of their parents, forming instead their own views of the world.

This growth process, however, can be interrupted by depression or mania in people with bipolar disorder. The impact this has on the individual is delayed or retarded social, psychological, and emotional growth. What therapists often see in these patients are poor interpersonal skills, limited coping skills, immature views of relationships, a failure to separate sufficiently from parents, or poor problem-solving skills.

The relevance of these developmental delays to the therapy process is in the choice of interventions. As therapists, we often assume that our patients have basic social skills such as how to get information, how to cope with stress, how to interact with others in various social situations, or how to make decisions about activities of daily living. With some patients who have had bipolar disorder since prior to adulthood, it may be necessary to help them develop these basic skills. This can take extra time in therapy. Patients may not know that they are lacking in basic life skills until they attempt new tasks or engage in unfamiliar social activities.

> Mr. Brewster had not had contact with his parents for several years. One of his goals in therapy was to talk with them and help them to understand his illness and what he had been through since they last heard from him. He had been hospitalized twice since leaving home, had been married and divorced, and had recovered from a drinking problem. "I'm going to go in there and make them understand where I'm coming from. I'm doing fine. They have no reason to be afraid of me. I'm going to set the record straight." He was ready to charge in unannounced, sit them down, and talk until they listened.
>
> His enthusiasm was great. He had come a long way through treatment. He wanted to mend the problems of the past and make peace with his family that had rejected him when he was a young man. Mr. Brewster's episodes of mania and frequent use of street drugs had frightened and frustrated his family. They saw their only option to be to force him out of the house and to discontinue any contact with him.
>
> In planning Mr. Brewster's family visit, it became clear that he did not have very well developed social skills. He did not appear to have the ability to evaluate or to anticipate the impact of his actions on others. He did not see anything wrong with barging into his parents' home, lecturing them, and demanding that they accept him as a new man. The therapist worked with Mr. Brewster on basic social skills, working toward a more diplomatic approach to reengaging his family.

To accomplish the goals of this treatment manual, therapists must assess and teach patients skills necessary to carry out each intervention.

When basic skills training is needed to best execute an intervention, take time to teach. It will be time well spent and will provide patients with basic skills they may be able to apply to several aspects of their lives.

"I Can't Do It"

Living through several episodes of depression and mania leaves most people with bipolar disorder feeling fearful and lacking in confidence. The fear is that the symptoms will return, especially if they stress or push themselves. The setbacks, losses, and devastation that many people experience affects their self-esteem. When working with these individuals, clinicians must find a place between pushing too hard and underchallenging. Particularly with the behaviorally oriented interventions, where therapists are asking patients to act, there may be resistance from those patients who are either fearful of the consequences or lack confidence in their abilities. "I can't do it" is a negative cognition that can be addressed with the cognitive restructuring exercises presented in Chapter 6. With this cognition, it may be particularly helpful to frame the behavioral interventions as experiments to test the validity of the cognition "I can't do it." These experiments should be easy to accomplish. Take time to explore the potential obstacles to success of the intervention (see Chapter 5 for guidelines) with adjustments or precautions made as needed. After the intervention has been executed, the cognition "I can't do it" should be reevaluated given these new experiences.

Denial

Some people with bipolar disorder are not ready to accept their diagnosis or participate in treatment. This is typically labeled as denial. Denial of this severity must be addressed before CBT can be maximally effective. Sometimes the first four sessions when patients are educated about the symptoms and treatment of bipolar disorder is all that is needed to open the discussion that helps them accept the fact that they have a mental illness. When people agree that they have an illness, but deny that it is bipolar disorder, it is usually because they have attached a specific and negative meaning to having bipolar disorder. People have negative beliefs about this disorder, many of which are false.

The more complicated patient is the one who reports to fully accept the fact that he or she has this terrible illness, yet demonstrates denial in other ways.

> "I used to be that bad, but I don't get like that anymore. I don't have mood swings. Mood swings landed me in the hospital. I'm under control now since I started taking my medication."

Teaching these people to monitor mild, subsyndromal symptoms is difficult because the fear of recurrence is so great that any admission of even mild symptoms means to them that they are getting sick. When technical labels are used to describe symptoms, these patients will deny their occurrence (e.g., "I do not have insomnia, I'm just having a little trouble falling asleep"). The therapist can work with their denial by using more palatable labels. For a few patients we relabeled the anchors on the Mood Graph using words that were easier to acknowledge (e.g., "down in the dumps" instead of mild depression). The fear underlying the denial can be addressed with the cognitive interventions described in Chapter 6.

FALSE ASSUMPTIONS OF THE THERAPIST

CBT is for intelligent and verbally skilled patients. Because of the emphasis on cognition, many therapist assume that CBT is designed for patients who are verbally skilled or highly intelligent. Our experience to date has been with patients with varying levels of intelligence, education, and verbal skills. We have not seen a strong relationship between how well people can execute the CBT interventions and these characteristics. As with any form of therapy, the presentation of the interventions by the therapist must be tailored to the needs of each patient.

One of the verbal skills we have found to be important in this intervention is the ability to label emotional experiences. Some people have limited emotional vocabularies (e.g., they either feel good or bad). Refining these evaluations takes time and practice. Therapists will have to listen to patients' descriptions and help them to define the emotions they experience, thus building their emotional vocabulary.

If my explanations are clear, patients will understand them. Clarity in receiving information is only partially dependent upon clarity of sending information. The therapist may feel that he or she is conveying information clearly, when, in fact, the patient does not understand. Common mistakes include giving too much information at one time, talking too fast, speaking too softly for the patient to hear clearly, or using slang, jargon, or words that exceed the sophistication of the patient's vocabulary.

Patients will often be too kind to tell their therapists that they talk too much, too fast, or are otherwise difficult to understand. Their lack of understanding will show when expected to use or repeat the information conveyed by the therapist, for example, when attempting to complete a homework assignment. Rather than being a problem with homework compliance, the real problem may be that the homework was not adequately explained. *Assuming* the patient understands without asking is the therapist's first mistake.

Patients will recognize the value of homework. For many people, the term *homework* has a negative connotation. It reminds them of grade school, punitive teachers, and interruptions in their play time. The value of homework may be appreciated logically, but emotionally the notion of homework may continue to be tied to old and negative memories. The therapist using this treatment manual must take time to resocialize patients to the concept of doing weekly homework. The ultimate goal of this therapeutic intervention is to teach skills that patients can use on their own in attempting to combat symptoms of bipolar disorder. Therefore, practice at home, between sessions, is essential to the learning process. Unfortunately, just because the therapist believes that homework is important and assigns tasks each week does not mean that patients will accept the instruction and comply with their therapists' requests. Before giving the first homework assignment, take time to ask patients how they feel about doing homework between sessions. If their response is negative, ask them to tell you more about it. Listen for negative automatic thoughts about homework. Help the patient to compare homework given in therapy to homework given in school. Underscore the critical difference that there will be no evaluation or "grade" given to therapy homework. Therapy homework is more like practice exercises done regularly to acquire a skill, such as shooting baskets or going to the batting cages to improve athletic skill. The practice itself is not graded, but it does influence the ability to acquire or refine a skill.

Use the compliance intervention each time you give a homework assignment. First, make sure that the patient understands how to do the homework. Second, help the patient to anticipate things that might interfere with completing the homework assignment—"What could keep you from filling out your Mood Graph this week?"Third, develop a plan for avoiding or overcoming the obstacles when they occur. Patients will quickly learn this intervention and will walk through the three-step process with little assistance from the therapist.

A related dysfunctional belief of therapists is that if patients have the skill to do the homework, they will do it. As suggested above, many things can keep a person from completing homework assignments. Reread Chapter 5 on treatment compliance obstacles for a summary.

This intervention will work with all patients. The development of this treatment manual was based on a prototypical patient with bipolar disorder. The individual interventions should be applicable to the majority of patients with bipolar disorder. It is likely that in working with each individual patient, the procedures in this manual will not be inclusive enough to cover all patient presentations at all times. Therefore, the therapist will need to use other CBT methods.

It is also possible that for some patients, this form of treatment will not be helpful at all. This may be particularly true when the patient presents with a substance abuse problem that is more severe than the bipolar disorder. In this case, treatment of the substance abuse problem may be needed before this manual can be effectively used with a patient.

This intervention is simple and does not require a lot of training. Our goal in writing this manual was to make the instructions easy to follow. We assumed that clinicians with varying clinical backgrounds will read the manual; therefore we tried to be explicit with directions and limit the "psychobabble" in the text. We also wanted patients and their family members and friends to be able to read along and understand the interventions. Sometimes our descriptions of interventions sound so simple that it would seem that patients could follow the directions on their own. In fact, this may be possible in some cases. The intention of the manual was to provide a package of interventions that addressed each of our treatment goals. We knew that to be successfully administered, clinicians would have to "improvise" to personalize the procedures to the special needs of their patients. Therefore, considerable clinical skill is needed to adequately administer this intervention. Trainees should seek supervision from trained cognitive therapists when learning this intervention.

CHAPTER SUMMARY

We recommend that you follow the session-by-session structure of this treatment manual as much as possible; however, patients' personal needs are more important than following the structure. We have attempted to build flexibility into the manual's structure so that the methods are similar to what would be done by a well-trained and thorough cognitive therapist without a manual. Newer therapists will try so hard to follow the procedures that they forget about the basics of good therapy (e.g., rapport, good listening skills). Following the protocol of this treatment manual is not an all-or-nothing phenomenon. If you find that you must deviate from the protocol and feel bad about it, reread the introduction to Chapter 5 on compliance. Full compliance with this manual is our intention. Approximating this as much as possible is the goal. Obstacles will arise that interfere with following the manual like a cookbook. The session instructions at the beginning of each chapter cannot replace good clinical judgment and a general understanding of cognitive-behavioral therapies. When there are any questions about how to administer this treatment manual, the answer is simply to do what is in the best interest of your patients.

Educational Materials and Related Associations

National Mental Health Information Center
National Mental Health Association
1021 Prince Street
Alexandria, VA 22314-2971
(800) 969-6642
(703) 684-7722
American Psychiatric Association: Facts about Manic Depression

National Institute of Mental Health and the D/ART Program
National Institute of Mental Health
Public Inquiries Branch, Room 7C02
Mail Code 8030
Bethesda, MD 20892
(800) 421-4211; (301) 443-4513

Depressive Disorders

Depressive Illness: Treatments Bring New Hope. DHHS Publication Number (ADM) 89-1491

Depression: What You Need to Know. DHHS Publication Number (ADM) 87-1543

Helpful Facts about Depressive Disorders. DHHS Publication Number (ADM) 87-1536

Helping the Depressed Person Get Treatment. DHHS Publication Number (ADM) 90-1675

If You're Over 65 and Feeling Depressed: Treatment Brings New Hope. DHHS Publication Number (ADM) 90-1653

Depression/Awareness, Recognition, and Treatment (D/ART) Fact Sheet. OM 88-4034

Depression/Awareness, Recognition, and Treatment (D/ART) Program: National Education Program on Depressive Disorders. OM 88-4035

Depression, Manic--Depressive Illness, and Biological Rhythms. ADM 82-0889

Depression in the Elderly: A Fact Sheet. ADM 80-0932

Information on Lithium. ADM 81-1078

Mood Disorders: Pharmacologic Prevention of Recurrences. OM 84-4015

Special Report on Depression Research. ADM 81-1085

Using Drugs to Lift That Dark Veil of Depression. FDA 84-3140

What to Do When a Friend Is Depressed: A Guide for Teenagers. OM 88-4036.

General Mental Health

Careers in Mental Health. ADM 84-0250

Plain Talk about Aging. ADM 85-1266

Plain Talk about Biofeedback. ADM 85-1273

Plain Talk about Handling Stress. ADM 85-0502

Plain Talk about Mutual Help Groups. ADM 83-1138

Plain Talk about Physical Fitness and Mental Health. ADM 84-1364

Plain Talk about the Art of Relaxation. ADM 85-0632

Useful Information on . . . Anorexia Nervosa and Bulimia. ADM 87-1514

Useful Information on . . . Medications for Mental Illness. ADM 87-1509

Useful Information on . . . Phobias and Panic. ADM 87-1472

You Are Not Alone: Facts about Mental Health and Mental Illness. ADM 85-1178

Institute for Rational Emotive Therapy
45 East 65th Street
New York, NY 10021
(800)323-IRET

Coping with Depression (Beck & Greenberg)

S. Karger Publishers
P. O. Box CH-4009
Basel, Switzerland

Lithium Treatment of Manic Depressive Illness: A Practical Guide (Schou)

National Depressive and Manic Depressive Association (NDMDA)
730 N. Franklin, Suite 501
Chicago, IL 60610
(312)642-0049 (800)826-3632

Moodswing. Item No. 1001

Sad to Glad. Item No. 1002

Broken Brain. Item No. 1003

Feeling Good. Item No. 1004

Your Brother's Keeper. Item No. 1005
Leading Self Help Groups. Item No. 1006
Overcoming Depression. Item No. 1007
Call Me Anna. Item No. 1008
Lithium Treatment of Manic Depressive Illness, A Practical Approach. Item No. 1009
Do You Have a Depressive Illness, How to Tell, What to Do. Item No. 1010
Lithium and Manic-Depression, A Guide. Item No. 1011
Carbamazepine and Manic Depression, A Guide. Item No. 1012
Depressive Illness, A Guide for Patients and Families. Item No. 1013
Manic Depressive Illness, A Guide for Patients and Families. Item No. 1014
Feeling the Rainbow. Item No. 1015
American Psychiatric Glossary. Item No. 1016
Rights of the Mentally Disabled. Item No. 1018
Breaking the Silence, Spiritual Help When Someone You Love Is Mentally Ill. Item No. 1019
Suicide: Why? 85 Questions and Answers about Suicide. Item No. 1020
Good News about Depression. Item No. 1021
The Good News about Panic, Anxiety and Phobias. Item No. 1022
High Times/Low Times: The Many Faces of Adolescent Depression. Item No. 1023
Nothing to Be Ashamed of: Growing Up with Mental Illness in Your Family. Item No. 1024
Beating Depression. Item No. 1025
About Manic-Depressive Illness. Item No. 1026
About Prescription Medications for Mental Health. Item No. 1027
How to Cope with Depression, A Complete Guide for You and Your Family. Item No. 1028
Diagnostic and Statistical Manual of Mental Disorders. Item No. 1029
Stress and the Family of the Manic Depressive. Item No. 2002
Manic Depressive Illness: Understanding and Coping: A Bibliography for the Layman. Item No. 2003
Helping Others–Helping Ourselves: A Guide to Starting Mutual Aid Self-Help Groups for Manic Depressive and Depressive Disorders. Item No. 2004
Guide to New Medicines of the Mind. Item No. 3002
Sixty Ways to Make Stress Work for You. Item No. 3003
Honk If You're on Lithium. NDMDA bumper sticker. Item No. 8001

Fifth Annual Convention of the National Depressive and Manic-Depressive Association at Northwestern University, Evanston, IL, July 22–24, 1988

Audiocassettes
Opening Plenary Session. Invocation. Item No. 4001
What Psychiatry in the 1990's Will Bring to Us, Part 1. Item No. 4002

What Psychiatry in the 1990's Will Bring to Us, Part 2. Item No. 4003
Interpersonal Therapy. Item No. 4004
Antidepressants and Lithium Therapies. Item No. 4005
Anxiety and Panic Disorders. Item No. 4006
Pathology and Blood Levels. Item No. 4007
Fundraising. Item No. 4008
D/ART's on Its Way. Item No. 4009
Public Relations and Communications. Item No. 4010
Childhood Affective Disorders. Item No. 4013
Family Interrelationships. Item No. 4015
Public Policy and Concern. Item No. 4016
Legal Aspects of Chapter Operations. Item No. 4017
Awards Presentation. Item No. 4018
Family Psychoeducation: A Blueprint for Patient Advocacy. Item No. 4019
Alternate Therapies in Affective Disorders. Item No. 4020
Closing Announcements. Item No. 4021

Videocassette
Segments of 5th Annual Convention. Item No. 5001

Sixth Annual Convention of the National Depressive and Manic–Depressive Association at Astro-Village Hotel, Houston, TX, October 26–29, 1989

Audiocassettes
"Ask the Doctor" Panel (Part 1). Item No. 4022
"Ask the Doctor" Panel (Part 2). Item No. 4023
Overview of Basic Psychopharmacology. Item No. 4024
The Diagnosis of Masked Depression. Item No. 4025
Facilitator Training, Part 1. Item No. 4026
Advocacy, Part 1. Item No. 4027
Stress and the Family of a Depressive or Manic–Depressive. Item No. 4028
Legal Issues, Part 1. Item No. 4029
Depression and Manic Depression in Adolescence. Item No. 4030
Dual Diagnosis: Alcoholism, Drugs, and Manic Depression. Item No. 4031
Facilitator Training, Part II. Item No. 4032
Advocacy, Part II. Item No. 4033
Legal Issues, Part II. Item No. 4034
How to Regain Employment. Item No. 4035
Coping Effectively with a Manic Depressive. Item No. 4036

Clarke Institute of Psychiatry
Department of Social Work, 8th Floor
250 College Street

Toronto, Ontario, Canada M5T 1R8
(416)979-2221, Ext. 2576

Paranoid Conditions: A Guide for Families
Depressive Illness: A Guide for Patients and Families
Manic--Depressive Illness: A Guide for Patients and Families

National Clearinghouse for Alcohol
and Drug Abuse Information (NCADI)
P.O. Box 2345
Rockville, MD 20857
(800)729-6686

Publications on Drug Abuse and/or Alcohol Abuse and Alcoholism

Hazelden Educational Materials
Pleasant Valley Road
P.O. Box 176
Center City, MN 55012-0176
(800)328-9000

Understanding Depression and Addiction

Other Associations

Lithium Information Center
Dean Foundation
2711 Allen Boulevard
Middletown, WI 53562
(608) 827-2390

National Alliance for the Mentally Ill
2101 Wilson Boulevard, Suite 302
Arlington, VA 22201
(800)950-6264

National Mental Health Association
1021 Prince Street
Alexandria, VA 23314-2971
(800)969-6642

National Foundation for Depressive Illness
20 Charles Street
New York, NY 10014
(800)248-4344

References

References in bold are recommended homework readings. They are available through the NDMDA Bookstore at discounted rates or through their publishers as indicated in the Appendix.

Aagaard, J., & Vestergaard, P. (1990). Predictors of outcome in prophylactic lithium treatment: A 2-year prospective study. *Journal of Affective Disorders,* *18,* 259–266.

Akiskal, H. S., Djenderedjian, A. H., Rosenthal, R. H., & Khani, M. K. (1977). *American Journal of Psychiatry, 134,* 1227–1233.

Altamura, A. C., & Mauri, M. (1985). Plasma concentration, information and therapy adherence during long-term treatment with antidepressants. *British Journal of Clinical Pharmacology, 20,* 714–716.

Altshuler, L. L., Post, R. M. Leverich, G. S., Mikalauskas, K., Rosoff, A., & Ackerman, L. (1995). Antidepressant induced mania and cycle acceleration: A controversy revisited. *American Journal of Psychiatry, 153*(8), 1130–1138.

Ambelas, A. (1979). Psychologically stressful events in the precipitation of manic episodes. *British Journal of Psychiatry, 135,* 15–21.

American Psychiatric Association. (1990). *Facts about manic depression* [Pamphlet]. Washington, DC: American Psychiatric Press.

American Psychiatric Association. (1994). *Diagnostic and statistical manual of mental disorders* (4th ed.). Washington, DC: Author.

Angst, J. (1981). Clinical indications for a prophylactic treatment of depression. *Advances in Biological Psychiatry, 7,* 218–229.

Arancibia, A., Flores, P., & Pezoa, R. (1990). Steady-state lithium concentrations with conventional and controlled release formulations. *Lithium, 1*(4), 237–239.

Aronson, T. A., & Skukla, S. (1987). Life events and relapse in bipolar disorder: The impact of a catastrophic event. *Acta Psychiatrica Scandinavica, 75,* 571–576.

Baastrup, P. C., & Schou, M. (1967). Lithium as a prophylactic agent: Its effect against recurrent depression and manic–depressive psychosis. *Archives of General Psychiatry, 16,* 162–172.

Basco, M. R., Birchler, G. R., Kalal, B., Talbott, R., & Slater, M. A. (1991). The Clinician Rating of Adult Communication (CRAC): A clinician's guide to the assessment of interpersonal communication skill. *Journal of Clinical Psychology, 47,* 368–380.

Basco, M. R., & Rush, A. J. (1995). Compliance with pharmacotherapy in mood disorders. *Psychiatric Annals, 25,* 78–82.

Bauer, M. S., & Dunner, D. L. (1996). Validity of seasonal pattern as a modifier for recurrent mood disorders in DSM-IV. In T. A. Widiger, A. J. Frances, H. A. Pincus, R. Ross, M. B. First, & W. Davis, (Eds.), *DSM-IV sourcebook* (Vol. 2, pp. 281–314). Washington, DC: American Psychiatric Press.

Beck, A. T. (1976). *Cognitive therapy and the emotional disorders.* New York: International Universities Press.

Beck, A. T., & Greenberg, R. (1974). *Coping with depression* [Booklet]. New York: Institute for Rational Living.

Beck, A. T., & Rush, A. J. (1995). Cognitive therapy. In H. I. Kaplan, & B. J. Sadock (Eds.), *Comprehensive textbook of psychiatry/VI* (6th ed., Vol. 2, pp. 1847–1857). Baltimore: Williams & Wilkins.

Beck, A. T., Rush, A. J., Shaw, B. F., & Emery, G. (1979). *Cognitive therapy of depression.* New York: Guilford Press.

Benson, R. (1975). The forgotten treatment modality in bipolar illness: Psychotherapy. *Diseases of the Nervous System, 35,* 634–638.

Billings, A. G., Cronkite, R. C., & Moos, R. H. (1983). Social environmental factors in unipolar depression: Comparisons of depressed patients and non-depressed controls. *Journal of Abnormal Psychology, 92,* 119–133.

Blackburn, I. M., Evanson, K. M., & Bishop, S. (1987). A two year naturalistic follow-up of depressed patients treated with cognitive therapy, pharmacotherapy and a combination of both. *Journal of Affective Disorders, 10,* 67–75.

Bowden, C. L., Brugger, A. M., Swann, A. C., Calabrese, J. R., Janicak, P. G., Petty, F., Dilsaver, S. C., Davis, J. M., Rush, A. J., Small, J. G., Garza-Trevino, E. S., Risch, S. C., Goodnick, P. J., & Morris, D. D. (1994). Efficacy of divalproex sodium vs. lithium and placebo in the treatment of mania. *Journal of the American Medical Association, 271,* 918–924.

Brown, G. W., & Harris, T. (1978). *Social origins of depression: A study of psychiatric disorder in women.* London: Tavistock.

Caldwell, H. C., Westlake, W. J., Schriver, R. C., & Bumbier, E. E. (1981). Steady-state lithium blood level fluctuations in man following administration of a lithium carbonate conventional and controlled-release dosage form. *Journal of Clinical Pharmacology, 21,* 106–109.

Clancy, J., Crowe, R., Winokur, G., & Morrison, J. (1973). The Iowa 500: Precipitating factors in schizophrenia and primary affective disorder. *Comprehensive Psychiatry, 14,* 197–202.

Cochran, S. D. (1984). Preventing medical noncompliance in the outpatient treatment of bipolar affective disorders. *Journal of Consulting and Clinical Psychology, 52,* 873–878.

Cohen, D. (1983). The effectiveness of videotape in patient education on depression. *Journal of Biocommunication, 10,* 19–23.

Connelly, C. E. (1984). Compliance with outpatient lithium therapy. *Perspectives in Psychiatric Care, 22,* 44–50.

Connelly, C. E., Davenport, Y. B., & Nurnberger, J. I. (1982). Adherence to treatment regimen in a lithium carbonate clinic. *Archives of General Psychiatry, 39,* 585–588.

Cooper, T. B., Simpson, G. M., Lee, J. H., Bergner, P. E. (1978). Evaluation of a slow-release lithium carbonate formulation. *American Journal of Psychiatry, 135,* 917–922.

Danion, J. M., Neureuther, C., Krieger-Finance, F., Imbs, J. L., & Singer, L. (1987). Compliance with long-term lithium treatment in major affective disorders. *Pharmacopsychiatry, 20,* 230–231.

Davenport, Y. B., Ebert, M. H., Adland, M. L., & Goodwin, F. K. (1977). Couples group therapy as an adjunct to lithium maintenance of the manic patient. *American Journal of Orthopsychiatry, 47*(3), 495–502.

Dunner, D. L., Murphy, D., Stallone, R., & Fieve, R. R. (1979). Episode frequency prior to lithium treatment in bipolar manic–depressive patients. *Comprehensive Psychiatry, 20,* 511–515.

Floyd, F. J., & Markman, H. J. (1984). An economical observational measure of couples' communication skill. *Journal of Consulting and Clinical Psychology, 52,* 97–103.

Frank, E., Prien, R. F., Kupfer, D. J., & Alberts, L. (1985). Implications of noncompliance on research in affective disorders. *Psychopharmacology Bulletin, 21,* 37–42.

Gelenberg, A. J., Carroll, J. A., Baudhuin, M. G., Jefferson, J. W., & Greist, J. H. (1989). *Journal of Clinical Psychiatry, 50*(Suppl.), 17–22.

Glassner, B., & Haldipur, C. V. (1983). Life events and early and late onset of bipolar disorder. *American Journal of Psychiatry, 140,* 215–217.

Glassner, B., Haldipur, C. V., & Dessauersmith, J. (1979). Role loss and working-class manic depression. *Journal of Nervous and Mental Disease, 167,* 530–541.

Goddard, G. V., McIntyre, D. C., & Leech, C. K. (1969). A permanent change in brain function resulting from daily electrical stimulation. *Experimental Neurology, 25,* 295–330.

Gold, M. (1986). *Good news about depression.* Bantam Books.

Goldfried, M. R., & Davison, G. C. (1994). *Clinical behavior therapy.* New York: Wiley.

Goodwin, F. K., & Jamison, K. R. (1990). *Manic–depressive illness.* New York: Oxford University Press.

Gottman, J. M. (1979). *Marital interaction: Experimental investigations.* New York: Academic Press.

Hall, K. S., Dunner, D. L., Zeller, G., & Fieve, R. R. (1977). Bipolar illness: A prospective study of life events. *Comprehensive Psychiatry, 18,* 497–502.

Hammen, C., Ellicott, A., Gitlin, M., & Jamison, K. R. (1989). Sociotropy/autonomy and vulnerability to specific life events in patients with unipolar depression and bipolar disorders. *Journal of Abnormal Psychology, 98,* 154–160.

Himmelhoch, J. M., Yhase, M. E., Mallinger, A. G., & Houck, P. (1991). Tranylcypromine vs. imipramine in anergic bipolar depression. *American Journal of Psychiatry, 148,* 910–916.

Hollister, L. E. (1982). Plasma concentrations of tricyclic antidepressants in clinical practice. *Journal of Clinical Psychiatry, 43,* 66–69.

Hops, H., Wills, T. A., Patterson, G. R., & Weiss, R. L. (1972). *Marital Interaction Coding System.* Unpublished manuscript, University of Oregon, Eugene.

Jacob, M., Turner, L., Kupfer, D. J., Jarrett, D. B., Buzzinotti, E., & Bernstien, P. (1984). Attrition in maintenance therapy for recurrent depression. *Journal of Affective Disorders, 6,* 181–189.

Jamison, K. R., Gerner, R. H., & Goodwin, F. K. (1979). Patient and physician attitudes toward lithium. *Archives of General Psychiatry, 36,* 866–869.

Joanning, H., Brewster, J., & Koval, J. (1984). The communication rapid assessment scale: Development of a behavioral index of communication quality. *Journal of Marital and Family Therapy, 10,* 409–417.

Johnson, D. A. W. (1973). Treatment of depression in general practice. *British Medical Journal, 2,* 18–20.

Johnson, D. A. W. (1974). A study of the use of antidepressant medication in general practice. *British Journal of Psychiatry, 125,* 186–192.

Johnson, D. A. W. (1981). Depression: Treatment compliance in general practice. *Acta Psychiatry Scandinavica* (Suppl.), *290,* 447–453.

Keller, M. B., Lavori, P. W., Kane, J. M., Gelenberg, A. J., Rosenbaum, J. F., Walzer, E. A., & Baker, L. A. (1991). Subsyndromal symptoms in bipolar disorder: A comparison of standard and low serum levels of lithium. *Archives of General Psychiatry, 49*(5), 371–376.

Keller, M. B., Shapiro, R. W., Lavori, P. W., & Wolfe, N. (1982). Relapse in major depressive disorder: Analysis with the life table. *Archives of General Psychiatry, 39,* 911–915.

Kennedy, S., Thompson, R., Stancer, H., Roy, A., & Persad, E. (1983). Life events precipitating mania. *British Journal of Psychiatry, 142,* 398–403.

Kraepelin, E. (1921). *Manic depressive insanity and paranoia* (R. M. Barclay, Trans., G. M. Robertson, Ed.). Edinburgh: E & S Livingstone. (Reprinted New York: Arno Press, 1976)

Krishnan, K. R. R., Swartz, M. S., Larson, M. J., & Santoliquido, G. (1984). Funeral mania in recurrent bipolar affective disorders. Report of three cases. *Journal of Clinical Psychiatry, 45,* 310–311.

Kryger, M. H., Roth, T., & Dement, W. C. (1989). *Principles and practice of sleep medicine.* Philadelphia: Saunders.

Kucera-Bozarth, K., Beck, N. C., & Lyss, L. (1982). Compliance with lithium regimens. *Journal of Psychosocial Nursing and Mental Health Services, 20,* 11–15.

Leverich, G. S., Post, R. M., & Rosoff, A. S. (1990). Factors associated with relapse during maintenance treatment of affective disorders. *International Clinical Psychopharmacology, 5,* 135–156.

Lyskowski, J., & Nasrallah, H. A. (1981). Slowed release lithium: A review and a comparative study. *Journal of Clinical Psychopharmacology, 1,* 406–408.

Marston, M. V. (1970). Compliance with medical regimens: A review of the literature. *Nursing Research, 10,* 312–323.

McElroy, S. L., Keck, P. E., & Pope, H. G. (1987). Sodium valproate: Its use in primary psychiatric disorders. *Journal of Clinical Psychopharmacology, 7*(1), 16–24.

McElroy, S. L., Keck, P. E., Pope, H. G., & Hudson, J. O. (1988). Valproate in the treatment of rapid cycling bipolar disorder. *Journal of Clinical Psychopharmacology, 9*(5), 382–384.

Meichenbaum, D., & Turk, D. (1988). *Facilitating treatment adherence: A practitioner's guidebook*. New York: Plenum Press.

Morrison, J. (1995). *DSM-IV made easy: The clinician's guide to diagnosis*. New York: Guilford Press.

Murphy, D. L., & Beigel, A. (1974). Depression, elation, and lithium carbonate responses in manic patient subgroups. *Archives of General Psychiatry, 31*, 643–648.

Murphy, G. E., Simons, A., Wetzel, R., & Lustman, P. (1984). Cognitive therapy and pharmacotherapy: Singly and together in the treatment of depression. *Archives of General Psychiatry, 41*, 33–41.

National Institutes of Health/National Institute of Mental Health. (1985). Consensus Development Conference Statement. Mood disorders: pharmacologic prevention of recurrences. *American Journal of Psychiatry, 142*, 469–476.

Overall, J. E., Donachie, N. D., & Faillace, L. A. (1987). Implications of restrictive diagnosis for compliance to antidepressant drug therapy: Alprazolam versus imipramine. *Journal of Clinical Psychiatry, 48*, 51–54.

Parks, L. C., & Lipman, R. S. (1964). A comparison of patient dosage deviation reports with pill counts. *Psychopharmacologia, 6*, 299–302.

Paykel, E. S., Myers, J. K., Dienelt, M. N., Klerman, G. L., Lindenthal, J. J., & Pepper, M. P. (1969). Life events and depression: A controlled study. *Archives of General Psychiatry, 21*, 753–760.

Peet, M., & Harvey, N. S. (1991). Lithium maintenance: 1. A standard education program for patients. *British Journal of Psychiatry, 158*, 197–200.

Perris, H. (1984). Life events and depression: Part 2. Results in diagnostic subgroups, and in relation to the recurrence of depression. *Journal of Affective Disorders, 7*, 25–36.

Persons, J. B., Burns, D. D., & Perloff, J. M. (1988). Predictors of dropout and outcome in cognitive therapy for depression in a private practice setting. *Cognitive Therapy and Research, 12*, 557–575.

Physicians' Desk Reference (16th ed.). (1995). Montvale, NJ: Medical Economics.

Post, R. M. (1992). Transduction of psychosocial stress into the neurobiology of recurrent affective disorder. *American Journal of Psychiatry, 149*, 999–1010.

Post, R. M., Roy-Byrne, P. P., & Uhde, T. W. (1988). Graphic representation of the life course of illness in patients with affective disorders. *American Journal of Psychiatry, 145*, 844–848.

Post, R. M., Rubinow, D. R., & Ballenger, J. C. (1986). Conditioning and sensitization in the longitudinal course of affective illness. *British Journal of Psychiatry, 149*, 191–201.

Post, R. M., Uhde, T. W., Ballenger, J. C., Chatterji, D. C., Greene, R. F., & Bunney, W. E. (1983). Carbamazepine and its -10, 11- epoxide metabolite in plasma and CSF: Relationship to antidepressant response. *Archives of General Psychiatry, 40*(6), 673–676.

Powell, B. J., Othmer, E., & Sinkhorn, C. (1977). Pharmacological aftercare for homogeneous groups of patients. *Hospital and Community Psychiatry, 28,* 125–127.

Prager, K. J., & Basco, M. R. (1995). *Negative thinking and marital communication of depressed patients and their spouses.* Unpublished manuscript, University of Texas at Dallas.

Preston, J., O'Neal, J. H., Talaga, M. C. (1994). *Handbook of Clinical Psychopharmacology for Therapists.* Oakland, CA: New Harbinger Publications.

Prien, R. F., Caffey, E. M., Jr., & Klett, C. J. (1973). Prophylactic efficacy of lithium carbonate in manic–depressive illness. *Archives of General Psychiatry, 26,* 146–153.

Prien, R. F., Klett, C. J., & Caffey, E. M., Jr. (1973). Lithium carbonate and imipramine in prevention of affective episodes: A comparison in recurrent affective illness. *Archives of General Psychiatry, 29,* 420–425.

Prien, R. F., Kupfer, D. J., Mansky, P. A., Small, J. G., Tuason, V. B., Voss, C. B., & Johnson, W. E. (1984). Drug therapy in the prevention of recurrences in unipolar and bipolar affective disorders: Report of the NIMH Collaborative Study Group comparing lithium carbonate, imipramine, and a lithium carbonate–imipramine combination. *Archives of General Psychiatry, 41,* 1096–1120.

Pugh, R. (1983). An association between hostility and poor adherence to treatment in patients suffering from depression. *British Journal of Medical Psychology, 56,* 205–208.

Rabin, A. S., Kaslow, N. J., & Rehm, L. P. (1985). Factors influencing continuation in a behavioral therapy. *Behaviour Research and Therapy, 23,* 695–698.

Robins, L. N., Helzer, J. E., Weissman, M. M., Orvaschel, H., Gruenberg, E., Burke, J. D., & Regier, D. A. (1984). Lifetime prevalence of specific psychiatric disorders in three sites. *Archives of General Psychiatry, 41,* 949–958.

Rosenbaum, J. F., Fava, M., Nierenberg, A. A., & Sachs, G. (1995). Treatment resistant mood disorders. In G. O. Gabbard (Ed.), *Treatment of psychiatric disorders* (2nd ed., pp. 1275–1328). Washington, DC: American Psychiatric Press.

Roy-Byrne, P., Post, R. M., Uhde, T. W., Porcu, T., & Davis, D. (1985). The longitudinal course of recurrent affective illness: Life chart data from research patients at the NIMH. *Acta Psychiatrica Scandinavica, 71*(Suppl. 317), 1–34.

Rush, A. J. (1988). Cognitive approaches to adherence. In A. J. Francis & R. J. Hales (Eds.), *American psychiatric press review of psychiatry* (Vol. 7, pp. 627–642). Washington, DC: American Psychiatric Press.

Rush, A. J., Beck, A. T., & Kovacs, M. (1977). Comparative efficacy of cognitive therapy and pharmacotherapy in the treatment of depressed outpatients. *Cognitive Therapy and Research, 1,* 17–37.

Rush, A. J., Cain, J. W., Raese, J., Stewart, R. S., Waller, D. A., & Debus, J. D. (1991). Neurobiological bases for psychiatric disorders. In R. N. Rosenberg (Ed.), *Comprehensive neurology* (pp. 555–603). New York: Raven Press.

Schou, M. (1989). *Lithium treatment of manic depressive illness: A practical approach*. Basel, Switzerland: Karger.

Schwarcz, G., & Silbergeld, S. (1983). Serum lithium spot checks to evaluate medication compliance. *Journal of Clinical Psychopharmacology, 3,* 356–358.

Scott, J., Byers, S., & Turkington, D. (1993). The chronic patient. In J. H. Wright, M. E. Thase, A. T. Beck, & J. W. Ludgate (Eds.), *Cognitive therapy with inpatients: Developing a cognitive milieu* (pp. 357–390). New York: Guilford Press.

Seltzer, A., Roncari, I., & Garfinkel, P. (1980). Effect of patient education on medication compliance. *Canadian Journal of Psychiatry, 25,* 638–645.

Shakir, S. A., Volkmar, F. R., & Bacon, S. (1979). Group psychotherapy as an adjunct to lithium maintenance. *American Journal of Psychiatry, 136,* 455–456.

Simons, A. D., Levine, J. L., Lustman, P. J., & Murphy, G. E. (1984). Patient attrition in a comparative outcome study of depression: A follow-up report. *Journal of Affective Disorders, 6,* 163–173.

Snyder, D. K. (1979). *Marital Satisfaction Inventory (MSI)*. Los Angeles: Western Psychological Services.

Spalt, L. (1975). Sexual behavior and affective disorders. *Diseases of the Nervous System, 36,* 974–977.

Stallone, F., Shelley, E., Mendlewicz, J., & Fieve, R. R. (1973). The use of lithium in affective disorders: III: A double blind study of prophylaxis in bipolar illness. *American Journal of Psychiatry, 130,* 1006–1010.

Stephen, T. D., & Harrison, T. M. (1986). Assessment communication style: A new measure. *American Journal of Family Therapy, 14,* 213–233.

Suppes, T., Phillips, K. A., Judd, C. R. (1994). Clozapine treatment of nonpsychotic rapid cycling bipolar disorder: A report of three cases. *Biological Psychiatry, 35*(5), 338–340.

Thompson, R., Stancer, H., & Persad, E. (1984). *Manic depressive illness: A guide for patients and families*. Toronto: Clarke Institute of Psychiatry.

Thomsen, K. C., & Hendrie, H. C. (1972). Environmental stress in primary depressive illness. *Archives of General Psychiatry, 26,* 130–132.

Van Gent, E. M., & Zwart, F. M. (1991). Psychoeducation of partners of bipolar manic patients. *Journal of Affective Disorders, 21,* 15–18.

Vestergaard, P., & Amdisen, A. (1983). Patient attitudes toward lithium. *Acta Psychiatrica Scandinavica, 67,* 8–12.

Wallis, J., Miller, R., & McFadyen, M. L. (1989). A comparative study of standard and slow-release oral lithium carbonate products. *South African Medical Journal, 76,* 618–620.

Wehr, T. A., & Wirz-Justice, A. (1982). Circadian rhythm mechanisms in affective illness and in antidepressant drug action. *Pharmacopsychiatry, 15,* 31–39.

Wehr, T. A., Sack, D. A., & Rosenthal, N. E. (1987). Sleep reduction as a final common pathway in the genesis of mania. *American Journal of Psychiatry, 144,* 201–204.

Weissman, M. M., Leaf, P. J., Bruce, M. L., Florio, L. (1988). The epidemiology of dysthymia in 5 communities: Rates, risks, comorbidity and treatment. *American Journal of Psychiatry, 145*(7), 815–819.

Winokur, G., Clayton, P. J., & Reich, T. (1969). *Manic depressive illness.* St. Louis: C. V. Mosby.

Wulsin, L., Bachop, M., & Hoffman, D. (1988). Group therapy in manic–depressive illness. *American Journal of Psychotherapy, 2,* 263–271.

Youssel, F. A. (1983). Compliance with therapeutic regimens: A follow-up study for patients with affective disorders. *Journal of Advanced Nursing, 8,* 513–517.

Zis, A. P., & Goodwin, F. K. (1979). Major affective disorders as a recurrent illness: A critical review. *Archives of General Psychiatry, 36,* 835–839.

Zis, A. P., Grof, P., Webster, M., & Goodwin, F. K. (1980). Prediction of relapse in recurrent affective disorder. *Psychopharmacology Bulletin, 16,* 47–49.

INDEX

Index

Page numbers in italics refer to tables or figures.